Jefferson and the Press

President Thomas Jefferson. Copy of portrait by Rembrandt Peale.
Courtesy of the Library of Congress

Jefferson
and the Press

Crucible of Liberty

JERRY W. KNUDSON

UNIVERSITY OF SOUTH CAROLINA PRESS

© 2006 University of South Carolina

Published in Columbia, South Carolina,
by the University of South Carolina Press

Manufactured in the United States of America

10 09 08 07 06   5 4 3 2 1

Library of Congress Cataloging-in-Publication Data

Knudson, Jerry W.
    Jefferson and the press : crucible of liberty / Jerry W. Knudson.
        p. cm.
    Includes bibliographical references and index.
    ISBN 1-57003-607-1 (cloth : alk. paper)
    1. Jefferson, Thomas, 1743–1826—Relations with journalists. 2. Press and politics—United
States—History—19th century. 3. United States—Politics and government—1801–1809.
I. Title.
    E332.2.K58 2006
    973.4'6'092—dc22

                                                                            2005020245

Earlier versions of three chapters were published elsewhere. The author gratefully acknowl-
edges the permission to reprint the following:
    "The Rage around Tom Paine: Newspaper Reaction to His Homecoming in 1802," *New-
York Historical Society Quarterly* 53 (January 1969): 34–63. Courtesy *New-York Historical Soci-
ety Quarterly,* The New-York Historical Society.
    "Newspaper Reaction to the Louisiana Purchase: 'This New, Immense, Unbounded World,'"
Missouri Historical Review 63 (January 1969): 1823–213.
    "The Jeffersonian Assault on the Federalist Judiciary, 1803–1805: Political Forces and Press
Reaction," *American Journal of Legal History* 14 (January 1970): 55–75.

for
Julie, Kim, and Tom
and in memory of Todd

The collision of opposite opinions produces the spark
which lights the torch of truth.

—Resolution of the Patriotic Society
of Newcastle, Delaware

Contents

Illustrations

Introduction

The statement "Every generation writes its own history" has been attributed to John Bowman, although others have echoed his premise, including Elizabeth Janeway, who wrote in *Between Myth and Morning* (1974), "If every nation gets the government it deserves, every generation writes the history which corresponds with its view of the world."[1] Thus, what seems true to historians of one generation, immersed in their own culture and environment, may be rewritten by another. This practice may occur even among towering figures of American historiography, as Merrill D. Peterson has so ably pointed out in *The Jefferson Image in the American Mind* (1962). He traces the peaks and valleys of interpretations of Jefferson by such well-known historians in their times as Henry S. Randall, Henry Adams, Vernon Louis Parrington, and Claude Bowers. Thus, interpretations may come and go, but newspapers, the daily history of a people, remain constant.

Newspapers of any period have frequently been misused by historians, some of whom still view them as factual sources—a highly dubious premise—and by others who skim through them to find a dramatic quotation and lift it out of context to enliven the pages of their already completed research. It is my purpose here to examine the interaction between the press and the administration of Thomas Jefferson (1801–9) by studying representative periodicals of the period.

Newspapers in Jefferson's time were the major means—almost the only means—of public communication. Historians sometimes ignore this fact. As with the Watergate investigation two centuries later, the question might be posed about Jefferson's time, "What did the people know, and when did they know it?"

Scholars have long debated whether mass communications merely reflect society or in fact play a role in shaping it. In the age of Jefferson—saturated with politics and the emergence of political parties, as the Whigs and Tories in England earlier—the new nation was finding its way, channeled to a certain extent by a partisan press. The issues were clearly drawn by newspapers and pungently presented in the vernacular of the people, stimulating discussions and arguments in taverns and coffeehouses throughout the land.

Frank Luther Mott, early authority on the American press, calls the period from Jefferson to Jackson the "Dark Ages" of American journalism because invective and personal attacks marked this era of intense political warfare. Yet was it really that bad, viewed in the context of its time? One must remember the nation was a semiliterate society, with considerable secondary circulation of newspapers, whose ideas also were spread by word of mouth among those who could not read, what Richard D. Brown has called the "dynamics of contagious diffusion."

Yankees everywhere, including those who owned shoestring printing shops, did not hesitate to speak their minds, and they did so with all the coarse vocabulary at their disposal. Few read the patrician prose of Federalist Joseph Dennie's *Port Folio,* preferring the scathing attacks of William Duane's *Aurora.* They relished political jousting, which they could understand—and even be entertained by—rather than weighty disquisitions over their heads.

Some modern readers may be put off by this verbal sniping, and yet it offers refreshing insights into the culture of the period. Editors did not consciously entice readers with this style—rooted roughly in English satire—because it was part and parcel of the American landscape and of themselves. The American press was forged by the events leading up to the Revolution, tempered with the great debate over the Constitution, and plunged into the political battles of the new Republic. In the struggle for supremacy headed by Alexander Hamilton for the Federalists and Thomas Jefferson for the Republicans, which culminated in the first transfer of political power in the young nation's history in 1801, the press was the ultimate weapon. The tirade against Jefferson was so intense that he became the most vilified president in America's history, with the possible exception of Abraham Lincoln.

Journalism historians have long thought that the partisan political press reached its acme during the presidency of Andrew Jackson (1828–37), but anyone who reads the newspapers of the Jeffersonian period knows it first reached this intensity during Jefferson's administration. When Jefferson was planning his epitaph, for example, he indicated that on the simple metal marker to be placed in the family cemetery at the foot of Monticello, he wanted only three things listed as the milestones of his life: author of the Declaration of Independence, author of the Virginia statute on religious freedom, and father of the University of Virginia. Because of the abuse heaped on this essentially shy man, he did not want to be remembered as the third president of the United States.

Do present-day readers understand this sometimes outrageous political language? J. G. A. Pocock put it best when he advised the modern historian to "read and recognize the diverse idioms of political discourse as they were available in the culture and at the time he is studying."[2]

Thus, newspapers should not be regarded as mere chroniclers or recorders of the time, but rather as reflections of the culture of which they were a part and possibly as actors in the unfolding drama. I described my approach in a 1993 *Perspectives* article for the American Historical Association:

> In my view, history is concerned—or should be concerned—not only with what actually happened in any given time or place, but also with what people *thought* was happening, as revealed through the means of mass communication available to them, which may have affected their subsequent actions. Thus, the perception of events as filtered through the press may have changed the historical outcome. According to this concept, it is immaterial whether the news is false or distorted as long as readers believed it and acted on their belief.[3]

Newspapers might therefore be considered original documents rather than secondary sources in the formation of public opinion—immutable and timeless, if science can find a way to preserve wood-pulp paper or combat microfilm virus.

Early on, newspapers were shunned as historical sources for generations. Not until John Bach McMaster began publishing his *History of the People of the United States* in 1883 did any prominent historian in this country make copious use of newspaper quotations.

Lucy Maynard Salmon, all but forgotten today, became the first American historian to use advertisements as indices of social history when she published in 1923 her lengthy two volumes, *The Newspaper and the Historian* and *The Newspaper and Authority*. In 1908 a session of the annual meeting of the American Historical Association discussed the use of newspapers by historians, but the topic was not broached again until my article appeared in 1993.

This book is based on my revised and expanded Ph.D. dissertation, written in 1962 under Dumas Malone and Bernard Mayo at the University of Virginia, where it was my good fortune to be one of the first seven Jefferson Fellows. To catch up on Jeffersonian scholarship since then has been a sheer pleasure, if at times overwhelming. Those interested in studying Jefferson further should consult Peter Onuf, "The Scholar's Jefferson," a selected bibliography since 1960 in *William and Mary Quarterly* (October 1993).

Mario Cuomo, three-time Democratic governor of New York, has written *Why Lincoln Matters Today More Than Ever* (2004), which gives us the essence of the man and his thought. Bernard Mayo did the same with *Jefferson Himself* (1942) more than half a century ago, and it is still in print. People hunger for accurate and meaningful history, but recoil when the past is enlisted for partisan causes in the present.

In a way, I was fortunate in doing my basic research on Jefferson in the mid-twentieth century because, in addition to my mentors, I could also seek the advice of Frank Luther Mott, winner of the Pulitzer Prize for his five-volume *History of American Magazines*. His factual work in newspaper history still stands up. When I first approached him, he replied (November 9, 1959), "I approve very heartily the subject you suggest [Jefferson and the press] for a doctoral dissertation. A good deal has been written loosely on this subject, but as far as I know, it has never been examined carefully."

We settled on intensive rather than extensive research, selecting four Federalist and four Republican newspapers ranging from Boston to Richmond, all of national influence. Smaller newspapers of the hinterlands usually republished items from the national leaders on the seaboard, as the concept of local news was practically unknown at the time. Mott responded (March 6, 1961), "I think you have made an admirable selection of representative newspapers." These, along with their printer-editors, were:

FEDERALIST NEWSPAPERS

Boston *Columbian Centinel* (Benjamin Austin Jr.)
New-York Evening Post (William Coleman)
Philadelphia *Gazette of the United States* (Enos Bronson)
Richmond *Recorder* (James Thomson Callender)

REPUBLICAN NEWSPAPERS

Boston *Independent Chronicle* (Thomas and Abijah Adams)
Philadelphia *Aurora* (William Duane)
Washington, D.C., *National Intelligencer* (Samuel Harrison Smith)
Richmond Enquirer (Thomas Ritchie)

Once the newspapers are selected, how does one best discern their contents? Sampling was rejected because, even with the most recent and sophisticated techniques, important material may inadvertently be skipped over. Likewise, other social-science techniques—such as content analysis or quantification— seem less appropriate or satisfying than a careful reading that captures the nuances and tone of the piece itself. As it turned out, I read my way through fifty-six years of issue (not all published the full eight years), page by page. Extensive surveys are another matter, such as Jeffrey L. Pasley's *"The Tyranny of Printers," Newspaper Politics in the Early American Republic* (200l), which lists 106 newspapers in the selected bibliography.

There were guideposts, of course, as I wanted to find the reactions of these eight newspapers to the six major issues of Jefferson's presidency—the election of 1800–1801, the return of Tom Paine, the Louisiana Purchase, the Hamilton-Burr duel, the Republican assault on the Federalist judiciary, the Embargo and commercial warfare of 1807–9. Other issues were perhaps more significant, and undercurrents then unknown to the public may have been flowing, but the topics selected were those that most interested public and officials alike and filled the newspapers at the time.

Still, my work began as a dissertation, and I must borrow a leaf from Wilson Carey McWilliams, who wrote in the preface to *The Idea of Fraternity in America* (1973), "to the usual faults of dissertations I have added other defects, nurtured in the intervening years and perfected by revision."[4] It should be noted also that three chapters of my dissertation have been published:

"The Rage around Tom Paine: Newspaper Reaction to His Homecoming in 1802," *New-York Historical Society Quarterly* 53 (January 1969): 34–63.
"Newspaper Reaction to the Louisiana Purchase: 'This New, Immense, Unbounded World,'" *Missouri Historical Review* 63 (January 1969): 182–213.
"The Jeffersonian Assault on the Federalist Judiciary, 1802–1805: Political Forces and Press Reaction," *American Journal of Legal History* 14 (January 1970): 55–75.

The legacy of Lucy Maynard Salmon, who first saw the inherent historical value of newspapers, became firmly established when she wrote in 1923, "the periodical press still remains the most important single source the historian has at his command for the reconstruction of the life of the past three centuries."[5] Perceptions of events or persons may change, but the newspapers themselves remain constant. My own work in the press of Jefferson's world has convinced me that we need to view newspapers and their editors with new eyes—but with theirs, not ours.

ONE

The Partisan Press, 1801–1809

The contradictions and inconsistencies of the Jacobins [Republicans] are a perfect chaos; bottomless and boundless. . . . [Republican newspapers] must have been written by mad-men for the use of fools.

—*Gazette of the United States,* July 25, 1801

. . . an everlasting outcry about royalists, or republicans, jacobins or tories is a reproach to the newspapers, and ought to be scouted from the land as a common nuisance.

—Boston *Independent Chronicle,* May 18, 1801

When Thomas Jefferson was born in 1743, the English-speaking population of North America consisted of about one million settlers along the Atlantic coast, and at the time of his death in 1826 there were at least ten million Americans.[1] According to Isaiah Thomas, founder of the American Antiquarian Society and witness to the Battle of Lexington and Concord, in 1754 there were only 4 newspapers printed in New England, all published in Boston. Moreover, only 39 newspapers were publishing at the beginning of the Revolution. In comparison, there were 360 newspapers in the United States by June 1810, two years after the close of Jefferson's administration.[2] To some Americans this proliferation was a mixed blessing.

"Never, since America was free, has there been in so short a period such an overwhelming torrent of falsehood [in the newspapers] has been seen deluging the nation for these five months past," exclaimed Thomas Jefferson's semiofficial newspaper, the *National Intelligencer,* in 1802, when his administration was scarcely underway.[3] In an age saturated with politics as the new nation was feeling its way, Jefferson realized that he needed all the newspaper support he could muster. Jefferson's leading editors of the emerging Republican Party were not only the sedate and gentlemanly Samuel Harrison Smith—a fixture of Washington,

D.C., society and editor of the *National Intelligencer*—but also the Irish fire-brand William Duane of the Philadelphia *Aurora*.

The period before and during Jefferson's term in office was a time of wrenching change, the first transfer of political power in the young nation's history. As Daniel J. Boorstin has so aptly summed it up, "The political bonds with Europe had been broken, a constitutional federal republic had been established, and a national political tradition had begun to emerge."[4] Moreover Lewis and Clark had penetrated the horizon to open up a whole new world. The reactions these almost overwhelming changes evoked were the most intense in the history of American journalism. This politically partisan press, although riddled with vituperation and abuse, was also a robust and vibrant vehicle for debating the issues in a young, semiliterate nation. Readers in taverns and coffeehouses—most of whom could not afford to subscribe to the newspapers of the period—could understand the thrust and parry of editors such as William Duane, while the words of erudite and cultured Samuel Harrison Smith sailed over their heads.

The partisan press—politicians owning newspapers to further their cause or using editors for this purpose—had roots embedded in the "newspaper war" of 1791–93 during George Washington's administration. The rivalry between Alexander Hamilton, secretary of the treasury, and Thomas Jefferson, secretary of state—each eventually with his own newspaper—metamorphosed into America's first political parties, the Federalists (Hamilton) supported by John Fenno's *Gazette of the United States,* and the Republicans (Jefferson) backstopped by Philip Freneau's *National Gazette.*

In his sweeping biography of Jefferson, Merrill D. Peterson took a cautious view of the extent of his subject's role in the partisan journalism of the period, perhaps because Jefferson, with an aristocratic bent (in this regard), preferred to work behind the scenes. It is true that Jefferson's entry into the arena of Philadelphia journalism was tentative. In his desire to give the public more foreign news, before the founding of the *National Gazette,* Jefferson arranged to provide John Fenno, editor of the *Gazette of the United States,* with extracts from the *Gazette de Leide* to counteract English news, but this arrangement lasted only three months.

At this point, the secretary of state probably decided he needed his own newspaper, and Freneau was brought on board, but Jefferson did not deign to write for the new newspaper.[6] Hamilton, on the other hand, wrote openly for the public. He used Latin pseudonyms, the custom of the period, but his pen names were well known to readers. He founded several newspapers, including the influential *New-York Evening Post* in 1801. Earlier, Hamilton had attacked the founding of the *National Gazette,* clearly his archrival Jefferson's attempt to counter John Fenno's Federalist *Gazette of the United States.* Peterson claimed that Hamilton "credited Jefferson with a larger part in the newspaper's establishment than was his due, with an editorial influence he never had, and a party leadership he neither coveted nor possessed."[7]

Specifically, Hamilton attacked Jefferson for the subterfuge of hiring Philip Freneau as a French translator in the U.S. State Department (at $250 a month) whereas his real job was to edit the newly founded *National Gazette*. As party lines were drawn, Jefferson's newspaper—and there is no question of his close connection with it—even attacked repeatedly the president of the United States, provoking an outcry from Washington against "that rascal Freneau!" Hamilton was furious, declaring in print, "Can he [Jefferson] reconcile it to his own personal dignity and the principles of probity to hold an office under [the government] and employ the means of official influence in opposition?"[8] Before the mayor of Philadelphia, Freneau signed an affidavit swearing that Jefferson "at no time urged, advised, or influenced" the establishment of the *National Gazette* or had "ever, directly or indirectly, written, dictated or composed for it."[9]

Freneau, of course, was protesting too much. As Michael Lienesch has pointed out, "From 1791 to 1793, Thomas Jefferson played a pivotal role in the creation of an American political experience whose most prominent features include a free and partisan press, a system of popular political parties, and an extensive role for organized public opinion."[10] Federalist editors were dismayed "at the number of Republican prints which were industriously disseminated in all the villages and hamlets in the country, [and] have become truly alarming and threaten more extensive mischief than is generally imagined."[11]

As the number of "Jacobin" journals increased, the *Gazette of the United States* issued a strident call to all like-minded printers everywhere to report any antigovernment newspaper items to its office. Within twenty-four hours, however, the Federalist newspaper abandoned its "truth squad" operation. Heading the most powerful newspaper of its time, Fenno explained to his readers: "Upon experiment, we find, that to notice everything which would come under the two heads of *folly* and *falsehood*, would be to copy every *original* article which appears in the Jacobin [Republican] papers the consequence is, that we must content ourselves with occasional *selections* fully persuaded that our readers will be satisfied with these, as specimens of the whole."[12]

Other editors found much to amuse them, and the temperate Samuel Harrison Smith much to distress him, as when James Thomson Callender, a convert to Federalism, delighted in referring to the *National Intelligencer* as "MISS Smith's Silky-Milky National Smoothing Plane."[13] Such rhetorical flourish and hyperbole were commonplace, and much of it seems to have been meant half in jest, so many notches on the old quill pen, so to speak. Verses with a political twist were printed frequently, most of them doggerel but some quite good, such as this Tory sample from the Revolutionary period:

> Behold yon Patriot bellowing loud
> For Liberty—that darling Theme
> Pull off the Mask—'tis private Grudge
> Or Party Rage that forms the Scheme.[14]

One telling paragraph in Hamilton's *New-York Evening Post,* edited by William Coleman, reveals much about the inner workings of the partisan journals. In answer to an irate reader who claimed that Coleman had wrongly attributed a statement to the Spanish minister, the editor briefly replied, in part, "We readily say that the paragraph to which [the reader] alludes is merely to be considered as an unmeaning pleasantry, a mere badinage, resorted to by way of saying nothing on a subject which we could not be supposed entirely to pass over."[15]

At the opposite extreme, when Jefferson was finally elected, ending twelve years of uninterrupted Federalist rule, political writing soared. It flared beyond satire or even the Pickwickian sense, the latter not intended to be taken in the obvious or literal way. These and other writers were prolific, however, reveling in the language. The Library of Congress, for example, before its catalog went online, had 306 entries in its card catalog for various editions of the works of William Cobbett.

Yet voices opposed to this verbal mayhem also were heard. In her biography of Jefferson, Joyce Appleby stated, "The Alien and Sedition Acts, were meant to rein in the routine invective found in newspaper columns."[16] This assertion ignores entirely the political motivation of the acts. Only Republican printers were prosecuted under the Sedition Act, and one would hardly describe the invective as "routine." Every writer tried to outdo his fellow printers or editors in verbal pyrotechnics, and readers frequently waited with anticipation for the biting reply to a particularly clever piece. It certainly was not all political entertainment in an otherwise drab world, but that element has been overlooked.

The polarization of Republicans and Federalists wrought partly by newspapers of the early years of the republic—an encore of the role of the press in the earlier definition of the Whig and Tory parties in England—has carried over, to some extent, to more-recent historians. Consider, for example, Frank Luther Mott's assessment in 1950:

> Indeed, the whole period of 1801–1833 was in many respects disgraceful—a
> kind of "Dark Ages" of American journalism. Few papers were ably edited; they
> reflected the crassness of the American society of the times. Scurrility, assaults,
> corruption, blatancy were commonplace. Journalism had grown too fast.[17]

More recently, William E. Ames claimed in 1972 that "political journalism, rather than being the dark ages of the American newspaper, offered a higher quality information and interpretation of American society than at any other time in American history."[18] It must be pointed out, however, that Ames's careful study of one responsible paper, the *National Intelligencer,* ignores a broader journalistic landscape filled with turmoil. It was open season on printers, who faced imminent seditious-libel prosecutions, whether under the federal Alien and Sedition Laws (1798–1801) or under state common law. They also faced possible duels, canings and beatings in the streets, or constant abuse from opposition printers. The Federalist *Gazette of the United States,* for example, once printed that William Duane of the Philadelphia *Aurora* "hurries back to lying like an old bawd not three weeks out of service."[19] When Duane attacked conditions in the Philadelphia jail, the *Gazette of the United States* commented, "What a pity there is no Gallows in Pennsylvania that he might have an opportunity of abusing his *last enemy* in this world.[20]

As in the colonial period, the battle spilled over into the pulpit. Shortly after Jefferson's inauguration on March 4, 1801, copies of the *New-England Palladium* were sent to clergymen in Boston with a request that the Federalist propaganda be read to their congregations. An indignant churchman wrote to the Boston *Independent Chronicle:* "Poor fools! What dismal situation, when you are obliged to confess, that the only support of your sinking party is a newspaper. Good God, how are the mighty fallen!"[21]

In one of the defining moments in the history of American journalism, news began to be separated from political jousting as embryonic editorial paragraphs first appeared at the beginning of the nineteenth century. The political press surfaced again during the administration of Andrew Jackson (1829–37).[22] At the age of seventy-five William Duane of the Philadelphia *Aurora,* faithful to his Jeffersonian principles and practices to the end, revived the *Aurora* in 1834 in a weak but courageous attempt to help Jackson fight the Second Bank of the United States.[23] Thus, Duane's career brackets what many consider the Jefferson-Jackson continuum.

Since Duane is usually remembered for his Irish brawls and proliferating libel suits (how easily we peg characters in history), it might be well to let the Philadelphia journalist and staunch Republican give his own assessment of his craft here:

> Every man of observation knows the fact, that public discussion, argument, and reasoning upon measures of policy, are not addressed to the intelligent and the virtuous part of the community; neither are they ever addressed to the hearts or heads of the depraved. There are in every society large masses of men, who never think or reason; some who have no capacity for thought; many whose judgments are too weak to be constant to any fixt [*sic*] ideas; and very many who assume a mask of moderation or liberality only to cover their diabolical selfishness and depravity; very unfortunately this mixture of ignorance, imbecility and hypocrisy is very numerous. It forms perhaps a full third of every society; and it is to the major part of this mass that all public discussions are addressed. They in fact make the majority in all critical times, and are as ready

to be thrown into the balance on one side or the other, according to the mode in which they are addressed."[24]

There is some confusion about what the designation *official newspaper* meant. It denoted simply that the paper was the recipient of the government-printing contracts. This practice was ended with the establishment of the U.S. Government Printing Office in 1860. Before that, political support was expected to follow government-printing contracts. Thus, the official designation came to mean *government spokesman* as well, although sub rosa as with Duane of the Philadelphia *Aurora*. Andrew Johnson was the last president to have an "official" newspaper, a pale image of its predecessors.

It was not only party loyalty to Jefferson that explains the proliferation of newspapers—from the 39 that survived the Revolution to 360 by June 1810.[25] Almost all newspapers in this period were founded for political reasons, and, after the election of Jefferson, Republican printers were for the first time getting patronage in the form of printing contracts. However, the florescence of these papers—many of them weeklies and a few published west of the Appalachians—were a prelude to the "Freedom's Ferment" Alice Felt Tyler found in the Jacksonian period.

Several other reasons suggest why the press ran rampant in this power struggle between Federalists and Republicans. Perhaps American printers were exulting in their regained freedom after the Alien and Sedition Laws (1798–1801) were allowed to expire under the Jefferson administration. Fines of not more than two thousand dollars and prison terms of not more than two years were repaid or canceled for those who had been convicted under the Sedition Law for making any "false, scandalous, and malicious" statement "against the Government of the United States, or either house of the Congress of the United States with intent to defame . . . or to bring them . . . into contempt or disrepute." There were twenty-five arrests under the Sedition Law, fourteen indictments, and eleven trials, resulting in ten convictions—eight of them Republican newspapers. Many of the printers were of foreign origin, and all were Republicans, suggesting the punitive nature of the Federalist assault.[26] The fact that there were some twenty-five thousand foreigners in the country at the time made their situation precarious. As the *Gazette of the United States* warned its Federalist readers after the expiration of the Alien and Sedition Laws in 1801:

> It is well known to all men of common discernment, Jacobins as well as others, that the present unhappy and perilous state of public affairs, in this country, is owing in a great measure, to the unrestrained licentiousness of presses imprudently suffered to remain in the hands of wicked and seditious foreigners. . . . Every avenue and every byway passage. . .will be seen thronged with motley gangs, whose faces we know not and whose languages we cannot understand, strangers, Jews, and proselytes, Cretes and Arabians.[27]

Furthermore, combative and largely anonymous printers of the colonial period and late eighteenth century continued to shape the political parameters of Federalists and Republicans in the early national period, just as newspapers had done earlier in England in delineating Whig and Tory parties. If anything, the transfer of power in the United States in 1801 fueled the controversy as the Federalists—the outs—wanted back in. As Samuel Harrison Smith lamented at the close of Jefferson's first term, "It is to be hoped that the annals of the American history will exhibit a few instances of a future administration being so unjustly calumniated as the present has been by the self-styled Federalists."[28]

Thus, in this highly charged political atmosphere, some printers became aware that their calling was something more than running off a few papers to sell in their shops along with the cider and home remedies. (William Parks in the colonial period had said he started a newspaper because "I had a prospect of getting a Penny by it."[29]) Of course, there were some clear-cut editors in the late eighteenth century as well, but the fact is that most were simply printers, which does not diminish their calling. The editor as a common entity had not yet appeared fully on the scene, but there were brilliant precursors such as the staunch Federalists John Fenno of the *Gazette of the United States* (which he edited between 1789 and 1796) and William Cobbett of *Porcupine's Gazette* (1797–99) and the Republicans Philip Freneau of the *National Gazette* (1791–93) and Benjamin Franklin Bache (grandson of Ben, who left journalism at the age of forty-two) of the Philadelphia *Aurora* (1790–98). The flood of political newspapers at the close of the eighteenth century may also be attributed in part to the fierce debate over the adoption of the Constitution and to the widening gulf between the two parties.

With the emergence of the editor came the fledgling appearance of the editorial, at first only a tenuous separation of comment from news. Was the device intended to siphon off opinion from news columns to make the latter more credible? That explanation would be the present day rationale, but more likely the editorial was simply meant to underline the political thoughts of the editor, which were also found liberally in all other parts of the paper. Who first came up with the editorial? There are as many explanations as scholars working in the field. According to Mott, Noah Webster first compartmentalized the newspaper, frequently placing editorials under the "New York" column of his New York *American Minerva*, founded in 1793.[30] Willard Grosvenor Bleyer maintained that it was James Cheetham of the New York *American Citizen* who first printed short editorials in almost every issue of his Republican paper.[31] Other newspapers soon followed the same line of development, including the Boston *Columbian Centinel*, and the *New-York Journal*, which set its editorials in italic type to differentiate them from the news. By 1800 the Philadelphia *Aurora* was using a column on its second page for editorial comment and was regularly employing the editorial "we." Editorial comment, unlike today, was limited to brief paragraphs.

All these changes—gradual but inexorable—happened on the threshold of Jefferson's presidency. Three-quarters of the 235 newspapers, mostly weeklies, that existed when Jefferson became president in 1801 were in the rapidly growing cities, where Federalists controlled the money and therefore the press.[32] Jefferson calculated that 4 percent of the citizens owed 75 percent of the newspapers, Federalists "swaying the government by their possession of the printing presses which their wealth commands."[33]

Without doubt journalism had become an expensive undertaking. Gone were the colonial days when printer Hugh Gaine had set up his shop with two thousand dollars from his savings as an apprentice. In 1801 Federalist Judge Samuel Chase had to raise eight thousand dollars from his friends to launch the Baltimore *Anti-Democrat*.[34] (Note the increasing use of the word *Democrat* for *Republican,* although usually in a derogatory sense, as here.) The immediate frontier beyond the Appalachian mountains opened up to printers, invariably Republican, after 1821, when Samuel Rust patented a less-costly, compact, hand-operated press that could be transported in a horse-drawn wagon and was capable of turning out 250 impressions an hour. Jefferson's dream of an agrarian democracy seemed less far away.

Meanwhile, printers felt the scourge of the times. No one was lower on the social scale than printers, except scruffy wandering minstrels begging for handouts, as the *Gazette of the United States* viewed with alarm. Its editor, John Fenno, abhorred the printers of the proliferating Republican papers that had "sprung up in every town and village." Fenno continued, "Those men who, in their own country, had been advanced to the rank of a secretary to a seditious club, or *strolling player upon the stage,* could write and harangue; while others could work a press or travel through the country and proclaim to the ignorant, that government is usurpation, that taxes are a robbery upon the poor to support the powerful, and that nothing but immediate opposition to their rulers can save them from the chains of slavery."[35]

In the partisan warfare of the period, denunciation knew no limits, ridicule no bounds. Duane delighted in listing the sins of the Federalists in neat, itemized columns in his Philadelphia *Aurora*.[36] Newspapers everywhere faced an endemic shortage of paper, so they went from 12-point Caslon type to the smaller 6-point Caslon, getting much more print onto a page, but also making it more difficult to read. Also, since paper mills were few, rag content was used, a boon to historians since wood pulp, which is acidic, lasts a much shorter time. Used clothing was also employed for the cause. As one ingenious printer made his pitch:

> Sweet ladies, pray be not offended,
>   Nor mind the jest of sneering wags;
> No harm, believe us, is intended,
>   When humbly we request your rags.[37]

Printers labored under other harsh conditions, including never-ending shortages of ink and type and dependable labor, as well as the difficulty of getting people to pay up their back subscriptions. Transportation was slow and hazardous —news of the death of Washington on December 14, 1799, for example, did not reach the pages of the Boston *Columbian Centinel* until eleven days later.

Moreover, Congress had to be convinced that the public was entitled to reports of its proceedings. Early newspaper editors fought a running battle with Congress for the right to report the lawmakers' debates. On December 2, 1801, William Duane announced in the Philadelphia *Aurora,* "The Editor proposes to give the proceedings in Congress with regularity and fidelity in the approaching important session."[38] Duane's first report from Washington, describing the opening of the congressional session, appeared in the *Aurora* on December 10. At about the same time, the *National Intelligencer* informed its readers, "It is the intention of the Editor . . . to present to his readers an abstract of the most interesting proceedings of the Legislature, as promptly as practicable. The detail of private business, or that of subordinate importance, will be given thereafter without much delay."[39]

Samuel Harrison Smith, editor of the *National Intelligencer,* experienced considerable difficulty in his modest aim, however. Early in January 1801 he was ejected from his customary place below the bar of the House of Representatives. He retreated to the gallery but was also denied a place there two days later.[40] Meanwhile, Smith stated in his newspaper:

> Uninfluenced by personal feeling, and guided by a *due* respect for the Speaker, and a *sincere* respect for the *People* of the United States, he will not, while he retains the power, cease, by publishing a record of truth, whatever or whomsoever it may affect, to manifest to the people, on *whose* support he relies, a spirit of dignity and moderation that the frowns of power can never dismay.[41]

Reporters had been allowed access to the House of Representatives since April 8, 1789, and to the Senate since December 9, 1795. A Senate resolution of April 30, 1790, to open the doors to reporters and later similar resolutions had been roundly defeated. When Congress moved from New York to Philadelphia, four seats on window sills were provided for stenographers, and here perched the first congressional reporters—Philip Freneau, John Fenno, James Thomson Callender, Joseph Gales Sr., and Samuel Harrison Smith. It has been claimed that James Gordon Bennett was the first Washington correspondent in 1827, but Frederic Marbut has found that the *United States Gazette* and *Freeman's Journal,* Philadelphia Federalist newspapers, maintained correspondents in Washington as early as 1808.[42]

The press greeted with jubilation a resolution passed by the U.S. Senate in early January 1802 by a vote of 17–9, which stated: "Resolved, that any Stenographer, desirous to take the Debates of the Senate on Legislative business, may be admitted for that purpose, at such place, within the area of the Senate chamber, as the President shall allot." This privilege was extended to any "note taker" in an amendment adopted by a vote of 16–12, but another amendment requiring each stenographer to give bond and two sureties in unspecified amounts was defeated by a vote of 18–10.[43] Samuel Harrison Smith had his "convenient place in the lower area" once again, which led the Republican editor to comment in the *National Intelligencer:*

> On the adoption of the above resolution, which opens a new door to public information, and which may be considered as the prelude to a more genuine sympathy between the Senate and the people of the United States, than may have heretofore subsisted, by rendering each better acquainted with the other, we congratulate, without qualification, every friend to the true principles of our republican institutions.[44]

Because of Samuel Harrison Smith's stenographic training, the reports of congressional debate in the *National Intelligencer* were unusually thorough and accurate. When the Baltimore *Anti-Democrat* charged that the reports in the *National Intelligencer* were "shamefully mutilated" and proceeded to send its own stenographer, the *New-York Evening Post* sprang to the defense of the *Intelligencer:*

> We are sorry to perceive in the editorial paragraph of the Baltimore Anti-Democrat, that the National Intelligencer has subjected itself to the charge of *shamefully mutilating* the speeches of the federal members in the House. It is there observed, that the Washington Federalist has provided a Stenographer of acknowledged abilities to take the speeches, which besides are corrected by the respective speakers. We are glad to hear this, because we have been not a little mortified that from the more ample and satisfactory manner in which the debates have hitherto appeared in the National Intelligencer, we have thought ourselves obliged to extract from that paper, instead of the Washington Federalist.[45]

In no other way did the newspapers from 1801 to 1809 show more enterprise than in the matter of reporting congressional debates, which illustrates the political tone of the age. One historian has stated that invective tapered off after Jefferson's overwhelming re-election in 1804 with 162 electoral votes against only 14 for Federalist candidate Charles C. Pinckney of South Carolina, but the record shows otherwise. Fighting for their political lives, the Federalists came on stronger than ever. As Thomas Ritchie, Republican editor of the *Richmond Enquirer,* observed in late 1806:

> It is impossible to peruse the federal papers of this country; and to observe their complete contempt for truth, their gross scurrility, their repulsive impudence, without feeling an aversion, which ought not to exist, against the very profession which they pursue. Is it possible, have I often exclaimed to myself, that Condorcet and Franklin could have been the *editors* of a newspaper?[46]

TWO

Republican Printers
"Immigrant Scribblers"

The American newspaperman is a touchstone of American civilization.

—Daniel J. Boorstin, preface to Bernard A. Weisberger,
The American Newspaperman

The newspaper editor writes in the sand when the flood is coming in.
If he but succeed in influencing opinion for the present,
he must be content to be forgotten in the future.

—Hugh Miller, quoted in Lucy Maynard Salmon,
The Newspaper and the Historian

Worthington Chauncey Ford once dismissed the Republican editors in the Jefferson years as "those scribbling immigrants,"[1] but it was to a newspaper edited by such a creature that Thomas Jefferson paid tribute in 1811: "This paper [the Philadelphia *Aurora*] has unquestionably rendered incalculable services to republicanism through all its struggles with the federalists and has been the rallying point for the orthodoxy of the whole Union. It was our comfort in the gloomiest days, and is still performing the office of a watchful sentinel."[2]

To perform the role of "watchful sentinel" in the first decade of the nineteenth century was no easy task, for editing a Republican newspaper during Jefferson's administration was hardly a serene and respectable occupation. Yet men were found willing to undertake this hazardous and thankless task, and on the whole they conducted themselves creditably. They seldom had the opportunity to praise the positive accomplishments of the Jefferson administration because they were so often employed in defending it from Federalist attacks. The Boston *Independent Chronicle,* edited by Abijah and Thomas Adams, defended the Embargo in the stronghold of opposition sentiment; the *Richmond Enquirer,* founded by Thomas Ritchie on May 9, 1804, defended Jefferson on the Virginia home front; the Philadelphia *Aurora* under William Duane continued as leader of the Republican newspapers, and the *National Intelligencer* in the capital, edited by the able Samuel Harrison Smith, served the administration as official reporter if not as partisan defender. Although the *Intelligencer,* so far as the public was concerned, was regarded as the administration's organ, it remained less partisan than any of its contemporaries.[3]

Samuel Harrison Smith (1772–1845), the son of a Philadelphia merchant, was graduated from the University of Pennsylvania in 1787 and first gained the attention of Thomas Jefferson by tying for the first prize offered by the American Philosophical Society in 1797 for the best essay on a system of education and a plan for free public schools.[4] Smith, secretary of the society, had admired Jefferson since Smith had become vice president of the American Philosophical Society at the same time Jefferson was elected to its presidency, which—as Bernard Bailyn has pointed out—was "a position he [Jefferson] enjoyed far more than he did the nation's vice-presidency and which he proudly and actively held for the next eighteen years."[5] As Margaret Bayard Smith recalled, her husband's winning the prize "led to a friendly intercourse which influenced the future destiny of my husband, as it was by Mr. Jefferson's advice, that he removed to Washington and established the *National Intelligencer.*"[6]

Smith had begun publishing a Jeffersonian newspaper, *New World,* in Philadelphia in the late summer of 1796 but discontinued it on August 16, 1797. In September 1797 he bought the *Independent Gazetteer* from the elder Joseph Gales and on November 16 brought out the first issue of the *Universal Gazette.*

On Jefferson's invitation, he moved his paper with the capital to Washington, D.C., where he established a triweekly, the *National Intelligencer and Washington Advertiser,* on October 31, 1800, retaining the *Universal Gazette* as a weekly edition of the same newspaper. Although the recognized administration newspaper under Thomas Jefferson, James Madison, and James Monroe, and heavily subsidized by public printing, the *National Intelligencer* showed little profit until after the War of 1812.[7]

When the national capital was moved to the banks of the Potomac in the summer of 1800, printers scrambled to establish journals in the wilderness clearing. Two newspapers that had been established there in 1795 and 1796 had failed because of insufficient support. After it was announced that Congress would meet in Washington on November 17, 1800, the triweekly *Washington Federalist,* with offices in Georgetown, was launched on September 25; James Lyon, son of the Vermont congressman jailed for violating the Sedition Law, started the *Cabinet of the United States* as a Republican daily about October 1, and Smith brought out his triweekly *National Intelligencer* on October 31. Also, the *Centinel of Liberty,* a Federalist paper that had been published for two years at Georgetown, established the *Museum and Washington and George-town Advertiser* on November 18. Thus, by the time Congress assembled, Washington had two Republican and two Federalist newspapers.[8]

The population of the District of Columbia was then 14,303—mainly concentrated in Georgetown—while Pennsylvania Avenue was but a mile-long trail between the unfinished Capitol and the President's Mansion, set in a cluster of fifteen or sixteen buildings.[9] Margaret Bayard Smith rejoiced at this setting along the "Beautiful banks of the Tiber!" but a later writer described Pennsylvania Avenue in rainy weather as "all but impassable because of the yellow clinging mud, and in dry weather the wind swirled blinding dust in the passer's eyes."[10]

It was an unlikely setting for journalism of any stature, but Samuel Harrison Smith nurtured the *National Intelligencer* through the years until it became a national institution. He fully exploited the role of editor as a man of position in the community by devoting equal attention to the social life of Washington. As William E. Smith has written, "Whether in the country or in town, his home was the rendezvous of statesmen, authors, musicians, politicians, and editors. He set a lavish table, filled his cellar with rare wines, attended an Episcopal church regularly, enjoyed chess and whist, and drove fine horses."[11] Smith was assisted greatly in his social ambitions by his Federalist-inclined wife, the former Margaret Bayard, who has been described as a "charming hostess, happy in her married life, capable, intelligent, vivacious, energetic, sympathetic, and positive."[12] Smith had married his cousin on September 29, 1800, and the couple had a son and three daughters. The Smiths often dined with Jefferson, and they visited him at Monticello. In 1804 the editor bought a country estate, Turkey Thicket, and renamed it Sydney.[13]

Overworked and in poor health, Samuel Harrison Smith considered selling the *National Intelligencer* in 1808 but decided to continue editing the newspaper until the Embargo crisis had passed. He sold the journal to Joseph Gales Jr. on August 31, 1810. Two years later Gales acquired a partner in his brother-in-law William Winston Seaton, and the newspaper under this famous pair became a daily in 1813.[14]

Samuel Harrison Smith devoted the remainder of his life to public service. In July 1813 he was appointed commissioner of revenue, and in 1828 he was chosen president of the Washington branch of the United States Bank. Before his death on November 1, 1845, he also served as a director of the Washington Library, as president of the Bank of Washington for nearly a decade, as treasurer of the Washington National Monument Society, and as a public-school trustee.[15] Smith was not successful in moderating the virulent journalistic abuse of the period, but he edited for ten years a newspaper thoroughly in keeping with the character of the administration it served.

In retrospect it seems strange that Jefferson would have selected the tri-weekly *National Intelligencer* as his official spokesman when the daily *Aurora* was readily available in Philadelphia. William Duane did establish a stationery store and printing shop in Washington, so he probably would have moved the

Aurora to the new capital if he had been asked to do so. The decision to keep the *Aurora* in Philadelphia and to make the *National Intelligencer* Jefferson's "official"organ in the capital may have stemmed from the maneuver to maintain a two-pronged partisan offensive in both major cities.[16]

William Duane (1760–1835) led the most colorful career of any editor of the period. Considered an Irish firebrand, he was kicked out of India, ignored in Great Britain, rejected once by Jefferson, and spent the last years of his life fighting the Second Bank of the United States and traveling in South America. Born near Lake Champlain, New York, of Irish parentage, he was taken back to Ireland by his mother after his father's death in 1765. Because William Duane married a Protestant girl, Catherine Corcoran, he was disinherited by his Catholic mother and was forced to learn the printer's trade. In 1787 He went to India, where he established the *Indian World* at Calcutta, which brought him prestige and fortune. But his denunciations of a scandal in the East India Company and his support of the grievances of some British army officers led to his arrest without charge and his deportation without trial. Returned to London, he worked as parliamentary reporter for the *General Advertiser,* later merged with the *Times,* and sought in vain for the restitution of his confiscated Indian property.

Disgusted with English justice, he sailed to America and took up residence in Philadelphia, where he easily fell in with the British-baiting Benjamin Franklin Bache, editor of the *Aurora.*[17] Duane assisted this grandson of Benjamin Franklin until Bache died during the yellow fever epidemic of 1798, whereupon the brash young Irishman took over Bache's newspaper and married his widow, Margaret Markoe Bache.[18]

In the opinion of Claude G. Bowers, "No single person [other than Duane] did more to discredit the projected war with France over the X.Y.Z. incident, to make the Alien and Sedition Laws abhorrent, to arouse and munition the masses, and make the triumph of Jefferson in 1800 inevitable."[19] Yet Bowers was mistaken in adding, "With Jefferson's election, the career of Duane moved toward an anti-climax,"[20] for the Philadelphia *Aurora* remained the mentor of the Republican press of the United States even after the national capital moved to Washington, D.C. Duane originally planned to move the *Aurora* to Washington to follow Jefferson, but was promised the printing of the House journals while still in Philadelphia if he continued marshaling the Republican press from there, the country's largest city.[21] The *National Intelligencer* was not an effective spokesman for Jefferson's administration during a violently partisan age, and William Duane retained the mantle of leadership that Samuel Harrison Smith declined to accept.

Whether caused by the scorching Philadelphia summers or by the clash of diverse national groups, the City of Brotherly Love early became a pest hole of partisan journalism. The population of Philadelphia increased from 28,522 in 1790 to 81,009 in 1800, and the city remained the largest in the United States until the census of 1830 revealed that New York had forged ahead.[22] Still, in 1800 Philadelphia was not too populous to start its annual fox hunt in January at the sign of the Liberty Cap on Coates Street between Third and Fourth or to have an annual spring deer chase at Bush Hill.[23]

On the death of Benjamin Franklin Bache from yellow fever on September 10, 1798, at the age of twenty-nine, his widow resumed publication of the daily on November 1 of that year.

On arriving in America on July 4, 1796, Duane had first edited the Philadelphia *True American,* published by Samuel F. Bradford. When Duane took over the duties of editing the *Aurora* from the widow Bache, he assumed great financial burdens. During the seven years that Benjamin Franklin Bache had edited the newspaper, he had lost $14,700.[24] Publishing a political journal in early America was not a lucrative business.

Along with debts, Duane inherited an editorial policy from his predecessor. The Irishman's role in the attempted destruction of the Washington legend began during Bache's lifetime. In 1796 Duane appears to have been the author of a diatribe against the first president entitled *A Letter to George Washington, President of the United States, Containing Strictures on His Address of the Seventeenth of September, 1796, Notifying His Relinquishment of the Presidential Office.* The pamphlet ostensibly was written by "Jasper Dwight, of Vermont," but it has been attributed to Duane.

Bache and the Washington administration had parted company over the celebrated Jay Treaty with England in 1795. Bache had lacerated the treaty and the President in his 1796 pamphlet, *Remarks Occasioned by the Late Conduct of Mr. Washington as President of the United States.* Viewed together, these two pamphlets of Bache and Duane were a formidable double-headed assault on the chief executive. If anything, Duane's pamphlet was more scurrilous than Bache's, although conceivably both men may have had editorial hands in each. To William Duane, Washington's farewell address to his countrymen reflected "the loathings of a sick mind."[25]

The *Aurora* bluntly charged that bribery had been perpetrated in high places in the Adams administration, to which the aging Washington replied:

> There can be no medium between the reward and punishment of an Editor, who shall publish such things as Duane has been doing for sometime past. On what ground then does he *pretend* to stand in his exhibition of the charges, or the insinuations which he has handed to the Public. Can hardihood, itself be so great, as to stigmatize characters in the Public Gazettes for the most heinous offences, and when prosecuted, pledge itself to support the allegations unless there was something to build on? I hope and expect that the Prosecutors will probe this matter to the bottom. It will have an unhappy effect on the public mind if it be not so.[26]

The former president had no cause to fear, for prosecutors were always concerned with the *Aurora*. A common-law action similar to prosecutions under the Alien and Sedition Laws of 1798 had been brought against Benjamin Franklin Bache, but his death precluded his being brought to trial. William Duane faced a double-barreled prosecution under both the Alien Law and the Sedition Law because of doubts raised by the Federalists concerning his citizenship.[27] Secretary of State Timothy Pickering wrote to President John Adams that although Duane pretended to have been born in Vermont, he was "really a British subject, and, as an alien, liable to be banished from the United States."[28] With his letter, Pickering enclosed a copy of the *Aurora,* which he said contained "an uninterrupted stream of slander on the American government." The secretary of state added that he would give the newspaper to William Rawle, a government attorney, "and, if he thinks it libelous, desire him to prosecute the editor."[29]

The president's reply to Pickering's letter indicated that John Adams was perfectly in accord with the spirit of the Alien and Sedition Laws:

> Is there anything evil in the regions of actuality or possibility, that the Aurora has not suggested of me. You may depend upon it, I disdain to attempt a vindication of myself against any of the lies of the Aurora, as much as any man concerned in the administration of the affairs of the United States. If Mr. Rawle does not think this paper libelous, he is not for his office; and if he does not prosecute, he will not do his duty. The matchless effrontery of this Duane merits the execution of the alien law. I am very willing to try its strength upon him.[30]

Duane's opposition to the repressive Alien and Sedition Laws had been organized from the beginning of this sad chapter in American history. On the second and third pages of the *Aurora* of December 18, 1798, were printed seven columns of the congressional debate on the resolution to print twenty thousand copies of the Alien and Sedition Laws to be distributed throughout the United States, and "Philodemus" attacked the Sedition Law as unconstitutional in a full-page essay in the issue of December 19, 1798.

William Duane, Dr. James Reynolds, and two other men were arrested and hustled off to jail on February 11, 1799, when Duane precipitated a riot by attempting to gather signatures for a petition to Congress favoring repeal of the Alien Friends Act.[31] The brawl took place in the churchyard of St. Mary's Catholic Church in Philadelphia, and at the ensuing trial in the State House on February 21, 1799, Duane and his accomplices were acquitted through the able pleading of their defense counsel, Alexander J. Dallas. Special state prosecutor was Joseph Hopkinson, author of "Hail, Columbia!," who argued, "aliens have no right whatever to petition, or to interfere in any respect with the government of this country—as the right of voting in elections is confined to our citizens, the right of petitioning is also—if aliens do not like the laws of this country, God knows there are ways and wishes enough for them to go back again."[32]

The scuffling in St. Mary's churchyard was followed by more serious violence three months later, when thirty officers of the Philadelphia militia—outraged over an item in the *Aurora*—confronted Duane with drawn swords and pistols in his office on May 15, 1799. The editor was held and beaten over the head with a pistol butt, knocked down, and kicked. He offered to fight any one of his assailants singly, but he was dragged downstairs into Franklin Court, where the brutal assault was repeated. Duane's sixteen-year-old son threw himself across his father's body, and reinforcements dispersed the attackers. That night armed Republicans maintained a vigil in the *Aurora* office, which prevented further bloodshed.[33]

Duane finally brought down the wrath of the Federalist Senate by exposing the notorious Ross electoral "reform" bill. Senator James Ross of Pennsylvania, defeated Federalist candidate for the governorship of Pennsylvania in 1799, introduced a bill in the U.S. Senate on January 23, 1800, that was clearly designated to wrest the election of 1800 from Thomas Jefferson if it became apparent the Virginian was going to win. The bill would have created a grand committee of six senators and six representatives presided over by the chief justice, to rule on electoral returns. The committee's decision behind locked doors was to be final. Although the Federalist majority tried to cloak the measure in secrecy, three copies of the bill were dispatched to the office of the *Aurora*. Duane printed the proposed bill in full on February 19, 1800, labeling it "a bill to influence and affect the approaching Presidential election, and to frustrate in a particular manner the wishes and interests of the people of Pennsylvania."[34] The Senate on March 14 adopted a resolution declaring that Duane's comments were "false, defamatory, scandalous, and malicious" and that publication of the proposed bill was a "daring and high-handed breach of the privileges of this House."[35]

Then began the comic-opera affair of William Duane versus the U.S. Senate. The Senate commanded Duane to appear and answer for his conduct. Duane replied that he would appear if he might be heard by counsel. The Senate agreed, but both Thomas Cooper and Alexander J. Dallas declined to appear for Duane before a Federalist Senate. The editor told the Senate that he considered himself "bound by the most sacred duties to decline any further voluntary attendance upon that body, and leave them to pursue such measures in this case as in their wisdom they may deem meet."[36] Thus, the Senate declared Duane in contempt on March 27, 1800, and issued a warrant to the sergeant-at-arms for the editor's arrest. The Senate spent three hundred dollars and employed twenty-two constables in an effort "to *ferret* out the obstinate democrat," while Duane lived in his own home at No. 106 Market Street and even led a parade of his Republican Greens through the streets of Philadelphia.[37]

Jefferson, as vice president and presiding officer of the Senate, signed the warrant for the arrest of William Duane for contempt of that body. On May 14, 1800, however, the Senate decided to have Duane prosecuted in a court of law rather than in the Senate, and the editor was arrested on a charge of seditious libel on July 30, 1800. On August 2, Duane was brought before District Court Judge Richard Peters, who bound him over to the October term of court and released him on bail of four thousand dollars. During the October term, Duane obtained a continuance until June 11, 1801, and again was released on three-thousand-dollars' bail. The action was still pending when Jefferson assumed office on March 4, 1801.[38]

The new president ordered the suit against Duane dropped, insofar as it was brought under the Sedition Law, but left the way open for a new action under whatever other law might apply. It was clear what Jefferson had in mind, however, for in a memorandum of 1801, he explained that he had abandoned the prosecution against Duane because the case rested mainly on the unconstitutional Sedition Act.[39] However, a grand jury called to enquire into the case failed to find a true bill.[40]

Although Jefferson adhered to orderly legal procedure in this case, he made his sentiments known to Duane in a letter of May 23, 1801, in which the president asked for "an exact list of the prosecutions of a *public* nature against you, & over which I might have control."[41] Jefferson also wrote to R. R. Livingston on behalf of Duane, and prepared a message to the Senate that never left his desk. Jefferson explained in greater detail in this message that he had endeavored

> to do the duty of my station between the Senate and Citizen, to pursue for the former that legal vindication which was the object of their resolution, to cover the latter with whatsoever of protection the Constitution had guarded him & to secure to the press that degree of freedom in which it remained under the authority of the states, with whom alone the power is left of abridging that freedom, the General Government being expressly excluded from it.[42]

The rival Federalist newspaper in Philadelphia, the *Gazette of the United States,* did not view the president's action on behalf of Duane in such a benevolent light. "Juris Consultus" stated:

> If he [Jefferson] has dared to STOP A PUBLIC PROSECUTION, carrying on by the *United States* in one of its *courts of law,* on presentment of a *grand jury,* in any *other* way than by PARDON of the offender, I pronounce that he is an *usurper,* that he has *broken the constitution!* [In that event] I shall raise my feeble voice, on the side of a *solemn protest;* I shall appeal to the *representatives of the people* as the *grand inquest* of the nation, and call on them to find a *bill of* IMPEACHMENT, for a HIGH CRIME against the *constitution* and *people* of the United States of America.[43]

Throughout his career, William Duane was in court more times as participant than as reporter. By 1806 sixty or seventy libel suits had accumulated against him. As Allen Culling Clark has noted, "In the docket the letter D had most entries."[44] The editor also feared for his personal safety. As he wrote to Dr. Caesar Rodney on January 28, 1807, "I have ... judged it more prudent to remain at home than go abroad much, because every idea of Justice is out of the question for me as you know, and tho' I might be killed and my family ruined without justice as was lately the case in Boston ... if I were to wound or kill one of them even in defending myself, a prison and a gibbet would be soon provided for me by corrupt sheriffs and marshals."[45]

At the same time that he feared the wrath of his enemies, Duane also incurred the displeasure of his friends. After the election of 1804, Alexander J. Dallas wrote to Albert Gallatin that Duane's editorial violence had produced "a fatal division" in Pennsylvania politics. Dallas added that he thought "there is reason for Mr. Jefferson himself to apprehend that the spirit of Callender survives."[46] Michael Leib, another Republican acquaintance of Duane's in Philadelphia, had written to Dr. Rodney in 1806: "How illtimed, how unfortunate, how ruinous ... must be these articles of reprobation which have appeared in the Aurora! This paper is considered as the mirror of the sentiments of our party, every thing, therefore, which is restated from it, the party is held responsible for."[47]

In later life Jefferson wrote to Monroe that Duane "is in truth the victim of passions which his principles were not strong enough to control."[48] Yet throughout his presidency and later, Jefferson maintained a continuous correspondence with Duane. In 1809 he wrote to the Philadelphia editor: "I cannot conclude without thanking you for the information you have usefully conveyed to me from time to time, and for the many proofs of your friendship and confidence. I carry into retirement deep-seated feelings for these favors and shall always recollect them with pleasure."[49] John Quincy Adams commented testily in his diary, "I had rather have Duane and his Aurora against me than for me."[50]

In Pennsylvania politics Duane led the radical or antijudiciary faction against Governor Thomas McKean. Duane ran for the Pennsylvania state senate in 1807 but was beaten badly in his only bid for public office.[51] He broke with Albert Gallatin on the issue of federal patronage and ultimately turned against Madison and Monroe. President Jefferson appointed him lieutenant-colonel of rifles in July 1808 and solicited funds to relieve him in 1811. Duane served as adjutant general through the War of 1812 and continued to edit the *Aurora* until 1822, when he made a trip to South America. On his return he tried to revive the *Aurora* to fight the Second Bank of the United States, but the newspaper's name had lost its luster, and the attempt failed. He was made prothonotary of the Supreme Court of Pennsylvania for the eastern district and held this position until his death on November 24, 1835.[52]

The Philadelphia *Aurora* was not without competitors for leading the Republican press of the nation. As the Federalist *Gazette of the United States* stated in 1801, "The two principal mediums through which [the Republicans] convey their poison to the community are the Chronicle, printed at Boston, and the Aurora."[53]

The Boston *Independent Chronicle,* founded in 1776, had also fought the Alien and Sedition Laws of 1798 "openly and with vigor."[54] During Jefferson's presidency the newspaper was a semiweekly published by Abijah Adams and Ebenezer Rhoades. The journal had been controlled by Adams's younger brother Thomas since 1784.

Abijah Adams (1754–1816) was a Bostonian throughout his life: he was born in the city, married the widow Lucy Ballard there on July 11, 1790, and died there at the age of sixty-two. No relationship between this Adams family and the more illustrious Braintree Adams has been traced. Abijah was trained as a tailor and first appeared on the public scene in 1799 as a clerk and bookkeeper in the office of the *Independent Chronicle.* Both brothers were arrested in 1799 for libeling the General Court, which had refused to endorse the Kentucky and Virginia Resolutions on the grounds that it had no right to decide on the constitutionality of an act of Congress.[55] The newspaper had printed on February 18, 1799:

> As it is difficult for common capacities to conceive of a sovereignty so situated that the sovereign shall have no right to decide on any invasion of his constitutional power, it is hoped for the convenience of those tender consciences who may hereafter be called upon to swear allegiance to the State, that some gentleman skilled in federal logic, will show how the oath of allegiance is to be understood, that every man be so guarded and informed, as not to invite the Deity to witness a falsehood.

Thomas Adams, already under federal indictment for violating the Sedition Law, was too ill to appear in court and was never tried on either charge. Abijah Adams received a sentence of thirty days in jail, and Thomas died soon afterward. In 1800 the newspaper passed into the joint control of Abijah Adams and Ebenezer Rhoades, and under these two men it became "the chief supporter in New England of Jeffersonian principles."[56] Principal authority for this statement was a Boston contemporary of Abijah Adams, Joseph T. Buckingham, who later wrote, "For a period of near thirty years, the Chronicle was the principal organ, in New-England, of a large and powerful political party [under] Thomas Jefferson."[57]

The congenital optimism of the Boston *Independent Chronicle* under editor Abijah Adams is evident in its comment on January 1, 1801, six weeks before the election of Thomas Jefferson had become a certainty: "The present era is important—it forms a conspicuous epoch in the American history—the government is to be administered in its Executive department, by THE MAN, whose sentiments are congenial with those manifested in the great instrument of our Independence. That Declaration is his political creed, and while he acts conformable to those principles, the citizens of the United States will have reason to bless the name of JEFFERSON."[58]

Benjamin Austin Jr. (1752–1820), a fellow Bostonian, was a frequent contributor to the *Chronicle* and perhaps its chief editorial writer until Abijah Adams's death in 1816. Descended from New England Tories on his mother's side and the son of a Boston merchant who was a member of the Council of Massachusetts, Benjamin Austin Jr. took a peculiarly independent view of politics when he became a champion of the Jeffersonian cause. During the Revolution he had written patriotic orations published in the Boston press, adding to his reputation in 1786 by proposing reforms in the Massachusetts law in his pamphlet *Observations on the Pernicious Practice of Law*. He was elected to the Massachusetts Senate in 1787 and also served there from 1789 to 1794. Defeated in 1795, he was again elected in 1796, but definitely lost his political control of Boston three weeks later at a town meeting attacking the Jay Treaty.

Austin was never again re-elected to any state government post, but civic activities kept him busy. He was Overseer of the Poor, manager of the Harvard College lotteries, and a leader of the Boston Constitutional Club, founded in 1794. John Quincy Adams described Austin's leadership of a mob of seven hundred democrats, who invaded a town meeting looking "as if they had been collected from all the Jails on the continent, with Ben. Austin like another Jack Cade at their head."[59] Federalists called the Republican writer "Lank Honestus with his lanthorn jaws." Samuel Eliot Morison has written: "Although regarded as a dangerous radical, Austin was essentially a conservative always opposing local improvements and changes. He liked the political vintage of 1775 (Sam Adams) too well to accept the new wine of Federalism."[60]

Austin's longer and more important contributions to the Boston *Independent Chronicle* were written under the pseudonyms of "Brutus" during the Revolution, "Honestus" in articles that ran from March 9 to June 15, 1786, "Old South" after 1795, and "Examiner" after 1812. His most famous nickname was "Old South," earned by his discussion of the town meetings held in the Old South Meetinghouse to argue the merits of the Jay Treaty. This series was republished in 1803 in an octavo volume of more than three-hundred pages, *Constitutional Republicanism, in Opposition to Fallacious Federalism; as Published Occasionally in the Independent Chronicle*. This production won him an appointment by the Jefferson administration as federal commissioner of loans in Boston.[61]

The most famous incident of Austin's journalistic career occurred in 1806, when he accused T. O. Selfridge, a Federalist lawyer, of barratry in the columns of the *Chronicle*. On August 4, 1806, his son Charles Austin assaulted Selfridge with a hickory stick and was shot dead. As Morison pointed out, "The trial of Selfridge for manslaughter developed into a contest of strength between Federalists and Republicans; his acquittal by a Federalist jury, following a charge by Justice Parker, added bitterness to the party conflict."[62]

Other writers for the Boston *Independent Chronicle* included Perez Morton, later attorney general of Massachusetts, and Dr. Charles Jarvis, often a representative from Boston in the General Court before the period of Federalist ascendancy, but none could match the flowing eloquence of Benjamin Austin Jr., who should be rated one of the most accomplished partisan journalists of the period. In his last years Austin was twice elected a member of the Board of Selectmen of Boston. Soon after his second election, he died at the age of sixty-nine on May 4, 1820.[63]

Throughout his career Abijah Adams was a staunch supporter of the Virginia Dynasty and "Mr. Madison's War," and after 1804 he was joined by the *Richmond Enquirer*'s Thomas Ritchie in defending and promoting the federal administrations guided by Virginians. Thomas Ritchie (1778–1854) became the prototype of the paternal editor who thought he guided the political thinking of an entire state, a type that became more common as the nineteenth century progressed and that survived into the twentieth century in such figures as William Allen White of Emporia, Kansas. Ritchie was born in Tappahannock, Essex County, Virginia, the son of Archibald Ritchie, a Scots immigrant and the community's leading businessman. Young Thomas Ritchie first tried his hand at reading law, studying medicine in Philadelphia, teaching in Fredericksburg, and running a small bookstore in Richmond before he found his calling in journalism.[64]

Ritchie moved to Richmond in 1803, four years after the town had become the state capital. The editor's biographer, Charles Henry Ambler, has written that Richmond at the time was a "Federalist stronghold" and that its leading citizens were "either soldiers or officers of the Revolutionary Army."[65] The previous Republican newspaper in Richmond, the *Examiner* edited by Skelton Jones, had folded because of lack of support; Judge Spencer Roane, under whom Ritchie had read law, wanted another partisan journal established, and Thomas Jefferson—interested always in Virginia affairs—promised federal support. Thus, the *Richmond Enquirer* first appeared as a biweekly on May 9, 1804. Editor Ritchie paid little attention to advertising, anchoring the newspaper on political patronage and subscriptions, which increased from 500 to 1,500 during the first eighteen months. "Without official patronage," Ambler remarked, "it could not have lived in so strong a Federalist atmosphere as Richmond and in competition with a well established and popular press," the Federalist *Richmond Gazette*.[66] Ritchie's business management of the newspaper was so successful that he continued to edit the newspaper for forty-one years.

Thomas Ritchie was a moderate conservative and a table aristocrat, a great compromiser and conciliator, and a strict-constructionist to the day of his death. It is impossible to measure the influence of the *Richmond Enquirer*, but it became one of the most powerful regional papers of its era. In the judgment of Ambler, "The first office of the *Enquirer* was to echo and re-echo the utterances of the *National Intelligencer* and the thoughts of the federal administration until they became the utterances and the thoughts of the common people."[67] C. C. Pearson has written, "Probably no other editor of his time was equally successful in holding in the bonds of friendship a varied host of men, and in securing for his paper discussions of the greatest public questions by men whose opinions carried the weight of authority."[68]

We have noted the reluctance with which Ritchie entered public debate on national issues, and the editor was grateful that the Louisiana Purchase was an accomplished fact when he started his newspaper so he would never have to comment on its constitutionality.[69] Nor did Thomas Ritchie feel that Thomas Jefferson could do no wrong. The president's method of dealing with Spain was judged by the *Enquirer* a "melancholy example" of Jefferson's human frailties, although he was still "a man of most unblemished integrity, a man whose administration had manifested no less vigilance than virtue."[70]

In July 1807—less than six months after his marriage to Isabella Foushee on February 11, 1807—Thomas Ritchie marched off to Norfolk with the Republican Blues. Ritchie and the militia unit were intent on redressing recent British outrages on American shipping. He served briefly in the War of 1812, and in 1814 the state legislature elected him state printer, a position he held for twenty-five years except for a short interval in 1834. He also edited the Richmond *Compiler* for several years around 1830, and he was in Washington from 1845 to 1851 publishing the *Union* as spokesman for the Polk administration.[71]

Thomas Ritchie has been described as "a tall, lean, quick-moving man, with brilliant eyes and striking profile, always clinging to the old low shoes and silk stockings, secretary of all the public meetings, toast-master of the dinners, leader of the dances, welcomer of distinguished guests, the state's 'Father Ritchie,' his intimates' 'Tom Ritchie.'"[72] He was the essence of the country gentleman, and he consciously edited the *Richmond Enquirer* for this class, to whom the newspaper was an "intellectual necessity."[73]

Like Samuel Harrison Smith of the *National Intelligencer,* Thomas Ritchie tried to keep his Richmond newspaper on a high moral plane. Ambler maintained, "To Ritchie more than to any one of his contemporaries the press of today owes a debt of gratitude for the high ethical conceptions which he brought to and made a part of his profession."[74] Yet even William Duane of the vituperative Philadelphia *Aurora* recognized the moral obligations of a newspaper editor, and late in life Duane felt he had discharged these obligations with honor: "I never admit into my paper accounts of murders, robberies, crimes and despertitions, because habits make good or bad news, and familiarity with tales of crimes will blunt the faculties and form habits of indifference to crime."[75] It is a curious fact that editors in the first decade of the nineteenth century felt no compunction about charging rival editors with every human and inhuman vice, yet daintily excluded accounts of the realities of American life from the columns of their newspapers.

Ritchie and Duane, the Republican editors of Richmond and Philadelphia, disliked each other with mutual relish. Duane seemed jealous of Ritchie's preferred position in the heart of the Virginia Dynasty country, and the Richmond editor condescended to answer Duane's sarcastic comments in a four-column reply on June 4, 1805. "You may think the comparison a vain one," Ritchie informed his readers, "but I feel at present like the traveller on the top of the Alps, who hears the thunders rolling beneath his feet without danger or without perturbation."[76]

It was perhaps inevitable that in an age of personal journalism the press should come to be regarded as a personal weapon, which some thought unfortunately obscured rather than enlightened public issues. As William Duane wrote to Thomas Jefferson in 1801, "I had determined before the election, that upon the success of the people's choice, I should dispose of the paper and pursue another profession, but I find the hatred so violent against me that it would follow me for ever, and in any other situation I should not possess such formidable means of defence."[77]

Yet, as we have noted before, the more or less violent tone of journalism in the first decade of the nineteenth century must be understood in its historical context. As Allan Nevins has commented:

> In noting this abusiveness it must be remembered that the press was the product and mirror of its time. Politics was conducted with far more scurrility and coarseness than now, and the newspapers were largely an appendage of politics. A day of backwoods gouging and fashionable dueling, of constant fighting between street gangs in all the large cities, of fisticuffs on the floor of the House of Representatives, of a low standard of manners everywhere, was not a day for refined newspaper methods.[78]

In the judgment of recent students of this topic, "the press always takes on the form and coloration of the social and political structures within which it operates."[79] Moreover, H. W. Boynton has pointed out, "Upon the character of the daily press . . . depends the character of our entire periodical product; and this means, in large measure, the character of the public taste."[80]

Republican editors were also driven to harsh language because of the overwhelming strength of the opposition press, for in some areas Federalist newspapers outnumbered their political rivals by as much as five to one.[81] Abijah Adams bravely commanded an outpost of Republicanism in Federalist Boston, and Thomas Ritchie defied the political mores of Richmond to present the Republican side of current discussions of public affairs. William Duane wrote recklessly, faced countless libel suits, and at one time feared for his life. Samuel Harrison Smith declined to enter debate on incendiary partisan issues, and his stature as an editor was not enhanced by this abdication. Partisan journalism demanded an active engagement in the events of the day that would brook no timidity or second thoughts.

These editors were the men who guided the major Republican newspapers during the first broadly defined period of partisan journalism in American

history. Some of them, notably Duane and Adams, entered the newspaper battles of the Jefferson years with previous scars and triumphs; others, Smith and
Ritchie, were relative newcomers to the trials of political journalism. It is significant that the latter two men remained somewhat aloof from the more virulent
engagements in newsprint, but as time progressed they too tended to fight on
the same terms with their more vigorous contemporaries.

Thomas Jefferson himself regarded the storm and fury as a necessary con-
comitant to the power and effectiveness of a political press. Jefferson's luminous
comments on the value of a free press in a free society are now well known to
all, and the unmerciful verbal flogging he received at the hands of Federalist editors makes more admirable his recovery of these sentiments in later life after a
period of profound disillusionment with the conduct of the press.[82] Two years
before his death, Thomas Jefferson wrote to William Duane:

> I am long since withdrawn from the political world. I think little, read less,
> and know all but nothing of what is going on; but I have not forgotten the past,
> nor those who were fellow-laborers in the gloomy hours of federal ascendancy,
> when the spirit of republicanism was beaten down, its votaries arraigned as
> criminals, and such threats denounced as posterity will never believe.[83]

Mark Twain once quipped that doctors bury their mistakes, while journalists
publish theirs. His point was well taken. Republican editors in the years between
1801 and 1809 revealed many instances of political mistakes and personal malice,
but they functioned in a society that could afford mistakes and tolerate malice.
Like their Federalist brethren, the Republican newsmen fought for a cause that
to them was noble if not ennobling.

THREE

Federalist Editors
"Monumental Columns"

There is not a single man of truth
among all the Jacobin Editors whose papers we see.

—*Gazette of the United States,* June 15, 1801

The fact is, too many of our presses are the exclusive property of sects and
parties, and their editors but the twilight shadows of bodies without souls.

—J. T. Buckingham, about 1830, quoted in Alfred McClung Lee,
The Daily Newspaper in America, The Evolution of a Social Instrument

Critics of the press point out the embarrassing fact that in some widely contested presidential elections in the United States, victory has gone to the candidate with decidedly minor press support. The first such upset in American
history occurred in 1800, when fully three-fourths of the country's 235 newspapers were controlled by the defeated Federalists. Alfred McClung Lee has endeavored to salvage the reputation of the press in such one-sided contests by
claiming that the Jeffersonian triumph of 1800 was "an indication of the [lack
of] power of the press when it does not represent mass interests."[1] Yet the fact
remains that not only did the overwhelmingly more powerful Federalist press
lose the election of 1800, it was also unable to stem the growing ascendancy of
Republicanism for the next twenty-four years. Moreover, the period of Jefferson's
presidency was also the brightest period in the development of the Federalist
press. During these eight years the *New-York Evening Post* was founded for partisan purposes and destined for a brilliant future. As Bernard A. Weisberger has
pointed out," the *Post* outlived Hamilton, outlived the battles of the Jeffersonian
era, outlived Coleman, and has in fact survived until the present day."[2]

During the years 1801 to 1809, the Federalist press also recruited for its cause
the erratic and unprincipled James Thomson Callender, a one-time Jeffersonian
who conducted a vendetta against his former benefactor in the columns of the
Richmond *Recorder* (1801–3). The Philadelphia *Gazette of the United States* during

Jefferson's administrations lacked the luster it had had under the leadership of John Fenno but continued to be spokesman for the Federalist press at large under the editorial guidance of Enos Bronson. And no newspaper in the country could match the imposing authority of the Boston *Columbian Centinel* under Major Benjamin Russell, who considered himself the keeper of the Federalist flame of truth and political righteousness.

It was during these years that the young *New-York Evening Post* (founded on November 16, 1801) successfully challenged the venerable *Gazette of the United States* (1790–1819) for the mantle of Federalist leadership. The decline of the Philadelphia newspaper began with the death from yellow fever of John Fenno in 1798 and was hastened by the removal of the national capital to Washington, D.C., in 1800. After the death of Fenno, his son John Ward Fenno published the newspaper until he sold it to Caleb P. Wayne in 1800. Frightened by the loss of political support and the removal of the capital, Wayne sold the *Gazette* in 1801 to Enos Bronson, who took Elihu Chauncey into partnership in 1802. Despite the frequent changes in editorial supervision, the *Gazette of the United States* continued to espouse the Federalist cause, and minor Federalist editors throughout the country continued to rely on the *Gazette*'s former prestige for cues on political issues of the day.

Enos Bronson (1774–1823) is one of the forgotten figures of American journalism. Neglected by the *Dictionary of American Biography* and unknown to writers about the press, Bronson was truly one of those powerful but faceless "twilight shadows" of Federalism noted by J. T. Buckingham. Yet he was a man of considerable accomplishments, one who could easily match the polished background of William Coleman of the *New-York Evening Post*.[3] Graduated from Yale College at the age of twenty-two, Bronson became the first principal of Deerfield Academy in Massachusetts before going to Philadelphia near the end of the century. He became associated with Caleb P. Wayne in editing the *Gazette of the United States* during the violent presidential election of 1800. Encouraged by his journalistic efforts, Bronson bought out Wayne, who had suffered seven libel prosecutions during his last year as editor of the newspaper, on November 2, 1801. Bronson inherited the once-proud *Gazette of the United States* in a weakened condition, with a subscription list that had dwindled from three thousand to eight hundred.

Yet Bronson interjected a new tone into the newspaper's columns and more money into the till by publishing such works as Roscoe's *Life of Lorenzo de Medici* (1797) and *Life and Pontificate of Leo X* (1805), and a multivolume set of the *Works of James Wilson* (1804). Dr. Nathaniel Chapman, his physician and friend, said that Bronson wrote editorials in the *Gazette*'s office, "a most aggressive Federalist headquarters," while surrounded by friends discussing politics; and as the printer's devil asked for more copy, Bronson would give him what he had written without corrections.[4]

Of retiring disposition, Enos Bronson made no great splash in journalistic circles, and he appears to have had little sense of business management, an aspect of the publishing enterprise that he left to his partner Elihu Chauncey, by far the more colorful of the two men. Chauncey was taken into partnership on May 19, 1802, and the two dissimilar men continued to edit and manage the newspaper until they sold it to the firm of Selden & Sanford on May 22, 1819.[5]

If Enos Bronson had an enemy in the world, it was "that prostitute and venal slave [William Duane]," editor of the rival Republican newspaper, the Philadelphia *Aurora*. On December 16, 1801, the *Gazette of the United States* commented: "It is said that Mr. Jefferson invited Duane to dine with him. We should be glad to know if the invitation was given for a public day; for it would be a curious sight to see the President of the United States of America sitting at dinner, with Duane on one hand, talking Irish, and Mr. Gallatin from Geneva, with his broken French, on the other." There was no love lost between the scholarly Enos Bronson and the robust William Duane, who spent his leisure hours composing military manuals.

Bronson was perhaps the most moderate Federalist who ever guided the policy of the *Gazette of the United States*. While the names of other editors were bandied about in the public prints frequently, Bronson seems to have drawn fire on only one occasion—a diatribe printed in the rival *Aurora* before Bronson took over control of the newspaper. William Duane, anxious to prove that the *Gazette* was a hireling of the British faction, stated in the *Aurora*: "The Gazette of the United States has about 800 subscribers—it has an idle young man of the name of *Wayne* as its nominal proprietor—a raw young man of the name of *Brinston* or *Brimstone* [Bronson] as its editor, and as a subordinate the *Chauncey*. QUERY—Who pays them? The profits of 800 subscribers to a daily paper would not buy *molasses* for their *mush*."[6] This meager subscription list was proof enough in Duane's eyes that the British paid the distressed young men of the foundering *Gazette,* and it was Bronson's misfortune that the Massachusetts pronunciation of his name led Duane to confuse it with "Brinston," an easy springboard to "Brimstone."

Never again did William Duane find occasion to ridicule his opponent, a modest young man who stated to his readers on taking over the newspaper: "I shall not fatigue [your] patience by a tedious recital of perfections, which one man might easily imagine, but which a hundred would not be able to attain."[7] This promise ranks as perhaps the only honest prospectus in the history of American journalism. But Bronson quietly edited a capable newspaper, one that tended to drift away from its earlier Federalist moorings. Under Bronson's editorship the *Gazette* even criticized the conduct of John Adams, both during and after his presidential term, a circumstance unthinkable to Timothy Dwight, who wrote Bronson on January 21, 1802:

I have, since my arrival in this town [Philadelphia], been informed, that some disadvantageous observations have been made concerning Mr. Adams in your paper. I cannot but think any such thing would better be wholly omitted. Were I present, I would, I think, persuade you of this truth. I know it to be the opinion of the most respectable Men, of my acquaintance, from Boston to New York. I think the most exact delicacy should be observed on this subject. I know you will believe this hint kindly given, & will therefore receive it kindly.[8]

Enos Bronson may be considered the last significant editor of the *Gazette of the United States*. That the newspaper continued to exert some influence in Federalist circles (who fielded their last presidential candidate in 1812) after the loss of political printing and close contact with government officials was the minor triumph of Bronson.

What happened to this once proud and powerful party? In the judgment of Daniel J. Boorstin, "The Federalist school—contemporary with the Jeffersonians—was not (except perhaps in those features which it shared with the Jeffersonians) especially qualified to express the American intellectual temper of the nineteenth century."[9] They had quality newspapers such as the *New-York Evening Post* and dominated what few magazines the country had because the latter were expensive and therefore limited to the upper classes. They did not reach the common people, whose tastes were neither literary nor politically conservative, as did the *New-England Palladium* or even more so Joseph Dennie's *Port Folio*, which has been described by William C. Dowling "as a last permanent sanctuary from Jeffersonian democracy."[10]

What else did Americans of that time have to read? The Library Company of Philadelphia, first in the city, was founded by Benjamin Franklin and friends in 1731, but it was not a lending library. Southern plantation owners maintained their own private libraries, which perhaps partly explains why literature has flourished in the South. An inventory of nine eighteenth-century Virginians' libraries reveals that the most frequent books found were Blackstone and Montesquieu, valued for their utility and prominence. After all, eight presidents came from Virginia, and Herbert E. Sloan, who did the survey, found "that gentry Virginians were, broadly speaking, familiar with major mid-century works of history and political economy and, moreover, that they thought it important—for whatever reason—to have such works in their personal collections."[11]

On the newspaper front, the *New-York Evening Post* was gaining steadily in circulation and prestige. Its origins were far from auspicious, however. As Allan Nevins has observed, "The spring of 1801, when plans were laid for issuing the *Evening Post,* was the blackest season the Federalists of New York had yet known . . . . [and] for [Alexander] Hamilton himself, inasmuch as many of his own party deemed him responsible for the disaster which had overtaken it, the hour was doubly black."[12] Hamilton needed to defend himself from the Adams wing of the Federalist Party, still outraged over Hamilton's imprudent letter that had found its way into the opposition press before the election of 1800. What better way to restore Federalist standing, and to attack the triumphant Republicans, than to establish a newspaper in New York City devoted to the Hamiltonian brand of Federalism?

Everything in Alexander Hamilton's background indicated that he would turn to the medium of the press to present his case. From his early youth he had been intimately associated with journalism. He had won his college education at Kings College, New York, by an impressive article in a St. Kitts newspaper, and he had contributed to John Holt's *New-York Journal* during the Revolution, while he was still a student. Hamilton's national reputation was established by his brilliant contributions to *The Federalist* series published in the New York *Independent Journal* in 1787–88 to drum up support for the new federal Constitution. Hamilton had encouraged the Boston schoolmaster John Fenno to establish the *Gazette of the United States* in 1789, and he had delved into his own pocket for one thousand dollars to save the newspaper in 1793. According to Nevins, "Hamilton also financially assisted William Cobbett, the best journalist of his time in England or America, to initiate his newspaper campaign against the Democratic haters of England." Moreover, Hamilton and Rufus King had provided part of the capital with which Noah Webster launched the *Minerva* in Philadelphia in 1793, for which Hamilton and King wrote the series of "Camillus" papers on the Jay Treaty. In short, Alexander Hamilton was never far away from some journalistic endeavor. Nevins believes, "If Hamilton's unsigned contributions to the Federalist press from 1790 to 1800 could be identified, they would form an important addition to his works."[13]

Newspapers had become expensive properties. As mentioned earlier, Judge Samuel Chase and others needed eight thousand dollars to establish the Baltimore *Anti-Democrat* in 1801, and that same year ten thousand dollars was required to launch the *New-York Evening Post*. Hamilton and his New York friends secretly circulated a founders' list among trusted Federalists, who were each expected to contribute a minimum of one hundred dollars.[14] Hamilton himself contributed not less than one thousand dollars. Other prominent backers were the businessman Samuel Boyd, the dismissed collector Joshua Sands, and one of the richest and most dignified of the New York merchants, Archibald Gracie. The money was not given outright but "loaned," and the debt was discharged without payment or protest in 1810. In the summer of 1801 a splendid brick office was prepared on Pine Street, and subscriptions were solicited soon after the first of November. The *New-York Evening Post* appeared on November 16, 1801, with a list of 600 original subscribers that read like a roster of the inner councils of the New York Federalist Party.[15]

Selected to edit the newspaper was William Coleman (1766–1829), who has been described as "the most effective Federalist journalist of the period of Hamilton's leadership."[16] Coleman became editor of the *New-York Evening Post* at the age of thirty-five after a somewhat unsuccessful earlier career. His unusual promise as a youth had won him funds to attend Andover Academy, and he later received an honorary degree from Dartmouth College. He studied law under Robert Treat Paine, signer of the Declaration of Independence and judge of the Massachusetts Supreme Court, interrupting his studies to march with the militia during Shays' Rebellion. Coleman began to practice law at Greenfield, Massachusetts, where he also established the *Impartial Intelligencer.* His articles in this newspaper won him a place in the Massachusetts legislature in 1795 and 1796, but unwise speculation in the Yazoo land frauds ruined him financially. He tried to recoup his fortunes in a business partnership with Aaron Burr—an association that Coleman regretted to his dying day—and in a law partnership with John Wells, a brilliant young Federalist attorney. Coleman had arrived in New York penniless, but Wells introduced him to members of the Federalist Friendly Club, and Alexander Hamilton—whom Coleman had first met when Hamilton toured New England in 1796—helped him to obtain a government position as clerk of the circuit court. Jefferson's election in 1800 cost Coleman this three-thousand-dollar-a-year job, and he became editor of the *New-York Evening Post.*[17]

The prospectus of the fresh young newspaper stated: "Though we openly profess our attachment to that system of politics denominated FEDERAL, because we think it the most conducive to the welfare of the community, and the best calculated to ensure permanency to our present form of government, yet we disapprove of that spirit of dogmatism which lays exclusive claim to infallibility; and willingly believe that honest and virtuous men are to be found in each party."[18] The mission of the *New-York Evening Post* was to supply the people of the country with "correct information, to enable them to judge of what is really best." The editor guaranteed that his newspaper would be "equally free to all parties . . . . But . . . we never will give currency to any thing scurrilous, indecent, immoral, or profane, or which may contravene the essential principles of social order."[19]

In its third issue the *New-York Evening Post* expanded on this theme, advising its patrons that it would strive for intra-party harmony:

> It has been long since observed, that the cause of FEDERALISM has received as much injury from the indiscreet contentions and bickerings among those who profess to be its friends, as from the open assaults of its enemies. . . . With sincerity then the Editor declares that it will always be his wish and endeavor to promote a spirit of harmony and conciliation among those who, forgetful of petty distinctions, little rivalships, or unessential shades of opinion, are disposed to unite in their exertions to maintain the CONSTITUTION AND LAWS. . . .[20]

One historian of American journalism has written that Alexander Hamilton founded the *New-York Evening Post* more to influence New York state politics rather than to establish a national organ.[21] Another historian has stated that none of the New York papers wielded much influence outside the city itself, pointing out that "the mentor of the Democratic Republican journals of the state was the Albany *Evening Register*.[22] Both scholars vastly underestimated the ambitions of Alexander Hamilton. One has only to read the columns of the *Evening Post* to realize how deeply the newspaper was enmeshed in national issues. The population of New York City in 1801 was sixty thousand persons living south of City Hall, certainly enough to support an urban newspaper, but this type of journal was unknown in the early nineteenth century. All newspapers other than purely local commercial and shipping sheets were concerned with national politics and aimed at an audience beyond their immediate environs.[23]

Other Federalist newspapers greeted the appearance of the *New-York Evening Post* with open arms and brotherly affection. Said the *Gazette of the United States*, with becoming generosity, "Federalism has much to hope and expect from this paper. The talents and activity of WILLIAM COLEMAN, Esquire, the Editor, are such as entitle him to the attention and liberal encouragement of all who realize the importance of well conducted papers."[24] In his enthusiasm, the *Gazette* writer couched his praise in a mixed metaphor, stating that the *New-York Evening Post* promised to become "a strong and ornamental pillar in the fabric of Federalism."[25] It was with a touch of envy that the *Gazette of the United States* added: "Those who look at the *advertisements* in that paper will perceive by what means such elegance can be afforded. The mercantile gentlemen of New-York deserve much commendation for the very prompt and liberal manner in which they have proffered their encouragement. . . . "[26]

Printers everywhere hailed the superb typography of the *New-York Evening Post.* From the columns of the Richmond *Examiner,* came words of praise from James Thomson Callender: "This newspaper is, beyond all comparison, the most elegant piece of workmanship that we have seen, either in Europe or America."[27] The *Gazette of the United States* agreed with Callender's judgment: "The Evening Post is printed upon a type entirely new, and in a style by far superior to that of any other news-paper in the United States."[28]

From its birth the *Evening Post* was an affluent newspaper, one that boasted four complete fonts of type in a period of publishing difficulties when most newspapers could hardly muster one set.[29] The weekly edition was sent for $3.50 a year, and the daily edition cost $8.00. Within a short time, the *Evening Post* outstripped the *New York Post*'s circulation of 1100 by 500 copies.[30] The subscription prices limited circulation more than anything else in a period when skilled workers such as journeyman printers received only six to eight dollars a week in wages. As Willard Grosvenor Bleyer has remarked, "Editors were no doubt glad to have politically minded workingmen and clerks read newspapers in taverns [a considerable secondary circulation], but they edited their journals for the classes and not for the masses."[31]

Less than a year after William Coleman started editing the *New-York Evening Post*, James Thomson Callender dubbed him "Field-Marshal of the Federalist editors."[32] Until that time, however, the exact status of Coleman was perplexing to his fellow editors. As James Cheetham commented in the rival Jeffersonian newspaper, the New York *American Citizen:*

> Mr. Coleman says that to pay a man for writing against the late Administration was a crime. He will allow that the application of the rule will be just when applied to the present Administration. We then say that Mr. Coleman receives the wages of sin; for he is in every sense of the word paid for writing *against* the present Administration. The establishment at the head of which he is, is said not to be his *own;* it is said to belong to a company, of which General Hamilton is one. The paper was commenced for the avowed purpose of opposing the Administration. Mr. Coleman, it is believed, receives a yearly salary for writing for it, and for his wages he is bound to write against the Administration, whether the sentiments he pens accord with his own or not. He runs no risk, he has no responsibility upon his shoulders. He may, in fact, be called a mere hireling.[33]

Coleman was not one to let such an insult pass unnoticed. He met the charge straight on, declaring that *"not one word of it is true."* Explained the editor, "The establishment of the *Evening Post* is, and always since its commencement has been, the sole property of the editor: it does not, or did it ever, belong to a company, or to General Hamilton, or to any one else but the editor; and lastly, the editor is not a *hireling,* nor has he at any period of his life received *wages for writing."*[34]

So it was that William Coleman declared his editorial independence. Yet no one doubted that Alexander Hamilton was the guiding light behind the newspaper's editorial policy and probably contributed rather frequently to the journal. Allan Nevins is the best authority on this topic:

> From 1801 to 1804 only a single bit of signed writing from Hamilton's pen appeared in the *Evening Post.* This was a communication denying the hoary legend, originally circulated in derogation of Washington and Lafayette, that at Yorktown Lafayette had ordered Hamilton to put to death all British prisoners in the redoubt which he was sent forward to capture and that he had declined to obey the inhumane command. But a much more important contribution was hardly concealed. This was a series of articles upon President Jefferson's first annual message, written under the signature "Lucius Crassus" and published irregularly from December 17, 1801, until April 8, 1802. They were eighteen in all, and not equal to Hamilton's best work.[35]

As for other writings by Hamilton in the *Evening Post,* "All other contributions must be sought for upon internal evidence, and such evidence can never be conclusive." It is possible that Hamilton dictated part or all of the attack of April 19, 1803, on the Manhattan bank founded by De Witt Clinton's faction; that he outlined an article of July 9, 1803, on neutrality, and that he assisted later in the same month in an article on the funding system, land tax, and national debt. "But it is bootless to pile up such conjectures. The editorials upon the diplomatic aspects of the Louisiana treaty, the Chase impeachment, and the navigation of the Mississippi certainly represented Hamilton's views," Nevins concluded[36]

Thus, Alexander Hamilton participated fully in the general conduct of the *New-York Evening Post,* but as Frank Luther Mott has pointed out, "Coleman was by no means a mere amanuensis."[37] He was of a far too vigorous cast of mind to accept the role of editorial yes-man or to be content with a purely mechanical role. The continued forceful leadership of the *Evening Post* after Hamilton's death in 1804 is the best evidence of William Coleman's own editorial strength and integrity.

Having studied classical Greek and Latin at Andover Academy did not prevent Coleman from meeting other editors in the arena of verbal fisticuffs common to the journalism of the day. Less than a year after the *Evening Post* was founded, the Philadelphia *Aurora* was complaining:

> The paper of *Alexander Hamilton* at New York has assumed the *full toned* grossness and vulgarity of *Porcupine* and *Callender*—their morals and their principles are congenial; to them nothing is so abhorrent as the Aurora. While we feel a pride in their hatred, and it is a just cause of pride to be an object of *fear* and *hatred* to the vilest men in a community—we shall pursue our course steadily, and laugh at the insolent stupidity which they substitute for argument, and the mendacity which they employ to escape from the exposure of their crimes.[38]

Yet Nevins observed, "It is evidence of the comparatively moderate tone of the *Evening Post* that no suit against it ever succeeded, though a number were begun."[39] The historian of the *New-York Evening Post* added, "Coleman's chief faults were three. His style, like Hamilton's was diffuse; he sometimes forgot taste and decency in assailing his opponents; and he was a wretched business man." The printer Michael Burnham corrected Coleman's business deficiency by becoming half owner a few years later after the newspaper was founded.[40]

Coleman continued to edit the *New-York Evening Post* until his death in 1829, and he left the newspaper in the hands of a young man named William Cullen Bryant, who saw it through a distinguished half century. During Coleman's editorship, the *Evening Post* wrested the leadership of the Federalist press in the United States from the declining *Gazette of the United States* in Philadelphia and the less active Boston *Columbian Centinel.* No newspaper editor in America rivaled the power and prestige of William Coleman except William Duane, his counterpart as undisputed leader of the Republican press. As James Thomson Callender commented in 1802, "The people of America derive their political information chiefly from newspapers. Duane upon one side, and Coleman upon the other, dictate at this moment the sentiments of perhaps fifty thousand American citizens."[41]

Frank Luther Mott has commented that in the early period of the party press, 1783 to 1801, "it was a Boston newspaper, the *Columbia Centinel,* which enjoyed the highest esteem of Federalist editors generally."[42] The newspaper was founded on March 24, 1784, by Major Benjamin Russell as the *Massachusetts Centinel and the Republican Journal,* but as the connotation of the word *Republican* changed, the journal was enlarged on June 16, 1790, and rechristened the *Columbian Centinel.*[43]

Frederic Hudson stated that the *Columbian Centinel* was after the Revolution what the *Massachusetts Spy* and the *Boston Gazette* were before the war—"the popular guide in Massachusetts."[44] No other newspaper of the period was so closely identified with the personality of the man who edited it for forty-two years, Major Benjamin Russell (1761–1845). The son of a Boston mason, Russell had learned the printing trade in the shop of Isaiah Thomas before the Revolution broke out. On April 19, 1775, he followed a detachment of patriot troops to Cambridge and was cut off from his home for three months. Soundly thrashed on his return, he enlisted in the army at the time of the Declaration of Independence, but since he was not yet sixteen he was soon released. In 1780 he joined the army at West Point, serving as a substitute for Isaiah Thomas. Russell was a member of the guard at the execution of Major John André but saw no military engagement. After his six months' enlistment expired, he married Esther Rice of Worcester on September 21, 1783, and founded the *Massachusetts Centinel and the Republican Journal* as a semiweekly on March 24, 1784. At the end of the second year, Russell bought out his partner, William Warden, and continued to own and edit the *Centinel* until his retirement from journalism in 1828.[45]

His newspaper has been called "the most enterprising and influential in Massachusetts."[46] Its first great cause was the adoption of the federal Constitution. Russell attended the sessions of the Massachusetts Constitutional Convention in a Boston church and reported the proceedings by using the pulpit for a writing desk.[47] He devised a masthead cartoon, adding each state as a column in the federal edifice to announce each new ratification. A devout Federalist, he delighted in dwelling on the funeral obsequies of the opposition on the inauguration of Washington and Adams.[48] When Thomas Paine (later Robert Treat Paine Jr.) showed Russell his poem "Adams and Liberty," the Federalist editor dismissed it with the comment, "You have not introduced the name of Washington."[49] He once declined payment for printing federal laws in the early days of the republic, prompting George Washington to assert, "This must not be. When Mr. Russell offered to publish the laws without pay, we were poor. It was a generous offer. We are now able to pay our debts. This is a debt of honor, and must be discharged." A check for seven thousand dollars was sent to Russell.[50]

On March 4, 1801, Major Russell published an epitaph for the tombstone of his own party:

Monumental Inscription.

———

"That life is long which answers Life's great end."

———

YESTERDAY EXPIRED

Deeply regretted by MILLIONS of grateful Americans,

And by *all* GOOD MEN,

The FEDERAL ADMINISTRATION

Of the

GOVERNMENT of the *United States;*

Animated by

A WASHINGTON, an ADAMS;—a HAMILTON, KNOX,

PICKERING, WOLCOTT, M'HENRY, MARSHALL

STODDERT and DEXTER.

Aet. 12 years.[51]

More than its contemporaries, the Boston *Columbian Centinel* was interested in literature as well as politics. Russell presented to his readers nearly all of Oliver Goldsmith's poems, the narrative of Captain James Cook's voyages, Allan Cunningham's pastorals, and portions of works by William Cowper, Thomas Gray, and other British poets.[52] Yet the *Columbian Centinel* was chief spokesman for the Federalist forces of Boston and much of New England, and the newspaper clearly recognized its political role. When Thomas Jefferson was inaugurated as the third president of the United States, the Boston *Columbian Centinel* declared, "As a Centinel, we will sound the alarm, and faithfully make report of our discoveries of the disposition, force, and movements of our country's foes. Further we need not say."[53]

Like the later Republican editor of Richmond, Thomas Ritchie, Benjamin Russell assumed an active role in the social life of Boston—serving as toastmaster at important public dinners, welcoming visiting dignitaries, planning civic improvements, and doing a great deal to advance the local prestige of the newspaper editor. A list of his civic functions is impressive; Russell seemed to be an inveterate "joiner." He joined others in founding the Massachusetts Charitable Mechanic Association in 1795, serving as president of this organization from 1808 to 1817. He was also president of the Faustus Association, a protective society of printers, and president of the Boston board of health from 1806 to 1810. Russell served as a member of the common council from the organization of this city government in 1822 until 1826. In 1829 he was elected alderman and re-elected for three successive years. First elected to the Massachusetts House of Representatives in 1805, he was re-elected every year up to 1821. In 1822 and 1825 he served as senator from the county of Suffolk, and he was a representative from Boston from 1828 to 1835. His last public service was as a member of the executive council, elected by the legislature for 1836–37. His wife died in 1837, after a married life of forty years, and Russell died on January 4, 1845, at the age of eighty-four.[54]

The *Columbian Centinel*'s partisan rival in Boston was the *Independent Chronicle,* edited by Thomas Adams and his brother Abijah. Frank Luther Mott has called the latter newspaper "the leading New England representative of the Republican party, as the *Centinel* was of the Federalists."[55] There was no love lost between Major Russell and the Adams brothers or their chief contributor, Benjamin Austin Jr., who referred to the *Centinel* editor as "that fellow, Ben Russell." The *Columbian Centinel* had its own choice stable of writers, including Fisher Ames, John Lowell, George Cabot, Stephen Higginson, and Timothy Pickering.[56] In a brief lull in the partisan warfare between the two newspapers, the Boston *Independent Chronicle* remarked, "We feel gratified, however, to perceive that the Editor of the *Centinel* has laid aside his *billingsgate*—we are not without hope of inducing him to treat his adversaries with some *decency;* though, at times, we are afraid of having undertaken *to white-wash a Moor*'s head."[57]

Benjamin Russell's rise to power and influence occurred at the wrong time, for throughout most of his editorial life he faced Republican administrations in the federal government. He regarded the election of Thomas Jefferson a national calamity, and not a single act of Jefferson's or Madison's administrations won a word of approval from the *Centinel.* As Frank W. Scott has commented, "during this period of verbal violence no paper was more vituperative in denouncing the Republicans and all their works."[58] Yet, although the fangs of the *Centinel* were always drawn, the body of the newspaper was withering away. As two journalism historians have written, the Boston *Columbian Centinel* "was a child of Federalism, and when the party began its decline, the child declined too."[59]

Of the Federalist editors, none gave President Jefferson more acute difficulty than James Thomson Callender, a Scots immigrant associated first with the Philadelphia *Aurora* and *Gazette* (1794–95), then with the Richmond *Examiner* (1799–1801) and *Recorder* (1801–3). Born in Scotland, James Thomson Callender (1758–1803) acquired a fair classical education before becoming a writer in Edinburgh in 1792. There his pamphlet *The Political Progress of Britain* (part 1) resulted in his indictment for sedition in January 1793. Failing to appear in court several times, Callender was declared a fugitive and outlaw. Like other journalistic novices in trouble before him, he fled to America, where he worked as congressional reporter for the Philadelphia *Gazette of the United States* until the spring of 1796, augmenting his slender income with paragraphs written for the Philadelphia *Aurora.*[60]

From this point on, Callender's career became increasingly stormy. Even as a congressional reporter he stirred up trouble, and he was eased out of that job at the insistence of William B. Giles of Virginia, Jefferson's champion in the House of Representatives. This loss of employment was the first injustice that Callender fancied he suffered at the hands of Jefferson, and he wrote his Virginia benefactor two years later, "A man has no merit in telling the truth but he may claim the privilege of not being the object of persecution from the hero of his encomium."[61] Disappointed and resentful, Callender left Philadelphia for Baltimore, where he published two volumes of *The American Annual Register,* a highly partisan account of national politics during the years 1796 and 1797. Although the first volume was better than its successor, it was dismissed by the *Gazette of the United States* as "the veriest catch-penny that was ever published, the mere tittle-tattle of Jacobinism."[62] Even Jefferson was disappointed in the production.[63] Still, the Virginian was sympathetic to destitute young writers—especially to one who had suffered persecution in Great Britain—and Jefferson from time to time advanced small sums of money to Callender and other young printers.[64] Opponents to Jefferson, both contemporary and later, not knowing his benevolent habits, tried to picture these payments as blackmail.

Meanwhile, Callender was writing additions to William Guthrie's geographies for Mathew Carey in Baltimore for two dollars a page. Early in 1797 Callender reappeared in Philadelphia, where he became acquainted with Thomas Leiper, a wealthy tobacco merchant, and Alexander Dallas, an enthusiastic Jeffersonian and later Madison's secretary of the treasury. "It was through these men that Callender's peculiar talents as a political writer were first recommended to Vice-President Jefferson," according to Charles A. Jellison. In June or July 1797 the vice president met Callender in the downtown printing office of Snowden and McCorkle.[65]

It was Callender's *History of the United States for 1796* that first established his reputation as a scandalmonger. John Beckley, clerk of the House of Representatives, had supplied Callender with documents implying that Hamilton had stolen from the U.S. Treasury. Callender's use of these documents in his *History* forced Hamilton to reveal his adulterous love affair with Mrs. Reynolds in order to vindicate his official honor.[66]

Wary of the Sedition Law and yellow fever, Callender journeyed to Loudoun County, Virginia, where he was taken into the home of Senator Stevens T. Mason in the late summer of 1798. From this refuge in what Callender considered "one of the vilest [counties] in America," the irritable Scotsman wrote petulant letters to Jefferson indicating that he would find a room at Monticello itself agreeable and stating:

> there is no more safety in Philadelphia than in Constantinople. Besides, I
> am entirely sick even of the Republicans, for some of them have used me so

dishonestly, in a word I have been so severely cheated, and so often, that I have the strongest inclination, as well as the best reason, for wishing to shift the scene. . . . I engaged in American controversies not from choice, but necessity; for I dislike to make enemies, and in this country the stile [sic] of writing is commonly so gross, that I do not think the majority of such a public worth addressing.[67]

Unhappily for Jefferson's future peace of mind, Callender did not return to Great Britain. Refusing to retrace his steps to Philadelphia, where the yellow fever "so justly deserved by all the male adults" was still raging,[68] Callender established himself in Richmond, where by the summer of 1799 he was working for the newly established Richmond *Examiner*, a semiweekly edited by Meriwether Jones that was the forerunner of Thomas Ritchie's *Enquirer*. Callender's paranoid personality soon embroiled him in a squabble with William Duane, editor of the Philadelphia *Aurora*. Callender considered himself "a stranger in the country, without 6 people in it, who care a farthing, if I were gibbetted,"[69] and he complained to Jefferson:

> I expected that Duane would copy from us more than he has done. I think some of our columns would have been more to the purpose than his endless trash about Arthur McConnor and Hindustan, of which I, for one, have never read a single line. He began to copy from us, and sickened I believe at hearing that the things were good. Thus the interest, or what I considered as the interest of the cause was betrayed from the meanest personal jealousy of me.[70]

It was in this splenetic mood that James Thomson Callender undertook his most famous political tract, *The Prospect before Us*, continuing to beg for periodic advances from Jefferson and endlessly complaining. "While I am in danger of being murdered without doors," he wrote on September 6, 1799, "I do not find within them any very particular encouragement to proceed."[71] From time to time he sent batches of proof sheets to Monticello, to which Jefferson responded, "Such papers cannot fail to produce the best effect."[72] In late January or early February 1800, Jefferson received a complete copy of *The Prospect before Us*.[73]

Public response to the pamphlet was enthusiastic. Callender wrote Jefferson on February 15, 1800, that "about 500 [copies] are sent off and many more bespoke, but not yet sent."[74] On March 14, 1800, he wrote that *The Prospect before Us* was more than half sold.[75] Yet the author was somewhat discouraged. He wrote to Jefferson on March 10, 1800, "I had once entertained the romantic hope of being able to overtake the Federal Government in its career of iniquity; but I am now satisfied that they can *act* much faster than I can *write* after them."[76]

But Callender had written enough. In *The Prospect before Us* the journalist had denounced John Adams as a "hoary headed incendiary . . . whose hands are reeking with the blood of the poor, friendless Connecticut sailor." Callender exhorted the people that in the election of 1800 they must make their choice between "paradise and perdition," between "Adams, war and beggary, and Jefferson, peace and competency."[77] John B. Walton, a federal-job aspirant, sent a copy of the booklet to Secretary of State Timothy Pickering, sedition watchdog for the Adams administration, and Callender audaciously sent a copy to President Adams himself—a gesture that upset Abigail Adams considerably.[78] On learning that the Federalists were attempting to suppress the sale of his pamphlet in Philadelphia, Callender issued a challenge to the authorities: "If the author has afforded room for *an action,* do prosecute him. But do not take such pitiful *behind the door* measures in order to stop the circulation of truth."[79]

The long arm of the Sedition Law was soon to snatch Callender from his Virginia retreat and make him face an action for seditious libel before the dreaded Federalist magistrate Justice Samuel Chase. While on his first tour of the Southern Circuit, Justice Chase received a copy of *The Prospect before Us* marked by Luther Martin, the Federalist attorney general of Maryland and an inveterate bloodhound of sedition. The "atrocious and profligate libel" of *The Prospect before Us* was too much for the excitable Judge Chase, who set off for Richmond with the intention of teaching state-rights Virginians a lesson in federal law enforcement. Thus, the scene was set for the last case tried under the Sedition Law of 1798 and the only one prosecuted in a southern state, a trial regarded later as the most important case brought under the Sedition Law "because it crystallized Republican hostility to the federal judiciary and later led directly to Chase's impeachment."[80]

Chase arrived in Richmond on May 21, 1800, and three days later the grand jury returned a presentment against Callender citing twenty offensive passages from *The Prospect before Us,* although the book was not specifically named. Callender was arrested in Petersburg on May 27 and was brought before the Circuit Court of the United States in Richmond on June 3. In the meantime, Governor James Monroe had written Thomas Jefferson, "Will it not be proper for the Executive to employ counsel to defend him, and supporting the law give an eclat to a vindication of the principles of the State?" Jefferson, as he summarized his reply in an abstract, stated his opinion "that Callender should be substantially defended, but whether publicly or privately till the legislature should meet, before whom he might lay it" was left to the judgment of Monroe.[81]

In the words of James Morton Smith, the eight-hour trial was "a head-on clash between Republicans and Federalists, between bar and bench, between state and federal authority."[82] Those charged with the difficult task of defending Callender were Philip Norborne Nicholas, attorney general of Virginia, William Wirt, clerk of the House of Delegates, and George Hay, destined to succeed Nicholas as attorney general. Each of the defense counsel was squelched in turn by the dogmatic and aggressive Judge Chase, and after deliberating two hours the jury returned a verdict of guilty. On sentencing Callender the next day, Judge

Chase lectured him on the folly of sowing "dissensions, discontent and discord among the people." Callender was sentenced to nine months in jail, assessed a $200 fine, and bound over on a $1,200 bond to good behavior for two years.[83]

Callender would not be silenced, however. While still in prison, he continued to write scathing articles for the Richmond *Examiner,* the *Virginia Argus* in Richmond, and the *Petersburg Republican.* Moreover, from his jail cell he published the second volume of *The Prospect before Us,* which condemned John Adams as "that scourge, that scorn, that outcast of America . . . a repulsive pedant, a gross hypocrite, and an unprincipled oppressor . . . one of the most egregious fools upon the continent."[84]

The last victim of the Sedition Law, Callender was released from prison on the day that statute expired (March 3, 1801). And on that day began an ordeal for Thomas Jefferson that continued until Callender's death on July 17, 1803. Callender had written to Jefferson from Richmond Jail on September 13, 1800, "If I live to see a republican president in the chair, I shall have a press of my own in Richmond, and give the aristocrats a cut and thrust volume per annum for some years to come [for] the federal viper will undoubtedly continue to hiss; but I make no doubt of living to trample him in the mire of universal detestation."[85] Again, in October 1800, Callender wrote Jefferson, "I have contemplated, for some time, the setting up, next summer, or autumn, a printing office in Richmond providing we succeed in turning out the aristocracy," and he added significantly, "2 or 300 dollars would be quite enough to buy a press &c."[86] The prisoner also complained because he had received no reply from Jefferson after sending him several installments of pages from the second volume of *The Prospect before Us.*[87]

Ten days before his release from jail, Callender asked Jefferson for the remission of his $200 fine, stating that he could not leave prison without paying it and that, if he did, he would have no money left for establishing his long-contemplated printing shop in Richmond.[88] On April 12, 1801, Callender repeated his plea, explaining that the former state marshal, Edmund Randolph, had refused to remit the fine, and adding:

> During the two years that I have been in Richmond, I was paid ten dollars per week as an editor for four months and a half; for a half of the rest of that time, I received victuals; and for what I did in the next nine months I neither received, nor do I ever expect to receive a single farthing. I mention these particulars as this is probably the close of my correspondence with you, that you may not suppose that *I,* at least, have gained anything by the victories of Republicanism.[89]

Callender concluded bitterly, "By the cause, I have lost five years of labor; gained five thousand personal enemies; got my name inserted in five hundred libels, and have ultimately got something very like a quarrel with the only friend I had in Pennsylvania."[90] Callender wrote to Madison on April 27 that he had again requested Jefferson to remit the fine, but "I might as well have addressed a letter to Lot's wife." In his letter to Madison, the querulous journalist also asked for the position as postmaster of Richmond.[91]

Refused this appointment, Callender hated Jefferson no less when his former benefactor and others repaid the court fine. Callender began threatening President Jefferson in a April 27, 1801 letter to Madison, noting that Jefferson had once offered to repay the fine and added ominously, "Does he reflect how his numerous and implacable enemies would exult in being masters of this piece of small history?"[92]

A flurry of letters passed among Jefferson, Madison, and Monroe on the delicate subject of Callender's demands and threats. The president recounted his relationship with the journalist in a July 17, 1802, letter to Monroe:

> I as well as most other republicans who were in the way of doing it, contributed what I could afford to the support of the republican papers and printers, paid sums of money for the Bee, the Albany register &c. when they were staggering under the sedition law, contributed to the fines of Callender himself, of Holt, Brown and others suffering under that law. I discharged, when I came into office, such as were under the persecution of our enemies, without instituting any prosecutions in retaliation.[93]

Two days previously, Jefferson had written to Monroe: "I am really mortified at the base ingratitude of Callender. It presents human nature in a hideous form. It gives me concern because I perceive that relief, which was afforded him on mere motives of charity, may be viewed under the aspect of employing him as a writer."[94]

But it was too late for self-justification. On July 11, 1801, James Thomson Callender and Henry Pace had established the weekly Richmond *Recorder*, which became in short time Callender's redoubt for the most vicious attack on a public figure in early American history. James Truslow Adams has written that Callender must be held responsible for "almost every scandalous story about Jefferson which is still whispered or believed."[95] The Richmond *Recorder* is still cited—even in supposedly scholarly works—as an authoritative source.[96]

Two examples of Callender's brand of journalism will suffice—in addition to his first charge, that Jefferson had fathered five children by his slave Sally Hemings at Monticello. The Richmond *Recorder* originated and scattered the gossip at that time of "Monticellian Sally" Hemings. A few samples of the verses of this song, republished in some Federalist newspapers, ignored by others, will give an indication of its tone:

A SONG.
Supposed to have been written by the
SAGE OF MONTICELLO.

And Venus pleases though as black as jet.
OVID.

Of all the damsels on the green,
 On mountain, or in valley,
A lass so luscious ne'er was seen,
 As the Monticellian Sally.
Chorus. Yankee doodle, who's the noodle?
 What wife were half so handy?
To breed a flock of slaves for stock,
 A blackamoor's the dandy.
Search every town and city through,
 Search market, street and alley;
No dame at dusk shall meet your view,
 So yielding as my Sally.
When press'd by loads of state affairs,
 I seek to sport and dally,
The sweetest solace of my cares
 Is in the lap of Sally.
Let Yankey parsons preach their worst—
 Let tory wittling's rally!
You men of morals and be curst,
 You would snap like sharks for Sally.
She's *black,* you tell me—grant she be—
 Must colour always tally?
Black is love's proper hue for me—
 And white's the hue for Sally.
What though she by the gland secretes;
 Must I stand shill-I shall-I?
Tuck'd up between a pair of sheets
 There's no perfume like Sally.
You call her slave—and pray were slaves
 Made only for the galley?
Try for yourselves, ye witless knaves—
 Take each to bed your Sally.[97]

More than other newspapermen of the period, Callender used the headline to heap abuse on the head of the president of the United States. Periodically he employed headlines such as "ANOTHER HOISTING OF THE BLACK FLAG; OR, THE PRESIDENT AGAIN" and "ANOTHER STROKE UNDER THE FIFTH RIB; OR, THE PRESIDENT AGAIN."[98]

Callender never attempted to conceal his motives for such unprecedented vilification. On September 22, 1802, he published a short warning:

How stands the great accompt 'twixt me and vengeance?
Much has been done, but much does still remain.
And I will not forgive A SINGLE GROAN.[99]

And in one of his last statements on the subject, before his drunken death by drowning in the James River on July 17, 1803, Callender wrote concerning Jefferson:

What would this unfortunate figure give to recall the moment, when he refused to pay Callender his fine? Chastisement was promised; and the promise has been kept with the most rigid punctility . . . and if we shall hear any more chirruping about BLACK SALLY, we shall bring down from Albemarle, a whole pamphlet of depositions. Such, O democrats! is the faithful portrait of your favorite hero![100]

Even with Callender's death—an occurrence almost completely ignored in all newspapers, Federalist or Republican—the ugly one-sided vendetta did not come to a close. Abolitionists later in the nineteenth century used Callender's allegations to further their cause, condemning both slavery and miscegenation. In her *Thomas Jefferson: An Intimate History* (1974) Fawn Brodie was the first professional historian to take the story seriously, also citing a late-nineteenth-century newspaper interview with Madison Hemings, son of Sally Hemings. Some critics questioned her use of psychoanalytical techniques when—unlike Erik Erikson in his *Young Man Luther: A Study in Psychoanalysis and History* (1958)—she was unqualified to do so. Brodie unfortunately opened the floodgates to pseudo-expertise when some biographers felt free to analyze their subjects, dead or alive, without consulting them.[101] An extreme example of this practice, although not by a professional historian, is the statement by Ismail Merchant, one of the producers of the film *Jefferson in Paris,* that Jefferson in France "doesn't know where to put his inappropriate feelings about his daughter," and by implication turned to Sally Hemings.[102]

Another defect in current historiography is that our work tends to tell us more about ourselves than the person or event we are studying. J. G. A. Pocock instructs the modern historian to "read and recognize the diverse idioms of political discourse as they were available in the culture and at the time he is studying."[103] According to Jefferson scholar Douglas L. Wilson, the contradiction between Jefferson and slavery and the role of Sally Hemings, requires some effort to understand these issues in their time.[104]

Almost all writers on the Callender-Jefferson dispute make this error, without knowing it, and it is not just a matter of semantics. Thus, Brodie speaks repeatedly of Callender's "exposé" of the Jefferson-Hemings liaison, a word that was not used at that time and that implies Callender uncovered the truth. It is also stretching the meaning of words to refer to *editor* rather than *printer* (for the most part), *reporter* or *journalist* rather than *writer,* the public's *right to know, investigating the news,* or to Callender as one of the *muckrakers,* that little band of reform journalists who flourished between 1902 and 1912.

All that can be said in Callender's defense is that he was abused as mercilessly by the Republican prints, which had once claimed him as their own, as he defamed Jefferson. The coolest and most reasoned defense of the president's character was conducted in the columns of the *National Intelligencer,* where Samuel Harrison Smith studiously ignored the calumnies, yet offered a positive defense. He once refused to print a letter from "Lucullus" on the subject because, although defending Jefferson, it would give wider circulation to the libelous remarks of Callender. Smith stated that he would observe "the duty of suffering these base aspersions to perish unnoticed in their own infamy."[105] The *National Intelligencer* also printed a letter from one Robert Lawson, who had also been befriended by Jefferson. Lawson's simple style of expressing himself constituted an eloquent plea for a return to standards of human decency, and, as such, it was one of the most effective replies to Callender that appeared in the newspapers of the time.[106]

In stark contrast to this method of dealing with Callender stood the equally incendiary language employed by William Duane in the Philadelphia *Aurora:*

> The noted *Callender* talks of bringing an action of *defamation*—and for what? Not for saying he suffered his wife to perish, or promoted her decay by administering *pint doses of brandy* by way of medicine—not for stating that his unfortunate wife was suffered by him to perish in her own filth until maggots were engendered beneath her, and along her spine! Not for stating that he lived in intoxication upon contributions levied upon the generosity of those who were strangers to his vice, and whom he never approached but in the deepest guise of misery and humiliation—not for stating that the fate of his unfortunate wife was hastened by his barbarity and brutality—nor that his children were left to wallow in filth, ignorance and misery, while he was indulging in intoxication on the money bestowed by blind and undiscriminating benevolence! No, this *apostate* and new *convert* of federalism passes all these *charges* over as trifles, and he fixes upon a petty theft. . . . he denies nothing of his barbarity to his wife or his perfidy to his children—but he calmly says he never stole any *mahogany.* . . .[107]

The number of historians and writers who have expressed their views on this matter—one way or the other—after DNA evidence seemed to link Jefferson to one child of Sally Hemings is truly astonishing. Two books at opposite extremes might be mentioned here. Michael Durey, an Australian professor, has given us a somewhat favorable biography, "*With the Hammer of Truth*": *James Thompson Callender and America's Early National Heroes* (1990). The title is misleading, however, because Callender used the phrase, "With the Hammer of Truth" when he printed, years later, that Jefferson had made "improper advances" at the age of twenty-five to his neighbor's wife, Mrs. Walker, which he publicly later acknowledged. Callender dredged it up to discredit the president, but the casual browser might think the cover phrase of the University Press of Virginia edition refers to the Sally Hemings affair, which at the time was gossip—if not malicious lies.

It is hard to see how anyone who has read the entire slender file of Callender's *Recorder* in the Virginia State Library could come to any other conclusion. Historians are notorious for quoting only that which suits their purpose, and it follows there was no concerted effort among early historians to ignore or vilify Callender—considering also his exchange of letters with Jefferson—to protect the president.

Annette Gordon-Reed's *Thomas Jefferson and Sally Hemings: An American Controversy* (1997) offers a fresh perspective. As a professor of law, she thoroughly presents the evidence both pro and con as it was known in 1997 and lets readers decide for themselves on the matter of Jefferson's paternity of Sally Hemings's children. Whatever the reality of the relationship between the two, the matter has been blown out of all proportion today. At the time, on the evidence of careful reading of eight newspapers—four Federalist and four Republican, all which republished many items from other newspapers, as was the custom, Callender's scandal did not create the splash he had hoped for. After all, although the scandal broke in 1802, Jefferson was overwhelmingly re-elected in 1804. The American public did not buy Callender's story (which some Federalist papers did not even mention) or simply did not care.

Actually, a greater explosion of public indignation in 1802 occurred not over the Sally Hemings story but over Jefferson's offer to send a warship to bring Tom Paine home from revolutionary France. Paine should have been regarded as a national treasure, but the old man was reviled because his *The Age of Reason* (1794, 1796) was regarded by many Americans as unholy and atheistic. The book was, of course, deistic and within the first few pages Paine clearly stated his position (which apparently few read, for as late as the beginning of the twentieth century, Theodore Roosevelt called Paine "that dirty little atheist"): "I believe in one God, and no more; and I hope for happiness beyond this life."[108]

All these Federalist editors had one characteristic in common—a devotion to a cause which would admit no trepidation, refuse no weapons, or grant any quarter to the Republican opposition. To them "every thorough Jacobin is, by necessity, a rogue and a liar."[109] To them an opponent's journal could be so vulgar that "there is only one other use the paper can be applied to."[110] In the twilight years of Federalism these journalists sometimes descended to a mean and vicious fight. But their brief hour had passed, for the sun of Federalism, in the words of the *Gazette of the United States,* was "indeed set for ever, and the luminary of Republicanism, in dim eclipse, disastrous twilight sheds o'er this devoted country."[111]

FOUR

Election of 1800–1801

Anguish and Triumph

The Sun of Federalism sets this day—would that its deliterous influence
were to die with it. But sufficient for the day is the evil thereof.

—Philadelphia *Aurora,* March 9, 1801

The Bay trees in our country all are wither'd. And meteors fright
the fixed stars of Heaven. Lean look'd prophets whisper fearful change.
Rich men look sad and RUFFIANS DANCE.

—*Gazette of the United States,* March 6, 1801

As the voting of 1800 approached, the Republicans faced formidable obstacles—
not only were three-fourths of the presses Federalist, but they were mainly in the
seaboard cities, where voting was likely to be the heaviest. Moreover, the Federalists had been entrenched in power for twelve years with all the patronage links
that entailed. On the other hand, the Republicans had ammunition against the
Federalists with their Alien and Sedition Laws, which were still in force and had
offended many Americans. Jefferson's Kentucky Resolutions against the Sedition Law became practically his platform in the election, declaring the right of
states to nullify oppressive federal laws.

On another front, Jefferson was attacked in the press for his religious views—
or what was perceived as his lack of them. As ambassador to France he formed
a firm attachment for that country and the French Revolution, which is why
Federalist editors frequently refer to Republicans as Jacobins. More deeply than
that, however, Jefferson was a child of the Enlightenment, a participant in the Age
of Reason. His introduction for the American edition of Thomas Paine's *Rights
of Man,* part one (1791) drew fire in the election of 1800. Religion was a domi-
nant theme in many papers, as in this—by no means atypical—paragraph from
the *New-England Palladium:*

Should the infidel Jefferson be elected to the Presidency, the *seal of death* is that moment set on our holy religion, our churches will be prostrated and some infamous prostitute, under the title of the Goddess of Reason, will preside in the Sanctuaries now devoted to the worship of the Most High.[1]

The day before Thomas Jefferson finally was named third President of the United States, the *National Intelligencer* with a somber sense of history noted: "All the accounts received from individuals at a distance, as well as the feelings of citizens on the spot, concur in establishing the conviction that the present is among the most solemn eras which have existed in the annals of our country."[2] For four days members of the House of Representatives had been voting as state units to break the unprecedented electoral tie of 73 votes each between Thomas Jefferson and Aaron Burr, and for four days the Republicans supporting Jefferson had mustered the votes of eight states—lacking only one state for the requisite majority—while the Federalists supporting Burr had controlled six states. Two states, Vermont and Maryland, were evenly divided and therefore cast blank ballots.[3]

"What will be the result?" asked the *National Intelligencer,* and the nation at large waited for the outcome of one of the most closely contested presidential elections in American history. Sober men of both political parties feared imminent violence and the possible disruption of the Union. The same day the *National Intelligencer* addressed its question to history, February 16, 1801, the Federalist *Gazette of the United States* reported with alarm a rumor in Philadelphia that the people had seized the public arms the preceding night. Thomas McKean, governor of Pennsylvania, had ordered all arms of the United States to be turned in to the brigade inspectors of the Pennsylvania militia.[4] In the same issue of the *Gazette of the United States,* "Ephraim" in a letter TO THE BUTCHERS OF PHILADELPHIA deplored the Republicans' intent "to cut the throats of the rulers of the people in council assembled!" and warned them:

> What! Lay hands on the Elders of the People, and smite them on the throat with your knives!!! Verily, verily, I say unto you, the news thereof, would go forth into the cities, and tidings would be carried into the deserts; the anger of the nation would be kindled forthwith, and become exceeding hot; there would be a rising of the people in divers places, and many tribes would be assembled in the North and the South, in the East and the West; and they would roll in like torrents of the mountains, arrest you in the center, and overwhelm you in the vortex, yea, verily, even unto the very last man.[5]

The country seemed to be careening on the abyss of civil war. On January 21 the *National Intelligencer* admonished its readers: "Until the Presidential election is passed, let every citizen realize that the country is in danger. Let him with prudence and firmness avow his opinions, that it may appear to the representatives of the people that the voice of the people is unequivocal, and that that voice shall not only be heard but obeyed."[6] In the same issue of the *National Intelligencer*, a "LETTER from a respectable citizen to a Member of Congress, on the ELECTION of a PRESIDENT" stated in part:

> I sincerely believe that all good men of both parties are inimical to a revolution, and that the warmest attachments to Mr. Jefferson have grown out of a hope, that under him moderate and orderly government may be expected, which will unite parties, at present so portentous to national prosperity, and constitute the best security against usurpation in whatever form she may attempt to exalt her crest. Towards this end, they must adhere to their motto, "The public will, and the supremacy of the constitution over government," to whatever individual it may apply.[7]

Of the Federalist newspapers, none was so violent in its reaction to the electoral crisis as the *Gazette of the United States* in Philadelphia. "Are they [the Republicans] then ripe for civil war, and ready to imbrue their hands in kindred blood?" the newspaper asked on February 16. The *Gazette* reported a threat by "the bold and imperious partisans of Mr. Jefferson" thrown *"in the Teeth of the assembled Congress of America—'Dare* to designate any officer whatever, even temporarily, to administer the government in the event of a non-agreement on the part of the House of Representatives, and we will march and *dethrone him as an usurper. Dare (in fact)* to exercise the right of opinion, and place in the presidential chair any other than the philosopher of Monticello, and ten thousand republican *swords will instantly leap from their scabbards,* in defence of the violated rights of the People!!!!!!'" But if it came to a showdown, the writer continued, Massachusetts alone had seventy thousand regulars under arms, whereas the Jeffersonians could command the loyalty of only Pennsylvania and Virginia. In fact, the *Gazette of the United States* invited a showdown:

> If the tumultuous meetings of a set of factious foreigners in Pennsylvania or a few *fighting* bacchanals in Virginia, mean the *people,* and are to dictate to the Congress of the United States whom to elect as President—if the constitutional rights of this body are so soon to become the prey of anarchy and faction—if we have already arrived at that disastrous period in the life of nations *"when liberty consists in no longer reverencing either the law or the authorities"*—in short the scenes which sadden the history of the elective monarchies of Europe are so soon to be re-acted in America, it would be prudent to prepare at once for the contest: the woeful experiment if tried at all could never be tried at a more favorable conjuncture![8]

Jefferson or Burr? The country rocked under the impact of the pending decision, and the turbulence was further agitated by the unexpected deadlock in the House of Representatives. On December 15, 1800, the *National Intelligencer* had stated: "The storm, which has so long raged in the political world, has at length subsided. Parties have tried their strength, and victory has crowned with success, in the Presidential election, the efforts of the REPUBLICANS."[9] This reaction followed on the heels of learning the results of the South Carolina election, but few persons suspected that Republican electors would uniformly cast their ballots for both Jefferson and Burr, causing the disputed election to be decided by the House of Representatives. Blissfully, the *National Intelligencer* in mid December 1800 congratulated itself and Jeffersonians everywhere on the outcome of the recent presidential election:

> To *Republicans* it must be a cause of sincere felicitation that their country has surmounted, without any other agitation than that of the public sentiment, the choice of their first magistrate. The example is auspicious to the destinies of the world. For while other nations, the victims of monarchical or aristocratical error, on similar occasions invariably appeal to the sword, America presents the august spectacle of a nation, enlightened and jealous of its rights, discharging with dignity the most interesting duty which republican institutions enjoin.[10]

Two months later the same newspaper was urging its readers not to take up arms to decide the issue by force! Such was the kaleidoscopic character of American politics in the formative years of the early Republic. But of course Burr would not possibly accept the presidency, when he had been so clearly intended for the vice presidency—or would he?[11] Samuel Harrison Smith of the *National Intelligencer,* like Republican editors elsewhere, was hard-pressed to avoid outright criticism of Aaron Burr. After all, the unpredictable New Yorker had been selected vice-presidential candidate by the high councils of the Republican Party, and he could not be repudiated at this surprising turn of events. As the *National Intelligencer* commented on December 24, 1800, when rumors began to circulate that the die-hard Federalists were planning to block the election of Jefferson by throwing their support to Burr:

> It cannot be supposed, however unlimited our candour, that a preference of Mr. Burr can arise from any sincere conviction of the superiority either of his talents or virtues to those of Mr. Jefferson. *Without drawing any invidious distinctions between the intellectual and moral qualities of these two gentlemen, which truth could not justify,* it may be affirmed that the private as well as public integrity of Mr. Jefferson are as untarnished as those of Mr. Burr, while the superior age, and the more extended field of political observation and action of the former justify an entire reliance in the general sentiment that ascribes to Mr. Jefferson the larger portion of information and experience.[12]

Burr was politically sound, but Jefferson was older and more experienced. On such tortured grounds was the Republican press forced to advocate the selection of Jefferson without derogating Burr. This position rested on partisan quicksand, and other editors floundered through it with as little enthusiasm as Smith had mustered. On the primary issue at stake, however, the *National Intelligencer* could afford to be more forceful: "Not a citizen of America is so ignorant as not to know that every vote given to Mr. Jefferson was as President, and every vote given to Mr. Burr was as Vice President. Now should the House of Representatives, *voting by states,* select a man not intended by the people, can the people be made to believe that such a selection carries with it any regard to the public will? Will they not, on the contrary, view it as an undoubted evidence of hostility to that will?"[13]

On January 1, 1801, the Philadelphia *Aurora* carried an essay under the title "WHO IS COLONEL BURR?" The writer stated pointedly, "Endowed with a mind vast, liberal, and comprehensive, America claims but few citizens as fit as Col. BURR to be placed second in her government."[14] "An American" in the *National Intelligencer* admitted: "Mr. Burr would certainly make an excellent President, and every man who voted for his electors, or for himself, will rejoice that he has been placed in the situation expectant, should any circumstance prevent Mr. Jefferson from finishing the term of the Chief Magistracy." But then the writer submitted "the apparent reasons for choosing Mr. Jefferson":

> He has filled the office of Secretary of State, and Vice-President under this constitution—his progress to the Presidency is therefore most happily and naturally gradual. In its deliberate course, maturing the stock of knowledge acquired in his libraries, his foreign missions, his offices of Governor, Secretary of State, Treasurer of the sinking fund, and President of the Senate, he is remarkably prepared for the duties of the Chief Magistracy. None of our concerns can be new to him—he has had frequent occasion to see and consider them all.[15]

The Boston *Independent Chronicle* decided that "Mr. Burr is just the sort of man that is wanted," but the newspaper was clearly referring to the office of vice president. In a rather obvious attempt to brace Burr for the blandishments of the Federalists, the *Chronicle* stated that Burr was "too wise to be duped, too honest to weaken his reputation, by an act even of equivocal merit, and too proud to submit to the leading-strings of the vilest faction that ever disgraced a *free country*."[16]

William Duane, editor of the Philadelphia *Aurora,* reported the Federalist "conspiracy" from Washington on January 10, 1801. At a caucus held at Judge Samuel Chase's house in Baltimore, a scheme was hatched to keep the Senate in session, obstruct the selection of Jefferson or Burr, and after March 4 install the president pro tem of the Senate as the president of the United States. To this end the Federalist-dominated Senate would continue debate on the French convention indefinitely, renew the Sedition Law, and push the judiciary bill—taking care to "call if required as considerable a portion of the Marines to headquarters as conveniently could be done." These *"few desperate characters"* in Baltimore had ascertained that Jefferson and Burr had 73 electoral votes each, and that the majority of members from eight states "have pledged themselves to make *no choice* of President."[17] The writer concluded, "By this means there would arise a case not provided for by the Constitution, and the government would be at an end!" Duane, however, saw a flaw in the Federalist scheme—in a time of such danger, Jefferson would not retire from the vice presidency before March 4, as customary, to allow the election of a chairman pro tem. "On this account," the writer continued, "it is that they wish to introduce a clause in the *projected bill,* in the face of the constitution, which goes to put the Chief Justice in the Presidential Chair!"[18]

The wildly improbable dimensions of Duane's "conspiracy" illustrates the uncertainty and suspicion that hovered over both political camps. The election in the House of Representatives marked the jittery climax of a long opposition to the administration of John Adams, which had inherited the furor over the Jay Treaty, had countenanced the Alien and Sedition Laws, and had waged the undeclared war with France. The Philadelphia *Aurora* under Benjamin Franklin Bache, Duane's predecessor, had denounced Adams as "President by three votes," "His Serene Highness of Braintree," "His Rotundity," and "Bonny Johnny Adams."[19]

The election of 1800 followed a hard-fought canvass in which the Federalists published more than a hundred anti-Jeffersonian pamphlets, several of which went through many printings. Federalist newspapers viciously denounced Jefferson for his alleged atheism, his philosophical attitude, his pro-French, revolutionary leanings, and his attachment to democracy—a scare word in 1800— and opposition to Federalism.[20] There were other charges in this most virulent of American presidential campaigns—that Jefferson had not paid his British debts, that he would emancipate southern slaves, that he maintained a "Congo Harem" at Monticello, and that he had revealed his cowardice by fleeing from the British in 1781. "Decius" in the Boston *Columbian Centinel* and "Burleigh" in the *Connecticut Courant* had lashed the Virginia candidate unmercifully in two long series of articles, but in the judgment of one scholar, "the anti-Federalist attacks were far more effective."[21]

"Quantitatively the charge of atheism was the most important attack made on Jefferson during the campaign," Charles O. Lerche Jr. has pointed out.[22] During the electoral process, the *Washington Federalist,* the Federalist paper Jefferson read most, hardly let a day go by without condemning his religious views, or republishing diatribes from other newspapers and magazines. Indeed, when it was all over, Jefferson wrote Joseph Priestley on March 21, 1801, "What an effort, my dear Sir, of bigotry in Politics & Religion have we gone through!" In his later years Jefferson came to the conclusion, "Say nothing of my religion: it is known to God and myself alone."[23]

In early November 1800 William Duane of the Philadelphia *Aurora* had tried to scotch the issue by writing, "The moment an attempt is made to impose any particular religious doctrines upon society, if not by establishments, by public opinions, *giving in elections a preference to one religion above another,* that instant you turn religion into a trade, and are sure to produce the most abominable hypocrisy and prevarication; instead of making men religious and honest, you make them knaves and hypocrites."[24] But the issue remained, and the *Aurora* was forced to meet it head-on:

> These observations have been occasioned by our unexpectedly finding, that the only charge which was brought by his enemies against Mr. Jefferson, is again produced:—that is, that he has no religion—a charge as false as it is weak and malicious, and which being brought at the eve of the last election prevented those enquiries and answers which have been already so fully given to it: enquiries, which have proved, that Mr. Jefferson was the most valuable and best friend that the true religion, and particularly the doctrines of the *Christian Religion,* ever had in the United States.[25]

The proof to William Duane was simple enough—had not Thomas Jefferson "first produced and carried thro' the act for establishing the freedom of religious opinions in Virginia, the first passed in the United States?"

Before the electoral votes were counted in joint sessions of Congress on February 11, 1801, both sides marshaled their forces. An aspersion on Jefferson's southern background was printed in the Boston *Columbian Centinel* on January 7, 1801. The writer was certain that neither John Adams nor Charles Coatesworth Pinckney would become president, "and it is certain that either Mr. JEFFERSON or Mr. BURR, will be, for they will have the suffrages of a minority of the free citizens, the weight of about half a million black cattle thrown into their scale."[26]

Also, on January 31, 1801, the *Gazette of the United States* had compared the election to a tobacco market: "The Demo's who have invested their whole interest in *Virginia fine,* are quite chap-fallen at the prospect of receiving returns in Burr-middlings.—It was a bad speculation at best. Every thing from Virginia savours so strong of French garlic, as to be worth little or nothing in the Northern market."[27] Earlier that month, on January 7, the Boston *Columbian Centinel* had published a brief poem that probably delighted the hearts of Bostonian Federalists:

> Stop—ere your civic feasts begin
> Wait 'till the votes are all come in;
> Perchance amid this mighty stir,
> Your Monarch may be—Col. BURR!
> Who, if he mounts the sovereign seat,
> Like BONAPARTE will *make you sweat,*
> Your Idol then must quaking dwell,
> Mid *Mammoth's* bones at *Monticello,*

His country's barque from anchors free,
On *"Liberty's tempestuous sea,"*
While all the Democrats will sing—
"THE DEVIL TAKE THE PEOPLE'S KING."[28]

On February 11, 1801, the electoral votes were counted in joint session, and Vice President Jefferson read the results—a tie between Jefferson and Burr at 73 votes each, 65 for John Adams, 64 for Charles C. Pinckney, and 1 for John Jay. On the same day, the House of Representatives began balloting between the two top contenders, and by midnight, after nineteen ballots, the results were still the same—eight states for Jefferson, six for Burr, and two evenly divided. Nathan Schachner has described the setting: "Washington, the new capital of the United States, raw, unfinished, its streets by turn mud-holes and knee-deep in snow, was jammed to bursting. Space in the boarding-houses was at a premium; prominent men slept on rude cots, on draughty floors, and were glad enough to obtain such accommodations. Intrigue was in the air, conspiracy stalked the passageways. Excitement, anxiety, showed on every face. . . . Outside, a snowstorm raged, the House was cold and draughty, but the members settled down to a long and weary balloting."[29]

At 8 A.M. on February 12, the tired Representatives adjourned, but resumed again at noon and continued voting for five more leaden days before the break came on February 17, only about two weeks before the new president was to be installed. On the thirty-fifth ballot, the members from the stalemated states of Vermont and Maryland, who had been voting for Burr, cast blank ballots, so these states slipped into Jefferson's column. Two states previously for Burr, Delaware and South Carolina, refrained from voting, making the final result ten states for Jefferson, four for Burr, and two not voting. Thomas Jefferson had become the third president of the United States.

A handbill rushed through the press of the Richmond *Examiner* proclaimed the news "by express from the City of Washington" at 2 A.M.:

THIS MOMENT THE ELECTION IS DECIDED, MORRIS, FROM VERMONT, ABSENTED HIMSELF, SO THAT VERMONT WAS FOR JEFFERSON. THE FOUR MEMBERS FROM MARYLAND, WHO HAD VOTED FOR BURR, PUT IN BLANK TICKETS. THE RESULT WAS THEN TEN FOR JEFFERSON. I HOPE YOU WILL HAVE THE CANNON OUT TO ANNOUNCE THE NEWS.[30]

The news reached Baltimore in a letter from General Samuel Smith, and on February 18 the Baltimore *American* announced:

JEFFERSON PRESIDENT!
BY EXPRESS.

Immediately on the arrival of the above highly pleasing intelligence, Capt. Porter, at the Observatory, (with a promptitude which did honor to his patriotism) announced it to the public by a discharge of sixteen cannon. Nothing could then equal the general joy which our citizens expressed. Huzzas echoed through the City until morning; many houses were illuminated, and the acclamations of the citizens answered through the night, by a discharge from the Observatory, of sixteen guns, at two hours interval, between each salute. At no period, and on no event, during the course of my short life, did I ever witness more general joy and satisfaction than was displayed on the above occasion by my fellow-citizens.[31]

In Philadelphia, the *Aurora* accompanied its announcement of the news with the simple statement, "The Revolution of 1776, is now, and for the first time, arrived at its completion."[32] The *Gazette of the United States* received the news by way of General Smith's letter to the mayor of Baltimore and printed the letter under the headline "MR. JEFFERSON, PRESIDENT!" The newspaper commented, "The question which has so long held the Union in doubtful suspense, was yesterday decided, by the election of the honorable Thomas Jefferson, as President of the United States, and Aaron Burr, Esq. as Vice-President," reporting the decision as "so grateful to many, and so anxiously anticipated by all. . . . "[33] An irate Philadelphian, disturbed by the ringing of the Christ Church bells to celebrate the occasion, wrote to the *Gazette:*

> Oh ye rascally Ringers and Jacobin foes,
> Ye disturbers of all who delight in repose,
> How I wish, for the quiet and peace of the Land,
> That ye had round your *necks* what ye hold in your *hands*.[34]

One Philadelphian who refused to abide by the decision of the House of Representatives wrote to the *Gazette of the United States* on February 21, 1801, as "A Freeman":

> That Thomas Jefferson is chosen President, I DO POSITIVELY DENY. The majority of the *Freemen* of the United States, have most indubitably given their suffrages for John Adams. The majority of the House of Representatives, have unceasingly preferred Mr. Burr, and the States, in their elective capacity, during a series of near 40 elective trials, have to the last pertinaciously refused to bestow on Thomas Jefferson a MAJORITY OF VOTES. It, therefore, follows, of necessary consequence, if he assumes the executive authority, that he and his faction have destroyed the Constitution of the Country, and proclaimed an absolute and notorious usurpation, against which all good men are bound to protest.[35]

On February 26, nine days after the event, the news reached Boston, and the Republican *Independent Chronicle* composed a headline reminiscent of the Revolution:

SPLENDID INTELLIGENCE!

———

THOMAS JEFFERSON
IS PRESIDENT, and
AARON BURR
VICE-PRESIDENT OF THE UNITED STATES.

The *Independent Chronicle* also received its information from General Smith's letter to Baltimore, noting: "An express from Gen. SMITH, arrived in this city three quarters past 7 o'clock this evening, announcing the election of Mr. JEFFERSON. —I have seen the letter, and you may depend on the information being correct.— The cannon are now firing."[36] The *Independent Chronicle* reacted to the "glorious information" by stating: "Thus it appears that this great Philosopher, Civilian and Patriot, is, after every effort which intrigue and malice could invent, at length announced PRESIDENT OF THE UNITED STATES."[37]

The *National Intelligencer*, at the seat of government, noted simply, "The voice of the People has prevailed, and THOMAS JEFFERSON is declared by the Representatives of the People to be duly elected President of the United States." Undoubtedly with a good deal of satisfaction, the newspaper added, "It follows, from the direction of the Constitution, that Aaron BURR is elected Vice-President." As was his wont, Samuel Harrison Smith could not refrain from pointing out the moral of the electoral crisis that had ended so happily for Republicans:

> In addition to the many evidences of the superiority of republican institutions, over those of the monarchic or aristocratic form, this honorable regard to the public will, expressed with calmness and intrepidity will produce an impression on the minds of the People of America, stronger than that attempted to be made by the unceasing eulogists of other systems. To those unfounded reproaches against republicanism, that ascribe to it the predominance of turbulent passions, and an imbecility to meet with effect a crisis of danger, it will with exultation oppose the proud example of a people of five millions, scattered over a wide extent of country, peaceably electing a chief magistrate, and the representatives of that people, constitutionally confirming the national will.[38]

The Philadelphia *Aurora* drew a more cogent moral from the affair: "It is to be hoped that at some convenient opportunity during the administration of Mr. Jefferson, the republicans will take care that the same disgraceful scene at the election of a President, shall not take place in future, which we have so lately experienced. However perfect the rest of the constitution may be, it ought no longer to be the means of rendering us the laughing stock of the civilized world."[39]

Some of the Federalist newspapers went to great lengths to deplore the election of Thomas Jefferson. On March 4, the Boston *Columbian Centinel* published the long "Monumental Inscription" (quoted earlier) bordered in black and intended as an epitaph for the Federalist Party. The *Washington Federalist*, in announcing the results of the election, placed a picture of the American eagle upside down over the caption "Pluria e Uno."[40]

Meanwhile, the Republicans joyously observed the victory celebrations that sprang up in all parts of the country. Jefferson's supporters in his home state of Virginia were so elated at the turn of events that they held an impressive celebration at Petersburg—probably the first in the nation—on January 29, 1801, two weeks before the balloting began in the House of Representatives.[41] In Philadelphia the *Gazette of the United States* announced grumpily on February 23: "The Democrats are this day going about the city soliciting subscriptions for the *Poor!*—Least the Public may be deceived, we think proper to inform them, that *two fifths* of all monies collected under this pretence, is to be appropriated to defray the expenses of celebrating the election of *Mr. Jefferson*."[42]

The *National Intelligencer* from its vantage point in the capital reported on February 27, 1801: "As far as accounts have been received from the various parts of the Union, the election of Mr. JEFFERSON to the Presidency has produced the liveliest feelings of joy. In Baltimore, Philadelphia, and New York, the bells have been rung, the artillery been fired, and convivial entertainments been given. In various places preparations are making for celebrating this great event on a scale proportionate to its magnitude."[43]

Word came from the Boston *Independent Chronicle* on March 5 that "Yesterday a number of *Republican Citizens* of this town announced their approbation of the choice of President and Vice-President, by a discharge of cannon, and other expressions of joy and congratulation." The *Chronicle* added, "The towns of Charlestown, Roxbury, and Brooklyne more particularly displayed those expressive feelings which operate in the breast of Republicans. . . . *Union, Republicanism,* and '*good order*' prevailed during their banquet[s]."[44]

In Virginia a pageant was held on the day of Jefferson's inauguration and described at great length in the *National Intelligencer:*

> The multitude appear irresolute and amazed—many busy figures are seen passing to and fro, soliciting their concurrence with the orator—some speaking in a foreign dialect, and most of them holding in their hands—commissions, diplomas, appointments, grants, contracts, warrants or accounts, relating to a multitude of dignities, officers and jobs, civil, military and religious, which had been or would be invented, for raising and expending public treasure to an incredible amount. The multitude are almost infatuated; the danger of liberty is imminent. At the moment a trumpet is heard, a courier arrives, he proclaims,—"Jefferson is President."[45]

Immediately Liberty stands erect once more, and the crowd cheers while the orator's papers are burned, the scepter is broken, the crown and miter are trampled into dust and ashes, the soldier is disarmed, and the statesman's papers are torn asunder. "Sixteen beautiful women now appear, each with a badge representative of a state, kneeling in a circle with arms locked, and directing the most fervent adoration towards the guardian angel of America, who is hovering over them, and pointing at UNION, which is seen in the centre of the circle, written in golden and capital letters." Amid general applause, the angel displays her label: *"Union can only be maintained by preserving liberty."*[46]

While the citizens of Virginia were participating in this way in the elevation of their own Thomas Jefferson to the presidency, the event itself was unfolding with simple dignity in Washington, D.C. As the *National Intelligencer* described an impressive moment in history:

> At an early hour on Wednesday the City of Washington presented a spectacle of uncommon animation, occasioned by the addition to its usual population of a large body of citizens from the adjacent districts. A discharge from the company of Washington artillery ushered in the day; and about 10 o'clock, the ALEXANDRIA company of riflemen, with the company of artillery, paraded in front of the President's lodgings. At 12 o'clock THOMAS JEFFERSON, attended by a number of his fellow citizens, among whom were many members of Congress, repaired to the Capitol. His dress was, as usual, that of a plain citizen, without any distinctive badge of office. He entered the Capitol under a discharge from the artillery. On his entry into the Senate chamber, where were assembled the Senate, and the members of the House of Representatives, the members rose, and Mr. Burr left the chair of the Senate, which Mr. Jefferson took. After a few moments of silence, Mr. Jefferson rose, and delivered his address before the largest concourse of citizens ever assembled here. Having seated himself for a short period he again rose, and approached the clerk's table, when the oath of office was administered by the Chief Justice; after which he returned to his lodgings, accompanied by the Vice-president, Chief Justice, and the heads of departments; where he was waited upon by a number of distinguished citizens. As soon as he withdrew, a discharge of artillery was made. The remainder of the day was devoted to purposes of festivity, and at night there was a pretty general illumination.

The account concluded with the brief notation that "neither Mr. ADAMS, nor THEODORE SEDGWICK, Speaker of the House of Representatives, were present at the Inaugural Ceremony; both those gentlemen having left the city at day light on that morning."[47]

Reports of Republican celebrations poured in from across the country. In Philadelphia the *Aurora* announced, "The happy event of a change in the administration of our government, and the placing the power thereof in the hands of the men whom 'the people' delight to honor and confide in, was celebrated in an unusual and merited degree, by all the republicans in this city and county;—The day was truly a day of jubilee and festivity."⁴⁸ Only a poem, "The People's Friend," could adequately express the *Aurora*'s overflowing emotions:

> REJOICE, ye States, rejoice,
>   And spread the patriot flame;
> Call'd by a Nation's voice;
>   To save his country's fame,
> And dissipate increasing fears,
> Our favorite JEFFERSON appears.⁴⁹

The concluding paragraph of an oration given in Philadelphia to celebrate Jefferson's inauguration reveals the unrestrained emotional fervor of the occasion: "Glorious morn of freedom, lightens, beautifies and adorns our political horizon; may its meridian splendor be reflected as the sun beams of heaven to vivify and preserve the ethereal flame; and may the sons of America feel its animating influences to the latest period of time; and do thou 'Almighty Being' on whose eternal fiat depends the fate of nations, and the destinies of the world, consecrate and perpetuate, the liberty, independence and happiness of our beloved country."⁵⁰

As usual, however, the festivities surrounding Jefferson's inauguration did not pass by in Philadelphia without an editorial exchange between the *Aurora* and the *Gazette of the United States*. The latter newspaper complained on March 9:

> At the entertainment given on Wednesday, at the Union Hotel, where several decent democrats dined, the toasts were in general moderate and such as might be drank by *Americans,* unless the *insipidity* of a number of them should render them objectionable. But at all the other feasts, so far as we can judge from the accounts with which the *Aurora* has favoured us, the sentiments expressed in the toasts were truly Jacobinical, and such as might be relished by any United Irishmen, French Jacobins, and fugitive members of the English Corresponding Society. Their music was Ca Ira, The Rights of Man, Marseilles hymn, &c. Among their toasts we find La Fayette, Logan, Buonaparte, Gallatin, and some other despots and fools.⁵¹

The *Aurora* shot back: "The Philadelphia Gazette of Friday, says, the procession on Wednesday was composed of *smiths, shoemakers,* and *tailors,* who have nothing to do with *politics;*—the cause of their rejoicing on that day, however, has proved the fallacy of this doctrine, for the republican smiths, shoemakers, and tailors formed a considerable portion of those who turned out the aristocratic *traitors, tories* and *defaulters,* who made themselves '*wealthy*' by the plunder of the *honest tradesman.*"⁵² Not content to let the matter rest there, the *Aurora* added in another editorial paragraph:

> Although the "*wealthy*" wise, and *virtuous aristocrats* disdained walking with the *mob-ility* on Wednesday last, they were not over-cautious in behaving like

gentlemen—two of them, wishing to *see* and not *be seen,* ran up stairs in a house in Race Street, opened the door of a room from the windows of which some ladies were looking at the procession, and without asking permission let down the curtains. An elderly lady who was present asked "Why [do] they let down the curtains?" to which one of them replied "we don't wish to be seen"— It is to be remarked that there were in the room none but females.[53]

The *Aurora* also remarked, with evident satisfaction, that "from every quarter we hear of the orderly and decent manner in which [the Republicans] conducted themselves" in celebrating Jefferson's inauguration. On the other hand, the "aristocrats" had done everything they could "to damp the joy" of the Republicans on March 4. The most notorious example was the Federalist gentleman of Burlington who removed the clapper from the church bell on the night of March 3. A Republican happened along and asked the portly gentleman why he did such a thing, and was answered, "lest the democrats should have the satisfaction of hearing the bell ring the next day." Replied the Republican, "That's the worst way to prevent it, for if you had suffered the bell to remain as usual it would be heard no where but in Burlington, but now it will be heard all over the continent."[54] William Duane would see to that.

In Boston, when the Republican *Independent Chronicle* republished the paragraph from the *National Intelligencer* noting the widespread nature of the victory celebrations, the rival *Columbian Centinel* replied, "we have yet to hear from the towns on the banks of *Connecticut-River;* whose stream, like the *Nile* in *Egypt,* fertilizes its banks from its source to the ocean, and causes them to produce abundant harvests of Federalism and unwavering attachment to the right principles." The Federalist newspaper added, "It is in seaports that Jacobinism and the yellow fever are endemical."[55]

As the celebrations dragged on and on, the Philadelphia *Aurora* defended them against Federalist complaints of noisiness and lack of propriety. Wrote Duane, "Where was the obstreperousness of the republican festival in this city of the Fourth of March, compared with the eternal din of cracked clarinets, and crazy fiddles, the yell that accompanied Hopkins and his savage song, in their midnight orgies with Hail Columbia[?]"[56]

But enough was enough. The tenor of the compliments and addresses rolling in on the president was becoming embarrassing even to Duane. The Philadelphia editor urged his readers: "It is sincerely to be hoped that in the future period of Mr. Jefferson's administration no more complimentary addresses may be presented. It is not on the *words,* but on the *actions* of his fellow-citizens, that he is to place his firm reliance, and on *his* actions must depend the measure of support he shall receive."[57] The *Aurora*'s plea did not stem the tide, however, for a month later the Boston *Independent Chronicle* stated: "Mr. Jefferson has endeavored to discourage addresses, which have become too common, to be flattering; but he has not had absolute success. The address from Fayetteville, in N. Carolina, gave him an opportunity to recommend that national jealousy and vigilance upon which the preservation of public liberty depends."[58] Almost three months after this statement, the Boston *Columbian Centinel* complained:

Mr. ADAMS was frequently the subject of anti-federal abuse for holding levees, receiving compliments, and permitting himself to be addressed. It was called aping royalty, sycophancy, and servile adulation. Nevertheless, we see his successor can thus ape royalty; can thus bear the sycophantic compliments of the Secretaries of the great departments, &c., and even the homage of a battalion of that standing military force, which one of his satellites denominated *"mercenary ragamuffins."* All this can be done by the *third* President without comment; which, in the *first* or *second*, would have furnished *Aurora* denunciations for a month.[59]

What about the defeated Federalists? The Philadelphia *Aurora* said on March 12, 1801, "Enamelling Mr. Adam's name as President, on TABLE China, was not a bad omen; for immediately after its arrival in this country, Mr. A was DISH'D!"[60] The *Gazette of the United States* wheeled into position to defend the ousted administration: "True it is, the real federalists stand convicted before the public . . . of raising their country from the lowest point of depression and weakness absolute and closely verging upon direful anarchy, to a state of wealth, security and happiness, for the space of time, unexampled in the annals of the world. . . ."[61] But the rival *Aurora* viewed matters differently, stating, "The history of the last American administration will be matter of astonishment to posterity."[62]

"Columbianus" in the Boston *Columbian Centinel* took a broad view of the Federalist upset:

It is the interest of the American people to form as many great CHARACTERS as possible: Mr. ADAMS has long been formed; he is full of years and full of glory. . . . Messrs. JEFFERSON and BURR, are candidates for fame; and who knows the harvest they may reap? If their heads are now bare of laurels, there is *room* for them to grow. . . . The eighteenth century, has been illuminated with a WASHINGTON, and an ADAMS; let the nineteenth be made resplendent by a JEFFERSON and a BURR. And per adventure other stars may arise before its close to add to the list of great names, and to gild its evening beams. The TEMPLE OF FAME is not yet crowded, come forward yet American geniuses and bend your course to its Portals![63]

The Philadelphia *Gazette of the United States* viewed such sentiments with alarm. After all, the newspaper maintained, "It is fallacious . . . to imagine that we shall experience only a change of men." The Federalists had nothing to fear from the conduct of one or two individuals, the *Gazette* continued: "It is the general ascendancy of the worthless, the dishonest, the rapacious, the vile, the merciless and the ungodly, which forms the principal ground of alarm."

These are the men who have incessantly maligned the officers of our Government collectively and individually, our courts of justice, our laws, our clergy and our seminaries of learning. These are the men who called WASHINGTON a *murderer;* and these are the men to whom Mr. *Jefferson* and Mr. *Burr* are indebted for the two highest offices in the nation. From such men we have everything to fear. They already proclaim in their appropriate jargon, that the "reign of terror" has ceased, and that the triumph of democratical and republic principles, over a tyrannical aristocracy, is commencing; in plain English, that the rabble has broken over all restraint, and are just preparing to imbrue their hands in the blood of those, who may attempt to stay their progress.[64]

For its part, the Boston *Columbian Centinel* feared the ascendancy of the South as much as the advent of the rabble. The leading Federalist newspaper of the North said, "*New York, Pennsylvania* and *Virginia,* with all the States to the southward, headed by JEFFERSON, will form a league as hostile to the interests of *New-England,* as it will be formidable in its duration."[65] Still, the *Centinel* found some solace in defeat: "However Painful the reflection must be that the United States are doomed to have a Jacobin President to rule over its destinies for the ensuing four years; we have yet one consolation remaining, that the event will unite and form into phalanx the upright, and the able, throughout the Union." If Federalists everywhere would only be on their guard, the *Centinel* advised, "Perhaps there is yet good sense and virtue enough remaining, if properly directed, to resist this overwhelming current, that threatens destruction to our Rising Empire." The administration had fallen into the hands of the Philistines, "but with proper exertions the chosen people will yet be saved."[66]

In retaliation the Republican newspapers gloated over the defeat of the Federalists and continued to abuse John Adams. No comments were more vindictive than those of Matthew Lyon, former Vermont congressman, addressed to Adams in the columns of the Philadelphia *Aurora:*

> By your administration you have rendered that vote fatal to your country and made it cost them millions.—You seem now more than ever bent on mischief: your vindictive spirit prompts you to do every thing in your power to give the succeeding administration trouble, but you are as unfortunate in this as in most of your calculations; your creatures are generally pliant reeds, they will bend to and fawn upon any body that is in power; it was power they worshipped in you, not John Adams.[67]

Lyon advised the last Federalist president to "cool yourself a little, don't coil round like the rattlesnake and bite yourself; no, betake yourself to fasting and prayer a while, it may be good for both body and soul, that is a safer remedy for an old man in your situation than the letting of blood." The writer concluded with an exhortation: "I hope and pray that your fate may be a warning to all usurpers and tyrants, and that you may before you leave this world, become a true and sincere penitent and be forgiven all your manifold sins in the next."[68]

The Philadelphia *Aurora* condemned the Federalist clergy of New England as well as John Adams for bringing the country so close to ruin:

> In the cup of mortification of which the ex-president hath been called to drink, ye are also partakers. Around this standard ye have rallied, expecting under its banners to see the salvation of God. They have now taken away your gods, and what have ye more? The wisdom of the wise hath failed, and the understanding of the prudent is brought to nought. The crown is fallen from the federal mount, and the face of Israel is turned away. Something must be wrong! There is a lie somewhere.—Those of you who have lifted up to heaven what is *now cast down;* and appointed to ruin that which is *now exalted,* ought, as Christians, to look about you! Ye cannot advance in your prospects! Some of you are astonished; others confounded, and the rest say, "the nation is ruined, and the end of the world is come!"[69]

John Adams, no longer backed by the Sedition Law, must have writhed under such attacks. The only balm to his pride came in an address from the legislature of Massachusetts, which stated in part, "The period of the administration of our General Government, under the auspices of WASHINGTON and ADAMS, will be considered as among the happiest eras of time." Yet former president Adams realized, as he said in his reply, that "the last scene, of the last act, of my political drama" was ended forever.[70]

Yet even the Republican *Independent Chronicle* of Boston labeled "INGRATITUDE!" a paragraph republished from William Cobbett's London newspaper: "Adams, it appears by the last advices, is sunk into complete contempt. He 'strutted his hour upon the stage,' sometimes performing very well, and sometimes very badly; the clap and hiss long contended for the preference; but the latter finally prevailed. Stript of his stage robes, and clad in the garb of simple citizen, the old man may now look back, and *make* a calm review of all the parts he has played, from the character of pettifogger to that of President."[71] Nothing as unkind as this appeared in the American press when Adams departed from office, and the man certainly deserved much better from a former Federalist supporter, the editor of the renowned *Porcupine's Gazette* of Philadelphia. The Boston *Independent Chronicle* seemed indignant at the jibe, apparently because it thought there should be honor even among Federalists.

The *National Intelligencer* was keenly interested in what the foreign press —especially the British—had to say about Jefferson's election and inaugural speech.[72] An unidentified London newspaper of April 18, 1801, was quoted as saying: "Notwithstanding what violent partisans have said, and continue to say respecting the Anti-Anglican politics of this gentleman [Jefferson], we can trace nothing in his speech (in a part of which he declares his political creed) that manifests an attachment to any one European nation more than another."[73] The *National Intelligencer* also republished a paragraph of comment from a British pamphlet that had reproduced Jefferson's first inaugural address:

> HAIL LIBERTY! Ye votaries or victims in her cause; whether homaging at her profaned altars, or expiring in unwholesome dungeons, ALL HAIL!!! The wished for event, in which philosophy and the lovers of human kind are interested, has occurred. Jefferson has been elected President of the United States of America, but which is more, an inauguration Speech, by way of address to the Senate, the members of the House of Representatives, the public officers, and a large concourse of citizens assembled on the occasion, proclaims those sentiments and dispositions his friends and admirers have long observed him to cherish.[74]

The Republican *Salem Gazette* noted: "By the foreign papers we find that President JEFFERSON's Speech has been translated into foreign languages. A Dutch Gazette remarks, while he assures his fellow citizens, that no change will be made in their happy Constitution, his tone and manner lead us to expect a distinct character will be given to his administration. Compliments are paid to his truly republican manners at home. United to his economy, his personal attractions will give him the public affections, and his personal safety will give dignity to the reputation of his country."[75]

Without doubt, Jefferson's inaugural address met its author's fullest expectations, for it gathered praise from friend and political foe in this country and abroad. As the early months of Jefferson's administration passed, the Republican press sought to sustain this ebullient mood against the growing uneasiness about federal patronage. The Boston *Independent Chronicle* risked Federalist censure when it pressed this point on May 25, 1801: "There appears at present to be a perfect tranquility throughout the continent—we hear of no riots, insults, or abuses, no standing armies to pillage and injure the inhabitants, no duty for Marshals, under the Sedition Law, nor any thing of the kind—but on the contrary, we see the people employed in industry, in perfect happiness and quietude. *Query*—Does this look like the reign of restless ambitious, disorganizing *Jacobinism,* or does it more resemble the reign of Republicanism in its purity?"[76] On June 18 the same newspaper stated:

> A daily change of sentiment in favour of Republicanism is visible, in almost all circles of company, and especially among the members of the Legislature. Many who brought to this town, on their late meeting, strong prejudices against Republican men and measures, have, by explanation and intercourse with Republicans, become sensible of the errors of their own party and appear disposed to renounce them, if they obstinately persist in their errors.[77]

Benjamin Austin Jr. proclaimed in the Boston *Independent Chronicle,* "The fact is, that 999 *real* citizens in a thousand throughout the United States, are in favor of Mr. Jefferson's administration. . . . "[78] To this journalistic outpost of Republicanism in Federalist Boston, no praise could be too lavish for Thomas Jefferson. In the same "Old South" series, Austin again stated, "we trust in that BEING who often relieved us when in trouble, and we console ourselves, that he has raised a JEFFERSON, who like Joshua, will conduct us to the promised land."[79]

The president's annual address to Congress in December 1801, delivered by message for the first time, met an enthusiastic response by Republicans and a more reserved reaction by Federalists. According to the Philadelphia *Aurora:* "The late communication of the president of the United States to Congress has deservedly met with the praise of every man, not prejudiced against every thing which bears the stamp of republicanism. In the different federal prints which have as yet reached us, it is spoken of, if not in very high terms, at least respect- ful. . . . "[80] The Boston *Independent Chronicle* noted a different reception in the Federalist North: "The masterly production, which has attracted so much of the censure of a party on one hand, and so much of the applause of the nation on the other, contains more considerations, worthy of the attention of a national legislature, than has ever been seen in the same compass of expression, in the English language."[81]

These varied comments were typical of the response by the press, Federalist and Republican, to the election and inauguration of Thomas Jefferson and to his first year in office. Republican editors were convinced that Jefferson "moves like the genius of America,"[82] while Federalist editors sickened at the unending stream of eulogium. The *Gazette of the United States* spoke for Federalist news- papers large and small when it printed a poem that stated in part:

> Columbia is ill at her ease,
> She a surfeit has got I can tell ye;
> And the cause of Columbia's disease,
> Is much turkey and goose in her belly.[83]

The Portsmouth (New Hampshire) *Ledger* added more rich dressing to the na- tional feast of praise by saying, "Jefferson's character shines clearer than the sun, for the sun has its spots, but the character of Jefferson has passed through the fiery furnace of Federal calumny, and come out without a spot."[84] Nor would the administration's semiofficial newspaper, the *National Intelligencer,* challenge such unrestrained comments. Samuel Harrison Smith wrote: "Thomas Jefferson has been called the man of the people. The title is the noblest that can be bestowed; nor will it cease to be continued, so long as his actions and principles remain truly republican."[85]

In conclusion, it seems evident that the Federalist press held the upper hand during the campaign, but after the election the Republican press seized the initiative and continued onward to splendid victory. Their addresses, poems, and words of praise were all pitched at too intense a level for sustained reader interest, but the Republican newspapers had much to celebrate. Unshackled from the hated Sedition Law, they reveled in their triumph. With few exceptions, they allowed the dispirited John Adams to retreat to Braintree in peace and dignity. Few epithets were hurled at the back of the former Federalist president, and none was as scurrilous as the abuse of Washington when he retired from office. In this respect, the first change in political power in American history passed off relatively smoothly in the press. John Adams was no longer to be dreaded, for he left no Federalist successor in the President's Mansion. Thomas Jefferson was president of the United States, and Republican newspapers everywhere rejoiced.

As for the remaining Federalist opposition, Republican editors hoped that time itself would take care of that. As the Boston *Independent Chronicle* stated late in 1801:

> Many honest people among us, who, not having the means of personal acquaintance, have received their information thro' discoloring channels, feel strong objections against JEFFERSON! but the personage, they thus implicitly oppose, is not the President of the United States. Nor is it his likeness; but a *caricature,* a creature of imagination, a mere image of party, dressed up and exhibited for an electioneering fright. The real *President* JEFFERSON, seen in his true character, would be the very man of their choice; and will be, as soon as time and cool observation shall present him fairly to their view, in the light of truth and reality. . . . They who knew him best, expect that he will overcome the *prejudices* of the misinformed, and *live* down the misrepresentations of his calumniators.[86]

What, after all, had the Federalist press gained by its virulent denunciation of Jefferson during the bitter campaign of 1800? One scholar has observed, "It is a demonstrable fact that Jefferson gained many votes through the excesses of his opponents."[87] In the congressional elections in the spring of 1802, the Republicans won a clear majority, gaining 66 of the 106 seats in the House of Representatives.[88] Yet Stephen G. Kurtz has pointed out that "Adams ran stronger in 1800 than in 1796 and appears to have been more popular than he had been four years previously."[89] If the Federalist press accomplished anything, it antagonized Republicans to the point that reconciliation was impossible, despite the gesture of Jefferson's inaugural address. By their obstreperous abuse, the Federalist editors invited the treatment they received on the issue of patronage, judicial or otherwise.

The Federalist press did not lose the election; on the contrary, it came remarkably close to winning it, although some have doubted whether "personal vilification has [ever] stopped the long-range trends of American political development."[90] Yet the Federalist press did lose the imposed Republican truce that followed the contest. Noble E. Cunningham Jr. has written that the election of 1800 "was a new experience in American political life, this transferring of political power from one party to another, and full proof that political parties had come of age."[91] Not quite. For the stumbling and half-hearted efforts of Federalist editors after Jefferson's electoral triumph revealed that they did not grasp a key concept of political life—the role of the active opposition. They learned quickly enough and refurbished old weapons for new purposes in opposing Jefferson's use of the federal patronage and the return of Thomas Paine.

Nevertheless, there was a period of grace. As the Philadelphia *Aurora* quoted a New York Federalist soon after Jefferson's first inaugural speech: "His public assurances . . . have inspired us with a hope that *he is not the man we thought him.*—We thought him a philosophist, and have found him a virtuous and enlightened philanthropist—We thought him a Virginian, and have found him an American—We thought him a partisan and have him a president."[92]

FIVE

Tom Paine Comes Home, 1802

Once more shall Paine a listening world engage;
From reason's source a bold reform he brings,
By raising up mankind he pulls down kings.

—New York *Daily Advertiser,* May 27, 1791

It is probable enough that the obscene old sinner [Thomas Paine]
will be brought over to America one more, if his carcase [*sic*]
is not too far gone to bear transportation.

—*Gazette of the United States,* July 22, 1801

No homecoming was more inglorious than that of Thomas Paine when that self-described "volunteer to the world"[1] returned to the United States in late 1802. The young Republic no longer needed an old revolutionary propagandist. On the contrary, Paine's esteem had fallen so low that his return triggered the first all-out attack on the administration of Thomas Jefferson, an attack that bordered on demolition. In Federalist newspapers throughout the country Paine was denounced as irreligious, depraved, unworthy to associate with the president of the United States, the assassin of Washington's character, and a journalistic hack who peddled his wares to the highest bidder.

The attack was aimed indirectly at Jefferson himself, because to many Paine represented the undiluted Republican philosophy. Jefferson did not abandon Paine, however. After his arrival in 1802 the two men could be seen strolling arm-in-arm on the grounds of the President's Mansion—while controversy raged around them. The defense of Thomas Paine was the first great test of the effectiveness of Jefferson's newspaper support, and the results boded ill for the future.

Fortunately for Federalist critics, the sixty-five year-old Paine had proved equal to the rigors of the Atlantic crossing, but it was a toughened Thomas Paine who returned to America after fifteen years in restless England and revolutionary France. Since leaving post-Revolution retirement at Bordentown, New Jersey, in 1787, Paine had experienced the best and worst of mankind in a Europe torn with turmoil, and this experience had changed him deeply. Gone forever was the idealistic firebrand who had prodded the reluctant colonies to independence with his *Common Sense* pamphlet in 1776 and had bolstered the patriot cause with the fifteen issues of the *Crisis* papers from 1776 to 1783. There returned another Tom Paine—old, wracked with the pain of illness, and not a little disillusioned. He had been made a French citizen by the Assembly on August 26, 1792, along with Washington, Hamilton, and Madison, but as one of the first internationalists, he could claim the protection of no nation.

To many Americans, he had forfeited his claim to United States citizenship—based on his service in the Revolutionary army—by agreeing in September 1792 to sit in the French Convention for Pas de Calais after having been elected from four departments. At the trial of Louis XVI, Paine pleaded for imprisonment and banishment rather than death, and after the fall of the Girondins in June 1793 he was deprived of his French citizenship and parliamentary immunity. Imprisoned on December 28, 1793, Paine spent eleven months of the Reign of Terror in the Luxembourg, where he composed part of *The Age of Reason* before being released in November 1794 on the intervention of the new American minister, James Monroe, who claimed Paine as an American citizen. Restored to his place in the Convention,[2] Paine continued to espouse the political faith stated in his *Rights of Man*, which had appeared in two parts in 1791 and 1792 in both France and the United States as a reply to Edmund Burke's *Reflections on the French Revolution* (1790). After his active political role ended, Paine lived quietly in Paris until the Peace of Amiens in 1802 made it possible for him to return to the land that had first launched him to international fame.

Most Americans might have forgiven Thomas Paine for his active role in the French Revolution—a cause that claimed the allegiance of the Jeffersonian Republicans, at least—but many could never forgive him for his last great work, *The Age of Reason*, published in two parts in 1794 and 1796. Although the opening paragraphs of this celebrated tract contained the statement, "I believe in one God, and no more; and I hope for happiness beyond this life," it was violently denounced throughout the Christian community as atheistic and considered a frontal attack on the Church itself.[3] Nor could some Americans forget Paine's bitter attack in 1796 on their prime hero in his "Letter to George Washington, President of the United States of America, on Affairs Public and Private."[4]

So it was that Thomas Paine, unknowingly facing such opposition, bade "adieu to restless and wretched Europe"[5] and turned his vision westward once more. The times were auspicious for his homecoming: Thomas Jefferson had been elected third president of the United States, and a new order was clearly in the air for the young nation. Paine had written to Jefferson from Paris on June 9, 1801: "I congratulate America on your election. There has been no circumstance with respect to America since the times of her Revolution that excited so much attention and expectation in France, England, Ireland and Scotland as the pending election for President of the United States, nor any of which the event has given more general joy."[6]

William M. Van der Weyde, editor of one of the early editions (1925) of the works of Thomas Paine, has written that "there is no evidence that Paine met with an actual open hostility on the part of his fellow-countrymen during the first years after his return."[7] Nothing could be further from the truth. From the first moment it became known that Jefferson had offered the author of *The Age of Reason* return passage on the warship *Maryland* until Paine's death on June 8, 1809, there was little peace for him or the Jefferson administration.

The clouds of controversy began to gather when Paine wrote to Jefferson on October 1, 1800, "If any American frigate should come to France and the direction of it fall to you, I will be glad you would give me the opportunity of returning."[8] Jefferson's reply of March 18, 1801, written only two weeks after he had assumed the presidency, was destined to become "one of the most famous documents of the decade."[9] The president extended his invitation to Paine in these terms:

> You expressed a wish to get a passage to this country in a public vessel. Mr. Dawson is charged with orders to the captain of the Maryland to receive and accommodate you back if you can be ready to depart at such short warning.
> . . . I am in hopes you will find us returned generally to sentiments worthy of former times. In these it will be your glory to have steadily laboured and with as much effect as any man living. That you may long live to continue your useful labours and to reap the reward in the thankfulness of nations is my sincere prayer. Accept assurance of my high esteem and affectionate attachment.[10]

Paine had attempted to return to the United States in 1795, 1797, and 1799, but each time he was deterred by the possibility of capture by a British ship, which would have returned him to England and death.[11] Paine had been outlawed and condemned for treason in December 1792 as the author of *Rights of Man,* an appeal to the English people to overthrow their monarchy and establish a republic. Thus delayed seven years in Paris, Paine decided he could wait for the westward sailing of a later ship that was to bring the new American minister Robert Livingston. This vessel, however, was ordered to the Mediterranean after leaving France, and when the Peace of Amiens was concluded soon afterward Paine no longer needed the protection of a national warship. He embarked from Le Havre on September 1, 1802, in a private vessel.[12]

The offer of government passage to Thomas Paine may seem an entirely proper gesture of gratitude today, for as John Bach McMaster has remarked, "It was a talent such as Paine's that enabled the United States to be a nation and have ships."[13] Even Henry Adams applauded the "earnestness and courage" of the president's action, but the great-grandson of John Adams also noted, "Had Jefferson written a letter to Bonaparte applauding his 'useful labors' on the 18th

Brumaire, and praying that he might live long to continue them, he would not have excited in the minds of the New England Calvinists so deep a sense of disgust as by thus seeming to identify himself with Paine."[14]

The first news of Jefferson's offer of a government ship for Tom Paine's return voyage appeared in the *National Intelligencer* on July 15, 1801. The newspaper republished Jefferson's letter to Paine as it had appeared in the Paris press, probably placed there by Paine himself to publicize the honor.[15] An almost immediate reaction was forthcoming from the Federalist kingpin of the Philadelphia press, the *Gazette of the United States,* which would not let this bit of news slip by without a slur on the Irish background of William Duane, rival Jeffersonian editor of the Philadelphia *Aurora:*

TOM PAINE AND PAT DUANE.

When the story arrived here, that the President of the United States had written a *very affectionate letter* to that living opprobrium of humanity, TOM PAINE, the infamous scavenger of all the filth which could be raked from the dirty paths which have been hitherto trodden by all the revilers of Christianity, Duane, instead of attempting to refute this scandalous charge upon the President, admits that it may be true, and even endeavours to justify it.[16]

Still the leader of the Federalist press, the *Gazette of the United States* was by no means alone in its attack on Jefferson's invitation. The *New-England Palladium,* pride and joy of the diehard Federalists of Boston, was even more vehement in its first reaction to the startling news: "What! Invite to the United States that lying, drunken, brutal infidel, who rejoiced in the opportunity of basking and wallowing in the confusion, devastation, bloodshed, rapine, and murder in which his soul delights?"[17]

This vicious language was only a mild preview of the calumny ahead for Paine and his presidential benefactor. Joseph Dennie's Philadelphia *Port Folio* jumped into the fray with all editorial guns trained on the Jacobin quarry:

If during the present season of national abasement, infatuation, folly and vice, any portent could surprise, sober men would be utterly confounded by an article current in all the newspapers, that the loathsome Thomas Paine, a drunken atheist and the scavenger of faction, is invited to return in a national ship to America by the first magistrate of a free people. A measure so enormously preposterous we cannot yet believe has been adopted, and it would demand firmer nerves than those possessed by Mr. Jefferson to hazard such an insult to the moral sense of the nation.[18]

From the first, the virulence of the attack by the Federalist press indicated that the return of Thomas Paine was to be treated as a purely partisan issue, the first great cause célèbre of Jefferson's administration. Indeed, in the thunderous roll of abuse lightened by flashes of vindictive humor, the figure of Paine himself almost became lost in the verbal histrionics. Such a fuss over the little fellow whom even the *Gazette of the United States* dismissed as a "revolutionary *bantam*" revealed that this was partisan warfare without quarter.[19] It seemed a harsh fate for the essentially gentle man who had confided to a friend before leaving Paris, "I had rather see my horse, Button, eating the grass of Bordentown, or Morrissania, than see all the pomp and show of Europe."[20]

Thomas Paine was but a pawn in the game, however. As the groundswell of protest increased against his return under any circumstances—and especially in a government ship—the *National Intelligencer,* which had unleashed the hounds of party malevolence in its seemingly innocuous republication of Jefferson's letter of invitation on July 15, 1801, noted the reaction with dismay two weeks later:

> It was not then believed that this short paragraph would be made the mighty instrument of calumniating, and even damning the character of the President. We possessed not the admirable penetration of discerning in such a measure a full demonstration that Mr. Jefferson entertained the same religious opinions with Mr. Paine, that he indiscriminately approved every act of Mr. Paine's life, and that he took this mode of evincing his secret pleasure in the calumny, alleged to have been cast by Mr. Paine upon the character of General Washington.[21]

The voice of reason could not mute the party zealots, however, at least not in this defensive posture. The Republican press at first denied and then cautiously admitted that the president may have invited Paine to return in a government vessel,[22] until the *National Intelligencer* was forced to confess on August 3, 1801, that this invitation had indeed been made.

If readers of Federalist newspapers expected a riot when Paine's ship docked at Baltimore on October 30, 1802, they were disappointed, for the arrival of the notorious figure provoked no incident. The Baltimore *American Patriot* reported that even Federalists "were the foremost to visit him, and with smiling friendly expressions, make him welcome in the city."[23] As the Baltimore *Anti-Democrat* announced Paine's arrival:

> The noted THOMAS PAIN [*sic*] arrived here on Saturday last. It is far from being the wish of the editor to speak of him in unbecoming terms, yet it is but Justice to observe that this man has some claims on our gratitude for his work entitled "Common Sense;" for, though the motives that induced him to collect together and publish the general arguments of the day, at that time, were, as might easily be proved, those of a hireling, yet that little work was of essential service in our revolution.[24]

The newspaper reported that a crowd of curious onlookers accompanied Paine to Fulton's tavern, where "after sipping well of Brandy, he became somewhat fluent in conversation, and readily declared that Mr. Jefferson's invitations were the cause of his returning to this country."[25] The *Anti-Democrat* briefly outlined Paine's itinerary—that he would go to Washington in a few days, then on to Fredericktown, Philadelphia, and New York, before returning to Washington—and concluded on a note of outraged indignation: "It is possible that Paine, like Jefferson, may visit the tomb of Washington.—Oh."[26]

Rather than simply announcing Paine's arrival, the Philadelphia *Aurora* took advantage of the occasion to weave an elaborate defense for the celebrated figure:

> Thomas Paine, the early and uniform asserter of the *Rights of Mankind*, and author of the immortal revolutionary papers called COMMON SENSE, and the CRISIS, arrived at Baltimore on Saturday last. The arrival of this interesting man, whose history as has been well observed, is interwoven with the immortality of *two revolutions* and *three nations* of the first distinction in human annals, was as might be expected, an object of interest and curiosity to the old who knew his services, and to the young who had heard of his fame in all the opposite modes which political sympathy or hatred could employ to express their respect or abhorrence of the asserter of freedom.[27]

The *Aurora* declared Paine's tranquil reception "a circumstance honorable to the character of Baltimore" and commended the fact that "the writings of Mr. *Paine* on religious subjects were not even mentioned, and the right of private opinion was neither assailed, nor brought into question."[28]

Like the good citizens of Baltimore, the Philadelphia newspaper also refrained from mentioning Paine's religious writings, especially *The Age of Reason,* which William Duane particularly disliked. In the same month that the above item appeared in the *Aurora,* Duane wrote to Jefferson:

> Paine's third letter ["To the People of the United States"] gives me considerable uneasiness, he has in fact commenced the subject of the Age of Reason in it. I have tried every effort of which I am capable to persuade him against it, but nothing will operate on him. I have fairly told him that he will be deserted by the only party that respects or does not hate him, that all his political writings will be rendered useless, and even his fame destroyed; but he silenced me at once by telling me that Dr. Rush at the period when he commenced Common Sense told him, that there were two words which he should avoid by every means as necessary to his own safety and that of the public,—*Independence* and *Republicanism.*[29]

As Duane clearly foresaw, the major attack on Paine would be on religious grounds, and such an attack would be dangerous to the Republican cause since it would reopen by association the scarcely healed wounds of the antireligious charges leveled against Jefferson in the months preceding his election. It was no time to talk about *The Age of Reason.* Duane would have slept better if Thomas

Paine had heeded the friendly advice of Robert Livingston when the newly arrived minister to France told Paine shortly before he left for America, "Make your will and leave the mechanics, the iron bridge, the wheels, etc., to America, and your religion to France."[30]

Duane had in fact braced for the assault on Paine's religious views as early as July 14, 1801, when the *Aurora* pointed out: "The pretended crime of Thomas Paine, is his *Age of Reason.* We do not mean to defend that work. That has been undertaken by hundreds, and the book itself is now thrown by among other lumber. We assert however that the writing of that book, is not a proof of his impiety, nor can it be a justification of any person in attempting to asperse the man."[31] In a later issue, the Philadelphia editor continued, "Any person who reads the *Gazette of the United States* and the *Washington Federalist* will soon be convinced that notwithstanding their clamour that they are as thorough-going deists, as the author of the *Age of Reason.*"[32]

One of the most caustic comments on Paine's arrival at Baltimore concerned the religious issue that Duane feared. Observed the *New-York Evening Post:*

> We request some correspondent to inform us how Mr. Paine will obtain a permit for the landing of his baggage. For this purpose, we know it is requisite to make oath at the custom-house, upon *the Holy Evangelists,* that the trunks contain no articles for sale. If Mr. P. takes the oath, he will give the lie to all he's said against the authenticity and sanctity of the bible; and if he will not take it, we apprehend he cannot get his baggage. But this is a difficulty from which Mr. Jefferson will probably relieve him, at the expense of—only a slight violation of the law.[33]

The *Gazette of the United States* denounced the *Aurora's* pleas for tolerance even more vigorously than Paine's religious thought itself. In a reply to Duane's early series of short paragraphs defending Paine's right of personal conscience, the *Gazette* exclaimed: "It is really an alarming thing to see almost every paper in the union which advocated the election of Mr. Jefferson, and commended his invitation to Tom Paine, now aiming their attacks, in a manner more or less direct, at the vitals of christianity."[34] This comment was headlined, "JACOBIN FAITH, OR DEATH AN ETERNAL SLEEP," ridiculing an earlier statement of the deist position on immortality printed in the *Aurora.*

Duane's fears were even more directly realized in the columns of the Richmond *Recorder* when the disgruntled James Thomas Callender wrote: "At the next election for president, it will be diverting to enquire what sort of Christian he must be, that votes either for Jefferson, or Madison? . . . Before proceeding to vote at the country court house, such of [the Republicans] as have Bibles must begin with burning the book. They have no other choice than that of renouncing their saviour, or their president, the son of the Virgin Mary, or the husband of black Sally."[35]

Shortly before Paine's arrival in the United States, the Philadelphia *Aurora* returned to its theme of 1801 in discounting the influence of Paine's religious writings. Commented the newspaper on October 13, 1802:

> The story about *Thomas Paine* is now contradicted by the tories, but they have founded another upon it—that he is coming to America to publish *the third part of the Age of Reason!*[36] what then? Has the christian religion been overturned, diminished or shaken by the first, or second part? There have been about fifty answers written to his former works, and the people go on without recollecting that such books ever existed, much less what they contained. If he writes, let him be answered. If he is wrong, of course he must be damned—and that surely is enough for the most pious and tender conscience. It is not easy to shake religion as fools and knaves believe or pretend to believe. There are many writings more violent against religion than Paine's books, and the majority of mankind appear never to have heard of them.[37]

Duane soon found that the most effective line of defense was simply to turn the charges back on the attackers. Could such outrageous calumnies be consistent with the genuine spirit of Christianity? The *Aurora* commented, "Are we to set down the multitude of *falsehoods* published against *Paine* about his passage and his refusals of passage—the pious wishes for his soul—and his body—as *evidences* of the CHRISTIAN *purity* of those who publish them; or of their mean subserviency and despicable hypocrisy."[38] The *Aurora* again pressed this line of argument about a week after Paine's arrival at Baltimore: "From the quantity of asperity employed against *Thomas Paine,* an enquiry naturally suggests itself— Is this *asperity* a criterion of *Christian piety*—or is not religion employed by hypocrites now, as in all former ages, as a MASK, to cover the attacks made on the man whose writings *vindicated America* and the *Rights of Mankind*."[39]

Yet the *New-York Evening Post* had a better time of it by appealing to the views of orthodox Christianity to discredit Paine and the administration that stood behind him. The *Post* commented in the satirical vein in which it excelled:

> The enemies of Mr. Jefferson may call his general political conduct into question—but surely they must at least be convinced of the *rectitude* of his intentions, and of his desire to *improve,* when they see him calling the virtuous Tom Paine to America to counsel, and perhaps to *decide*. Above all, that foolish sect, the *Christians* of the community, cannot fail to be grateful for furnishing them with an able preceptor to teach them the absurdity of their doctrines, and illuminate their minds. Some men have the happy knack of doing an honour while they confer a benefit; Mr. Jefferson is one of those; for by bringing Paine to America, he not only has procured the Christians the benefit of his pious advice, but done them the honor to treat their opinions, feelings, and prejudices with *becoming respect*.[40]

To appeal to that class of Americans that had little interest in things religious, the Federalist press at the same time carried on an unceasing attack on Paine's private moral character in terms that did not spare the vilest adjectives. Representative of this flank of the attack was a poem by "Stanley," which appeared in the *Gazette of the United States*, "Anticipated Elegy, A Parody on 'Tom Bowline'":

> HERE the fam'd Sot lies—poor Tom Ranter,
>   The darling of our crew!
> No more he'll hug his dear decanter,
>   For brandy brought him to!
> His face was of the manliest beauty,
>   With carbuncles beset:
> Faithful with us he did his duty,
>   And kept his ashes wet.
> *Tom* never from his club departed;
>   His prowess was so rare,
> Though often led or homeward carted,
>   In toping he was fair.
> And then he'd swear, and write so clever
>   Bl'phemy was his *fort;*
> But *Common Sense* is fled forever
>   Since *Tom* is turn'd to dirt!!
> Yet shall poor *Tom* not be forgotten,
>   For *Monticello*'s Sage
> Shall rank him though with tiplers rotting,
>   The wisest of the age.
> Thus brandy has in vain consign'd him
>   To death's unkind arrest;
> For while an Infidel's behind him,
>   His memory will be blest.[41]

The most incisive ridicule heaped on Tom Paine's moral character was contained in an anonymous letter printed in the *Gazette of the United States,* which at first appeared to be a defense of President Jefferson's attitude toward Paine, but concluded:

> It is well known that [Mr. Jefferson] is both a philosopher and an agriculturist.
> . . . I am inclined to think that it was in one of his meditations on manures that
> the idea of sending for Tom Paine first occurred to him; for I remember to have
> heard that *Paine* was half prepared for the compost bed two or three years ago;[42]
> and it is probable that a philosophical mind would suggest that by the time
> he could be brought hither, he would be fit to be used without mixture, and

furnish a fine opportunity for discovering, by actual experiment, whether infidel Philosophers (which are becoming plenty among us) will not form a new, and most valuable species of manure.[43]

The Boston *Columbian Centinel* channeled the smears against Paine's general moral character into a denunciation of his association with the president of the United States, and this sort of abuse was rapidly imitated by other Federalist newspapers. The *Centinel* commented, "But the importation of THOMAS PAINE, though he is clearly *a contraband* article, is most of all to be deprecated in a moral view—not on account of any ascendancy which *so notorious a drunkard,* and *so impious a buffoon* can be supposed to gain over the minds, or manners of *true Americans;* but because he comes under the sanction, and with the *co-operation* of the *highest officer* in the Union."[44] The newspaper continued, "Whilst these impressions lead the sober part of the community to *lament,* will they not embolden the licentious and abandoned to *rejoice,* that *the weight of presidential influence is thrown into the scale of infidelity and vice*?"[45]

Federalists shuddered when they learned that Paine had left Baltimore for Washington on November 9, 1802, expressly for the purpose of seeing the president. Cautiously the *National Intelligencer* announced Paine's appearance in the capital: "Thomas Paine has arrived in this city, and has received a cordial reception from the Whigs of Seventy-six and the Republicans of 1800, who have the independence to feel and avow a sentiment of gratitude for his eminent revolutionary services."[46] James Cheetham, editor of the New York *American Citizen*—which was an outlet for Paine's writings after he returned to the United States until Paine broke with Cheetham and then published his material in the New York *Daily Advertiser*—wrote later that Paine's "reception at Washington was cold and forbidding. Even Mr. Jefferson received him with politick circumspection; and such of the members of congress as suffered him to approach them, did so from motives of curiosity. Policy dictated this course. . . ."[47]

Others gave an entirely different account of the reunion between Paine and Jefferson. William Plumer recalled a visit to the executive quarters when "Thomas Paine entered, seated himself by the side of the President, and conversed and behaved towards him with the familiarity of an intimate and an equal."[48] John Bach McMaster has written, "The moment Paine landed he hurried to Washington and was warmly received by the President. Stories were afloat that he dined at the White House every day; that some lucrative office was soon to be given him; that he was at work on a defense of the administration."[49] Other members of the president's official family invited Paine to dinner, including Secretary of the Treasury Albert Gallatin and Secretary of War General Henry Dearborn.[50] Before leaving for New York in February 1803, Paine also visited Jefferson at Monticello—despite the protests of the president's daughters, Mrs. Randolph and Mrs. Eppes, both devout Episcopalians. Jefferson is supposed to have said,

"Mr. Paine is not, I believe, a favorite among the ladies—but he is too well entitled to the hospitality of every American, not to cheerfully receive mine."[51]

Jefferson's kindness to Paine found no favor among the Federalist prints,
however. The *New-York Evening Post* complained: "Our stomachs . . . nauseate at
the sight of their affectionate embraces, and we entertain no doubt that you, as
well as we, have become impatient to get out of such impious company. . . . We
leave them, then, to consummate their bliss."[52]

The Philadelphia *Aurora* answered these slurs with a barrage of editorial paragraphs. Typical were those of December 9, 1802, while Paine was still in Washington. According to one, "The *tory Gazette* is astonished that a president of the
United States should notice Mr. Paine—but they forget how intimate several
members of the last administration were with the avowed agent of the British
Cobbett [William Cobbett, Federalist editor of the Philadelphia *Porcupine's
Gazette*]—how convenient a *bad memory* is to the tories." Another paragraph in
the same issue stated: "The *tory Gazette* is very anxious for Mr. Jefferson's reputation—it deplores the circumstance of his having condescended to speak to
Mr. Paine; not reflecting that Mr. Jefferson and the other patriots who survive
the revolution in particular, and all friends to the rights of man are bound to
respect him for those services which received and merited the applause of all
independent Americans."[53]

The *New-York Evening Post* derisively identified Paine with Jefferson and the
entire administration in a poem of twenty-five stanzas, "Thomas Paine & the
King," which occupied considerable space in the four-page newspaper:

> . . . The ship came into port,
> King Thomas he sent his coach and six,
> To bring Tom Paine to court.
> Dearborn before him ran,
> All on the point of a glittering spear
> Carrying the Rights of Man.
> Monsieur Gallatin, from France,
> March'd on the right with a *pas vite* step,
> Carrying a flaggon of Nantz.
> Smith on the left did trot,
> The Age of Reason tied fast to his back,
> And tobacco and rum for the sot. . . . [54]

Having originated in James Thomson Callender's Richmond *Recorder,* the
charges of Jefferson's sexual relationship with his slave Sally Hemings were also
used by the *Federal Ark* to castigate the relationship between the two famous men:

> TOM PAINE
>
> That arch infidel, who has publicly declared to the world that he does not
> believe in any *creed* that he has read of, is now on a visit to

THOMAS JEFFERSON

the president of the United States, who wrote to him in France, and offered him a passage to this country in a national ship. It is said Paine has undertaken this journey to tender Mr. Jefferson his thanks for his polite letter to him while in France, and to request the *loan* of SALLY, as he has no female companion.[55]

It was the Richmond *Recorder* that ranted longest and loudest on the association between Jefferson and Paine, probably because of Callender's having felt abused by his relationship with the president. Paine's return was the first major issue that occurred after Callender and Henry Pace launched the weekly *Recorder* on July 11, 1801, and the irascible Scotsman made the most of the opportunity. In fact, it was Callender's comments on the Paine controversy that first marked the complete break between Callender and Jefferson. As the *Recorder* stated on September 15, 1802: "When it was first reported that Thomas Jefferson had invited Thomas Paine to return to this country, the Recorder affirmed that it was a federal fib; that the president never could have committed an action so imprudent. It has been our fate, however, to be deceived in every prediction which we had made in favor of the political sagacity of Thomas Jefferson."[56]

Callender admitted freely the literary power controlled by Paine, and this admission made the association between Paine and Jefferson appear even more formidable. In the opinion of Callender, Paine was "a man of superior, of gigantic, and Herculean intellect." The *Recorder* continued: "As a political gladiator, his merit is of the highest kind. He knows, beyond most men, both when and where to strike. He deals his blows with force, coolness and dexterity."[57] Yet, "Powerful and formidable as Mr. Paine is, he should not expect that five millions of people are prepared to fall on their knees before him" on his return to the United States. Indeed, if anyone were to fall it would be Jefferson himself. Callender condemned what he considered the greatest political blunder of the president's career in this manner:

> Mr. Jefferson had witnessed the unspeakable mischief that resulted to his party from Bache's publication of the second part of the Age of Reason. He knew that suspicions of atheism had been attached to himself. It seemed, therefore, incredible that the president, with his eyes open, should walk into such a gulf of reproach, as the invitation of Mr. Paine to return to this country. He could not have taken a longer step to destruction. . . . [58]

In short Callender saw the entire incident as evidence that "divine providence has predestined the disgrace and dismission of Thomas Jefferson." By accepting Paine as their friend, Jefferson and Madison had revealed that "they, as well as Paine, believe that the story of *the birth of Jesus Christ is an* OBSCENE BLASPHEMOUS FABLE . . . that the Virgin Mary was a woman of bad fame, and that her husband was cornuted [made a cuckold]."[59]

The outcry over Jefferson's association with Paine, denounced primarily on religious grounds, soon evolved into the story that Jefferson had brought Paine back from France to serve him as a partisan writer. It may have been the dramatic break between Jefferson and Callender that gave currency to this aspect of editorial comment on Paine's return. As the Federalist New York *Gazette* surmised, "A CORRESPONDENT says, that it is now easy to account for the anxiety of Mr. Jefferson, about bringing *Tom Paine* to this country—for his affectionate invitation and the offer of conveyance in a national ship. Mr. CALLENDER, whatever may be the cause, was no longer willing to write for him, and he might think that the pen of *Tom Paine* would be seasonable and useful."[60]

Callender, commenting on Paine's first letter to the people of the United States, called Paine the "*chosen vessel* of our beloved president! He sends twelve hundred leagues for an auxiliary writer, to tell his adversaries that they are *mad dogs!*"[61] According to this argument, Paine was not "invited" to return, he was "sent for." Joseph Dennie's *Port Folio* conjured up a quaint picture of Jefferson passing his editorial forces in review and then sending to Europe for Tom Paine:

THE TEMPTATION, AN EPIGRAM.
Wise Mammoth, in a chair of state,
  By slanders foul obtain'd;
How he should keep it, held debate,
  By the same arts 'twas gain'd.
He pass'd his forces in review;
  Smith, Cheetham, Jones, Duane,
  "Dull rascals—these will never do,"
Quoth he, "I'll send for *Paine.*"
Then from his darling den in France,
  To tempt the wretch to come,
He made Tom's brain with flatt'ry dance;
  And *took the tax from rum.*[62]

If Jefferson had actually hired Paine as a party writer, Callender predicted that their association would soon end in mutual recrimination. The *Recorder* observed, "It is quite as probable as otherwise that Jefferson will treat Paine, as he did Callender—He'll scarcely rent him a part of his house,—I tender you the homage of my high respects for the services you rendered me in vilifying Washington, Adams and the constitution, but, you see how 'tis, Mr. Paine; I–I-did not think you would come 'in event,'—I–I-should be happy to see your services rewarded—by 'the gratitude of nations,' the only reward a true philosopher wishes." But Callender added, "On second consideration, I think it more probable than otherwise, that Paine and Jefferson will not break friends: *the executive bought his wit dear enough in quarrelling with Callender.*"[63]

Other Federalist newspapers refused to pay Paine the indirect compliment that he was sought after as a writer. As the Boston *Columbian Centinel* saw the matter, "PAINE's abilities were always much overrated as his services. He was a bird of passage, and wrote for hire; and being a foreigner, all the coin he issued passed for sterling. The Congress of 1778, in their neglect of him, justly estimated his talents and integrity."[64]

The thinness of the charge that Jefferson had imported Paine as a party writer became apparent in November 1802, when Paine actually began to publish his series of "Letters to the People of the United States."[65] Paine obviously was more intent on talking about Thomas Paine rather than Thomas Jefferson. One mathematically inclined critic counted forty-four "I's" in the first letter alone, and historian John Bach McMaster has remarked, "As specimens of offensive egotism the letters are still unsurpassed."[66] In the first letter, Paine asserted, "I have no occasion to ask, and do not mean to accept any place, or office, in the government." After all, he already had "an established fame in the literary world,"[67] and a farm at New Rochelle, given him by the state of New York for his revolutionary services.

Curiously, in all the criticism raging around Tom Paine, his services as a French revolutionary were hardly brought into the indictment against him. Apparently the role of revolutionary agitator was still a respectable profession. The one exception that came to light was the story that Paine had tried to organize a French invasion force in 1794 for "revolutionizing" America. This story first gained wide circulation in the *New-York Evening Post* of February 4, 1803. The *Post* expressed initial disbelief in the story as it had appeared in the *Newburyport Herald* and waited to publish it until Paine had not refuted the story after it had been published in other papers. Since it was printed in the *Washington Federalist* while Paine was still in the capital, and no denial was forthcoming, the *Post* considered the story "genuine," but carefully added, "should any thing however at any time appear to disprove this, or even bring it into question, either from Mr. Paine or any of his friends, it shall readily have a place, and for the present we withhold all comment." Such editorial fastidiousness had the effect, deliberate or not, of lending greater authority to the story, which was headlined "PAINE'S PLAN FOR REVOLUTIONIZING AMERICA." To lend another touch of authenticity, the editor of the *Post* also republished the brief note from "A Customer" that had accompanied the original story in the *Newburyport Herald:* "In the *Public Ledyard* &c. of July 8, 1794, published in London, I met with a Plan proposed by TOM PAINE, to the French government, for revolutionizing the United States of America; a republication of which will oblige every friend to his country, whether Federalist or Democrat."[68]

Paine was quoted as saying, "Should George the Third be driven from his Throne, America will be his place of refuge; there he has deposited funds; and, incredible as it may appear, there he will be King." The article included Paine's detailed "plans" for the French invasion of the United States, and concluded with his words that "This is the only way to humble the British Lion, that now courts an alliance with the American Eagle, only to bring about its destruction."[69]

This story seems to have been too outlandish for even the most gullible readers, however, and it soon expired of its own patent falsity. The only other reference to Paine's revolutionary activities occurred in the *Port Folio,* which recounted this anecdote:

> During Tom Paine's stay in Philadelphia, he visited Peale's Museum; a young lady who happened to be there at the time, sat down to have her profile taken by the machine, called *phisognotrace.* Paine drew near to witness the operation, and when it was over he remarked to the lady—"They take off *heads here,* with great expedition Miss." "Not quite so fast sir, as they once did in France," was the reply, which so discomfited Paine, that he turned on his heel, and walked to another part of the room. An aged *friend,* who was present and heard the retort, stepped up to the young lady, and in a low tone of voice, exclaimed, "Excellent! excellent! young woman! The Lord is merciful, or the earth would open up and swallow up that wretch.[70]

While Paine's revolutionary services to France were glossed over, the Republican press did not neglect to recall his revolutionary services to America. Representative of this genre of comment was the following item from the Philadelphia *Aurora:* "The arrival of the asserter of the rights of man gives as much *pain* now to the *tories* as his *common sense* did during the war. The *tories* of that time denounced Mr. Paine for his political writings, and would have destroyed him as they did others, for his *whigism*—the *tories* of this day would do the same and for the same reasons, they now cloak their hatred upon pretence of revering *religion,* but *tories* will be *tories.*"[71]

On the other hand, one form of the Federalist attack was a denial of Paine's American citizenship. The *Gazette of the United States* voiced this complaint in a passage that echoes Federalist sentiment of the period of the Alien and Sedition Laws:

> Our government has so long permitted foreign convicts and renegades to go on, with impunity, in insulting the nation and dictating public measures, that they now seem to consider this country as the natural right and common property of all those who have shown themselves pre-eminent in baseness and impiety, of whatever nation they may be. The Aurora now talks of the services of Tom Paine to *his country!* and pretends to justify the President for making him the offer of a public vessel to convey him *home.* He says, "in offering him a passage, it was offering no more than Thomas Paine had an equal claim to with any OTHER AMERICAN CITIZEN." . . . If Tom is an American citizen and *this*

country is *his* country, we would fain be informed whether his letter to *"George Washington, Esquire,"* published at the office of the Aurora, was a letter to *his* President. It will not be pretended, that at *that time,* this was Paine's country, for then law and religion prevailed and were respected; and his motto is "where religion or law dwells there is *not my* country."[72]

In due course, this reminder of Paine's attack on George Washington evoked similar comment in other Federalist newspapers. The *New-York Evening Post,* reflecting Alexander Hamilton's political opinion if not direct editorial policy, was so enthralled with the subject that it republished three articles on this topic alone. It published a conclusion from the *Gazette of the United States* that Paine's services to Jefferson consisted of "his *exertions to destroy the reputation of* WASH-INGTON, *and with it the administration of our Government."*[73] Thus did Thomas Paine merit the "high esteem and affectionate attachment" of Thomas Jefferson, who had purchased these services "so grateful to his ambition and his envy."[74]

Not content with his past statements on the subject, Paine continued to heap abuse on the heads of Washington and John Adams in his "Letters to the People of the United States." The Philadelphia *Aurora* commented on the first letter with evident satisfaction: "We are pleased to see with what dignity the author before us, walks over the federal curs of America, scarce deigning to glance at this puny and bastard breed, which is only calculated to make a *noise* and wear *collars,* the badges of their slavery and *dependence."*[75]

After the fourth letter had appeared, the *Aurora* denounced Federalist opposition to Paine as attacks on a straw man: "Mr. Paine ought certainly to be thanked, and we make no manner of doubt that he is, in secret, by the *tory editors* throughout the union for the opportunity afforded them to keep up their clamour. If he had not arrived, what a miserable situation they would all have been in, where could they find a plot or massacre or any thing in short to keep them from sleeping at their posts?"[76] Nine days later, the *Aurora* again played a variation on this theme, claiming apparent victory where none actually existed:

> When Mr. Paine signified his intention, in his first letter to the citizens of the United States, of occasionally addressing them, we heard the *tory prints* rejoicing at the circumstance—he will, said they, afford us opportunity to write, and his writing will hurt only himself—since it has been stated by Mr. Paine in his fourth letter, that he would cease to write for the present, we have heard the same prints congratulating their readers that Mr. Paine has suspended his addresses . . . in fact the *tories* can make no more impression on Mr. Paine now than they did in '76, they find themselves engaged with no common antagonist, and are glad of the opportunity of making their escape.[77]

Contrary to expectations, Paine himself did not rush into the lists of partisan warfare where he was the primary target.[78] In his first "Letter to the People of the

United States," the beleaguered Paine noted—probably with secret satisfaction —the stir which his return to the United States had aroused: "In every part of the Union, this [Federalist] faction is in the agonies of death, and in proportion as its fate approaches, it gnashes its teeth, and struggles. MY arrival has struck it as with a hydrophobia; it is like the sight of water to canine madness."[79] With an air of patient suffering and superb condescension, Paine added, "as to the low party prints that choose to abuse me, they are welcome. I shall not descend to answer them. I have been too much accustomed to such common stuff to take any notice of them."[80]

Yet Paine found his natural champion in William Duane of the *Aurora*, and it must have been gratifying for the older man to notice the seriousness with which the Philadelphia editor undertook his task. In this controversy, at least, Duane kept his wits about him; he did not blindly strike back at every niggling criticism of Paine that came along; on the contrary, he more than anyone else realized the exact nature of the adversary and exposed the vilification of Paine for what it was:

> the clamor which is raised on [Paine's] arrival is by no means on Mr. Paine's account alone, no more than dread for religion is the motive for hostility, it is hoped to prejudice the president in the eyes of his constituents because he has not treated with indifference or contempt a man whose political services Mr. Jefferson had so good an opportunity to be acquainted with during the revolution . . . he has seen many good effects from Mr. Paine's early writings, he has seen him devoting his time, health, and talents to promote freedom, he has seen Mr. Paine's return to his country with pleasure, and will not by a line of conduct recommended, and which could only be pursued by *tories,* send him in his old age with sorrow to his grave; but by showing a respect, merited from Americans, will evince the goodness of his own heart, and fulfil the wishes of his constituents.[81]

Duane stated in late 1802 that "we doubt whether [the noise about Mr. Paine] will ever entirely cease,"[82] but by the summer of 1803 the bitterly fought controversy had blown over. In early 1803 Paine left Washington and arrived in Philadelphia on February 21 and at Bordentown, New Jersey, on February 24.[83] He reached New York on March 2, and according to an early biographer, his lukewarm popularity ceased with a New York dinner held at Lovett's Hotel.[84] William Plumer later recalled that Paine dined at the public table at Lovett's and "as a show, is as profitable as an *Ourang Outang,* for many strangers who come to the city feel a curiosity to see the creature."[85] Grant Thorburn, a minister in New York, was dismissed from his Baptist pulpit for shaking hands with Paine, and personal insults to the aged revolutionary were many. He was refused accommodations in taverns, once denied a seat on the Trenton stage, studiously avoided by his old friend Dr. Benjamin Rush, denied the right to vote on the grounds that he was not an American citizen, and bedeviled by crowds of young boys who pestered the old man on his farm at New Rochelle.[86] The young poet Thomas Paine petitioned the Massachusetts legislature to have his name changed to Robert Treat Paine Jr., "assigning as a reason, that he was desirous of being known by a *Christian* name."[87]

As Thomas Paine's notoriety eventually died down, he was allowed to lead a relatively peaceful if somewhat meager existence on his farm in New Rochelle or at boardinghouses in New York City. His obscurity became so pronounced, however, that on Paine's death on June 8, 1809, the *New-York Evening Post,* which had lavished so much space to revile Paine while living, took only this notice of his death:

> Died, on Thursday morning, the 8th inst. THOMAS PAINE, author of the Crisis, Rights of Man, &c. Mr. Paine had a desire to be interred in the Quaker burying ground, and some days previous to his demise, had an interview with some Quaker gentlemen on the subject, but as he declined a renunciation on his deistical opinions, his anxious wishes were not complied with. He was yesterday interred at New-Rochelle, Westchester county, perhaps on his own farm. I am unacquainted with his age, but he had lived long, done some good, and much harm.[88]

In conclusion, it was the Philadelphia *Aurora* that offered the most vigorous defense of Thomas Paine among the Republican newspapers. Except for its original announcement of Jefferson's invitation to Paine and subsequent apology for the gesture, the administration's semiofficial organ, the *National Intelligencer* remained aloof from the verbal combat. The Boston *Independent Chronicle* was removed from the scene of action because Paine did not visit that city, and the *Richmond Enquirer* was not yet in existence. William Duane of the *Aurora* loved the challenge of a good fight—or even a low and dirty fight—and the Philadelphia editor championed Paine's cause even through the thickest of the charges hurled at religious beliefs that Duane did not share. Unlike other newspapers, the *Aurora* did not rely on halfhearted apologies or squeamish distinctions, but boldly and forcefully claimed Thomas Paine as America's own, rum, rags and all. Here was, the *Aurora* proclaimed, "a distinguished and deserving revolutionary patriot," an outcast in the very country "that owes him so much, where every patriot heart ought to exult for the health and safety of this veteran, whose history is interwoven with two important revolutions, and an attempt at the third."[89]

On the other hand, the success of the Federalist attack on Thomas Paine has been evidenced by its long-range effects. In the words of Moncure Conway, Paine has emerged a "scarred monument to the Age of Unreason,"[90] and to this day there is no statue of the author of *Common Sense* and the *Crisis* series in Washington, D.C. Stephen Girard once said, "If they had only cut off Thomas Paine's head, he would then have been recorded in American schoolbooks as the

Honourable Thomas Paine, assistant savior of his country, instead of being exe-crated as Tom Paine, the infidel."[91]

Yet Paine lived to reap the bitter fruits of his controversial fame after he returned to the United States. The still-powerful Federalist press emerged the vic-tor in a one-sided and ominous test of strength. With the exception of the Phila-delphia *Aurora,* newspapers sympathetic to Jefferson failed to meet the challenge. Elsewhere there was almost no effective opposition to the blunt frontal assaults of the *Gazette of the United States* or to the clever satirical sniping of the *New-York Evening Post.* Most important, the controversy over Paine revealed the weak-ness of the *National Intelligencer* in a purely partisan contest.

One searches in vain for any recognition of Paine's patriotic services at the time of his death. There was one tribute, but it wasn't printed in any of the newspapers. Among the handful of persons at Paine's burial in the corner of a windswept farm field, only Madame Bonneville, a French émigré whom Paine had befriended, had the good sense to say, "Oh, Mr. Paine, my son stands here as testimony of the gratitude of America, and I for France!"[92]

Enos Bronson, editor during Jefferson's presidency of the once-powerful Federalist *Gazette of the United States.* The Historical Society of Pennsylvania (HSP), Enos Bronson, 1774–1823, Society Portrait Collection

Philip Freneau, editor of the *National Gazette,* sponsored by Jefferson in 1793. The Historical Society of Pennsylvania (HSP), Philip Freneau, 1752–1832, Gratz Collection, Case 6, Box 30

William Coleman, editor of the *New-York Evening Post,* founded by Alexander
Hamilton in 1801. Coleman was the only Federalist editor who supported
the Louisiana Purchase. The Historical Society of Pennsylvania (HSP),
William C. Coleman, Society Portrait Collection

Samuel Harrison Smith, editor of the *National Intelligencer,* Washington, D.C.,
Jefferson's official newspaper. The Historical Society of Pennsylvania (HSP),
Samuel Harrison Smith, 1772–1845, Leach Philadelphia Portraits Collection

William Duane, editor of the Philadelphia *Aurora* and leader of the Republican press. The Historical Society of Pennsylvania (HSP), William Duane, 1760–1835, Leach Philadelphia Portraits Collection

Thomas Paine, author of *The Age of Reason* and *Rights of Man*.
Collection of The New-York Historical Society, negative #58595

Thomas Ritchie, editor of *Richmond Enquirer.* The Historical Society of
Pennsylvania (HSP), Thomas Ritchie, Jr., Leach Philadelphia Portraits

Judge Samuel Chase. The Historical Society of Pennsylvania (HSP),
Samuel Chase, Society Portrait Collection

Federalists ridiculed Jefferson's philosophic "pretensions" as he sought re-election in 1804. © American Antiquarian Society

FACING: One of the earliest political cartoons (1793), this shows the contempt Federalists felt for the emerging Jeffersonian party. Jefferson exhorts, among others, Citizen Genet, New York governor DeWitt Clinton, naval hero Commodore Livingston, and Philadelphia astronomer David Rittenhouse, who peers through his telescope to find the "Creed of the Democratic Party." The Library Company of Philadelphia

A Peep into the Anti-federal Club

THE PROVIDENTIAL DETECTION

Divine intervention stops Jefferson from burning the Constitution on the "Altar to Gallic Despotism." Next to be sacrificed are Thomas Paine's *The Age of Reason* and the Philadelphia *Aurora* and Boston *Independent Chronicle*, Republican newspapers.
The Library Company of Philadelphia

SIX

Louisiana Purchase
"This New, Immense, Unbounded World"

... the acquisition of Louisiana will ... form the most important epoch
of Mr. Jefferson's administration.

Richmond Enquirer, February 19, 1805

This purchase has been made during the period of Mr. Jefferson's presidency,
and will, doubtless, give eclat to his administration [yet] the acquisition
has been solely owing to a fortuitous concurrence of unforeseen and
unexpected circumstances, and not to any wise or vigorous
measures on the part of the American government.

—*New-York Evening Post,* July 5, 1803

More than any other event in the springtime of the Republic, the purchase of
Louisiana from France by the United States in 1803 caused the already buoyant
spirits of Americans to soar to new heights of imaginative speculation. The very
thought of the vast reaches of Louisiana could be alluring—or daunting, and it
was the latter emotion that Senator Samuel White had in mind when he spoke
of the Louisiana territory as "this new immense, unbounded world" before the
Senate on November 2, 1803.[1] The acquisition of Louisiana was fraught with
momentous consequences for the future. In the opinion of Thomas M. Cooley,
the Louisiana Purchase "gave such direction to the subsequent thought of the
people and led to such marshaling of political forces, that nearly all the leading
events of later American history were either traceable to or in some measure
shaped or determined by it."[2] Walter Robinson Smith wrote that the acquisition
of Louisiana "marks the extent of the degradation of the Federalists and sounds
the death-knell of their party; and it begins an epoch of constitutional expansion by committing the Republicans to a liberal interpretation of the written
Constitution."[3] François Barbe-Marbois, the French official who concluded the
negotiations that gave a large part of America to the Americans, rejoiced at the
fate of Louisiana:

This colony, which had been always exposed to inevitable vicissitudes under the laws of a state, from which it was separated two thousand leagues, was now undergoing its last crisis. This event puts an end to uncertainties that had lasted for a century, and fixed for ever the fate of these fine regions. The spontaneous acknowledgment of the independence of Louisiana, its annexation to the confederacy of a prosperous people were the acts of the wisest policy; and those who shall hereafter be in a condition to observe their consequences, will admit that they ought to rank with the most important occurrences in the history of our times.[4]

In short, as the biographer of Barbe-Marbois, E. Wilson Lyon, has pointed out, "Rarely has a cession of such magnitude been accompanied by so much good will on the part of all concerned."[5]

All, that is, except the hard-core Federalists, who denounced the measure bitterly but to no avail. The price was not right. The territory was too large; the Union would be rent. Spain would never agree to the transaction; the United States would have to go to war to gain its new possession. The cities of the East would be depopulated; their streets emptied; their shops closed. The center of political power would drift southward and westward as new states were carved from the wilderness, each with two senators; New England would be ruined. The treaty of acquisition was a wild-eyed scheme adopted solely to advance the prestige of Thomas Jefferson; Virginia would be the real capital of a far-flung empire. Said William Plumer, Federalist senator from New Hampshire: "Admit this western world into the Union and you destroy at once the weight and importance of the Eastern States and compel them to establish a separate, independent empire."[6] Fisher Ames, the Federalist lion of New England, wrote: "Now by adding an immeasurable world beyond the Mississippi, we rush like a comet into infinite space. In our wild career we may jostle some other world out of its orbit, but we shall in any event quench the light of our own."[7]

President Jefferson had his doubts on the constitutionality of the transaction; Robert Livingston and James Monroe, the American envoys at Paris, went shopping for the city of New Orleans and doubled the size of their country, spending an unauthorized five million dollars; and Napoleon Bonaparte almost changed his mind—but the deed was done. Louisiana, from the bayous of the Gulf of Mexico to the peaks of the northern Rockies, was thenceforth and indisputably an American possession. In his final conversation with Livingston, French foreign minister Charles-Maurice de Talleyrand-Périgord said, "You have made a noble bargain for yourselves, and I suppose you will make the most of it."[8] This the United States was prepared to do.

By the time the United States had completed its westward expansion and nestled secure between two oceans and two weaker neighbors, it was difficult for Americans to imagine the fears and anxieties of early 1803, when Spain controlled the Floridas and France was soon to reoccupy Louisiana. For two years rumors abounded that Spain had retroceded Louisiana to France, a state of affairs President Jefferson contemplated with deep concern. As he wrote to Livingston on April 18, 1802: "The day that France takes possession of New Orleans fixes the sentence which is to restrain her forever within her lower water mark. It seals the union of two nations, who, in conjunction, can maintain exclusive possession of the ocean. From that moment we must marry ourselves to the British fleet and nation."[9] When Jefferson seriously considered an alliance with Great Britain, it was indeed a dark day for the young Republic. It was thought that French troops sent to quell the bloody racial struggle for independence in Santo Domingo would then proceed to invade Louisiana. "Every eye in the U.S. is now fixed on this affair of Louisiana," the president added. "Perhaps nothing since the revolutionary war has produced more uneasy sensations through the body of the nation."[10]

The worst feature of America's anxiety was the uncertainty concerning foreign news. The Philadelphia *Aurora* stated on March 26, 1802, "Concerning Louisiana, about which so much has been said . . . no definite knowledge can be possessed in America at this time." What was happening in Europe? "Whether [the cession of Louisiana from Spain to France] was finally agreed upon or not cannot yet be known, nor is it necessary to enter into anticipations, where so much depends upon interests, wherewith we cannot on this side of the Atlantic be very well acquainted."[11] Three days later, on March 29, 1802, the *Aurora* was able to announce the event with certainty and at the same time to deride the confusion in the opposition newspapers:

> The treaty between Spain and France which we publish this day, will afford the anti-republican scribes a new theme for the display of *their talents*—and the Boston Centinel and the Washington Federalist—and the Anti-Democrat and the New-York Evening Post, will unsay all their former sayings, and say a great number of things which they will have to unsay again. They will now discover that they were inspired by a prophetic spirit, and that the New-York Citizen, and the Boston Chronicle, and the Aurora, are all *false lights!* They will for example say, that they foretold the cession of Louisiana to France by Spain, three weeks ago; altho' they had formerly said that the First Consul usurped it without any treaty. They will say, that the N. York Evening Post was right in its first assertion, that Louisiana was ceded, though that paper afterwards declared that there was no foundation for the report. They will say that the present administration have been the promoters of this cession, though the treaty now given is dated when the present administration was not twenty days old. . . . They will now say further, that all the Aurora published concerning *Louisiana,* is not true, because what is in this treaty corroborates it![12]

When accused of "shuffling" and "contradiction" on the affair of Louisiana, the *Aurora* explained on March 30: "All that we have said on the subject we had thought perfectly consistent. The Philadelphia Gazette, either as an original or an echo, stated that Louisiana was, and afterwards that it was not ceded to France. We never said one or the other. We knew indeed that the cession had been made by Spain in May, 1800; but we also knew that subsequent negotiations had superceded that cession in January, 1802; we stated that general *Collot,* and citizen *Adet,* who had been appointed governor and prefect of Louisiana, had been suspended or removed from these appointments. Is there any thing shuffling or contradictory in this?"[13] At this point the newspaper's readers probably turned to less perplexing pastimes.

A few days later the *New-York Evening Post* shifted the grounds of argument by concentrating its verbal fire on the American ministers to France and Spain, Robert Livingston and Charles Pinckney:

> The Aurora has for some time past been vaunting about the extraordinary merit of our Executive, in appointing such immensely able and adroit Ministers to France and Spain; so active and so cunning that they effectually interposed and prevented the cessation of Louisiana to France. The Editor of that paper says, he *knows* that Mr. Livingston went at it in less than 48 hours after he got to Paris; and Mr. C. Pinckney gave the King of Spain no rest, night nor day, till he was enabled to *assure Mr. Duane* that the design was abandoned. All this, says the Aurora, was GLORIOUS *for our Executive, and happy for the country.* But while the garland, thus placed by Duane on the head of our illustrious President, was yet green, and the god-like man, proud and erect, bore
> *His blushing honors thick upon him;*
> *The third day comes a frost, a chilling frost,*
> *And* ————————————————— *nips his root.*[14]

The *Aurora* refused to admit any error, however, declaring, "We have repeatedly said that unless some new designs since the 4th day of February, 1802, have been formed; all that had previously taken place on the subject of Louisiana, was dissolved, and it remained upon the same footing as when it was ceded by France to Spain in 1767.[15]

While newspapers argued over who had ceded what to whom, matters took a decided turn for the worse in the autumn of 1802. On November 26 the *National Intelligencer* announced:

> We are informed that the Executive has received advice, that the port of NEW ORLEANS has been CLOSED against foreign vessels from the ocean, including American, and that the right of depositing American property there has been prohibited, without any other establishment being assigned in lieu of it [according to the provisions of the treaty of San Lorenzo between Spain and the United States, signed on October 25, 1795]. The right to export property before deposited was excepted from the prohibition. These regulations, so

contrary to our treaty with Spain, were published, at New-Orleans, by the Intendant [Morales], on the 17 October last.[16]

Thus did the foreign relations between the United States and Spain and France come to loggerheads in late 1802, bringing to a frustrating climax negotiations of the previous seven years. By the treaty of San Lorenzo of 1795—intended to complement the Jay Treaty with Great Britain—Thomas Pinckney had induced Spain to concede the free navigation of the Mississippi, so vital to western agriculture in the United States, and the right to deposit goods at New Orleans. Spain also conceded the thirty-first degree of latitude as the boundary line of Florida because she feared a possible alliance between the United States and England. Throughout the year 1796 France had sought to persuade Spain to cede Louisiana, but foreign minister Manuel de Godoy could not be moved.[17] When Talleyrand became minister for foreign affairs to the French Directory in July 1797, the French desire to reacquire Louisiana was greatly intensified. Even after the notorious X.Y.Z. affair ended in failure and disgrace, Talleyrand adhered to his larger purpose of rebuilding a New France. He thought that Louisiana and the Floridas united under one rule would be "a wall of brass forever impenetrable to the combined efforts of England and America."[18] But when Victor du Pont was sent in May 1798 as special commissioner to Philadelphia to study the general situation, he urged accommodation with America to prevent an alliance between England and the United States that would endanger the French and Spanish possessions in the New World.[19] Herein lay the seeds for the Louisiana Purchase five years later.

In January 1803, President Jefferson thought that immediate and decisive action was imperative. His plan was to buy the port of New Orleans and the adjacent Florida territory to settle the matter once and for all. On January 11, 1803, Jefferson nominated James Monroe "as Minister Extraordinary and Pleni potentiary to the First Consul of France, and to the Court of Madrid, in association with our Ministers to France and Spain, relative to the free navigation of the Mississippi."[20] Monroe, former minister to France, was an excellent choice for this trouble-shooting mission because he understood the problem of rights of navigation on the Mississippi thoroughly, having written a pamphlet on the topic in 1785. Moreover, Jefferson's appointment of a special envoy underscored the seriousness of his desire to come to a final settlement with the French and Spanish powers.

Meanwhile, newspapers speculated freely on the probable turn of events, once it was definitely known that Spain had retroceded Louisiana to France, from whom she had received the area by a secret treaty of 1762, on the eve of France's loss of her New World empire. Even before the closure of New Orleans, the Richmond *Recorder* commented: "The French are now masters of the Western waters. Tennessee and Kentucky cannot send a single barrel of flour to the

West Indies, if the first consul [Napoleon Bonaparte] chooses to forbid them. At least they cannot send it by the Mississippi, which is tantamount to prohibition."[21] Three weeks later the *Recorder* indulged in speculation: "Put the case that Mr. Jefferson shall, in the course of his duty, find it essential to refuse some demand which the first consul chooses to make. This is a thing very likely to happen. Well; and what then? Why then, Sir? Bonaparte sends two seventy-four gun ships to the mouth of the Mississippi, and there is *an end of your Western trade to the West Indies.*"[22] The Philadelphia *Aurora* countered this Federalist argument by reminding its readers of another matter: "The *tory* prints, have talked much about *Louisiana* and the *Mississippi,* but they have taken no notice whatsoever of the stipulations in the *British treaty* concerning that river, which may one day prove one of the most serious and injurious parts of that most imbecile or *wicked* of all our diplomatic transactions."[23] William Duane found the seven-year-old Jay Treaty still serviceable for partisan purposes.

The *New-York Evening Post* vehemently attacked the appointment of Monroe as special envoy to work with the resident American minister to France, Robert Livingston, in working out a settlement of the New Orleans problem. The *Post* stated, "the appointment of an Envoy Extraordinary, at this time, and under present circumstances, is in every respect the weakest measure that ever disgraced the administration of any country." In the same issue of the *New-York Evening Post,* "Pericles" declared, "Since the question of Independence, none has occurred more deeply interesting to the United States than the cession of Louisiana to France. This event threatens the early dismemberment of a large portion of our country; more immediately the safety of all the Southern States; and remotely the independence of the whole union." What should the United States do? The writer recommended seizing New Orleans and the Floridas at once and negotiating later. The *Post* itself noted that "Coriolanus" in the New York *Morning Chronicle* had written that negotiation by Monroe was preferable to war, "which he now deplores as the greatest calamity which can befall a nation. We, however, see no reason to alter our former opinions, nor shall we retract any thing that has been said in this paper.—War is undoubtedly a calamity, but national degradation is a greater, and besides, is always inevitably followed by war itself."[24] On February 21, 1803, the *New-York Evening Post* reported:

> We observe by the Morning Papers that Mr. Monroe arrived in town on
> Saturday, and will sail in a few days for Havre de Grace; but whether his depar-
> ture depends on the *secret affair* in the House as to the *Two Millions* of dollars
> [which Monroe was authorized to spend for New Orleans] we are not informed.
> By the extracts which we this day publish from London papers received by the
> last arrivals, we also perceive that the armament which is preparing in France
> under General Victor, and which our readers will recollect is destined for

Louisiana, is almost completed; that sailing orders had actually been issued, and that the fleet would put to sea early in January. It is possible therefore that about the same time that Mr. Monroe is making his first bow to the PREMIER CONSUL, if he indeed should be admitted to that honor at all, the French will be in quiet possession of New-Orleans.[25]

But the rapidly shifting political alignments of Europe caused Napoleon to decide not to dispatch the fleet supposedly bound for the invasion of Louisiana. In January 1803 Napoleon learned that his brother-in-law Charles Victor Emmanuel Leclerc had died from yellow fever while trying to put down the insurrection on the sugar island of Santo Domingo. Napoleon's Egyptian campaign had failed, and he was forced to consolidate his territorial holdings in Europe by giving up his grand design for a rejuvenated French empire overseas. War with Great Britain—and possibly with the United States—was once again imminent. In view of these circumstances, the sale of Louisiana to the United States would strengthen the American republic to counterbalance British power, would keep Louisiana out of British hands, and would provide funds with which to carry on the war against England.[26] As Napoleon told his advisers, "They ask for only one town of Louisiana; but I already consider the Colony as completely lost, and it seems to me that in the hands of that growing power [the United States] it will be more useful to the policy, and even to the commerce, of France than if I should try to keep it."[27]

Napoleon selected as his chief negotiator for the sale François Barbe-Marbois —a man who had served with the French forces in the American Revolution, was French chargé d'affaires in the United States for a time, married an American woman, and was the last intendant of the Old Regime in Santo Domingo. As a moderate in the French Revolution, he was deported to Guiana by the Directory but restored to favor under Napoleon as minister of the treasury.[28] The first interview between Barbe-Marbois and Robert Livingston took place on April 11, 1803; James Monroe arrived on April 12, and in fewer than three weeks the treaty was drawn up and signed.[29]

The American ministers were astonished at the unexpected offer to sell the whole of Louisiana when they had come only to buy the port of New Orleans and the adjacent territory of West Florida. Almost from the first, the American negotiators agreed between themselves to exceed their instructions by accepting the offer, and the conferences with French officials revolved primarily around the matter of price. Napoleon directed Barbe-Marbois to demand fifty million francs; the enthusiastic Frenchman raised this figure to one hundred million and the cancellation of the American claims that had arisen from shipping damages since 1800. Barbe-Marbois finally suggested a price of sixty million francs and settlement of the American claims by the United States. On April 15, 1803, the American ministers offered forty million; Napoleon drew up a treaty which demanded one hundred million; and on April 27 Barbe-Marbois dropped this figure to eighty million with the understanding that twenty million francs of this sum would be used to pay American shipping claims. Two days later Livingston and Monroe accepted these terms. The treaty itself and the two conventions that accompanied it—arranging for the amount and mode of payment and stating the terms for satisfying the American claims—were dated April 30, 1803, although the negotiations were actually completed a week later.[30]

James Monroe said at the signing ceremony on May 2, 1803: "We have lived long, but this is the noblest work of our whole lives. The treaty we have just signed was neither obtained by subtlety nor dictated by force. Of equal advantage to both parties, it will transform vast solitudes into thriving districts. The United States today ranks among the powers of the first order, and England's exclusive influence over American affairs has passed, never to return."[31]

Why did Napoleon forfeit a vast imperial domain in the interior of North America? Talleyrand summarized the reasons in writing to Denis Decres, minister of the navy, on May 23, 1803:

> The desire to spare the continent of North America from the war that threatened it, of settling various points of litigation between the Republic and the United States, and to remove all new causes for misunderstanding that their competition and neighborhood would have given rise to between them; the position of the French colonies, their need of men, agriculture, and aid; and finally, the force of circumstances, foresight for the future, and the intention of compensating by an advantageous arrangement for the inevitable loss of a country which war was about to place at the mercy of another nation [Great Britain]: all these reasons have decided the government to cause all the rights that it had acquired from Spain to the sovereignty and to the possession of Louisiana to pass to the United States.[32]

Was the price too high? In the opinion of E. Wilson Lyon, "A nation whose annual revenue of approximately $10,000,000 already bore a charge of $7,300,000 for the national debt was in no position to discharge immediately a further obligation of around $15,000,000."[33] A stock of $11,250,000 (sixty million francs) was created with a 6 percent interest rate payable semiannually at London, Amsterdam, and Paris. One-third of the principal was to be paid in 1819 and the remainder in the two successive years. Interest for the eighteen-year installment plan amounted to 59,140,000 francs, so the final cost was almost exactly twice that stipulated in the convention.[34]

The treaty itself, signed at Paris on April 30, 1803, stated: "The First Consul of the French Republic, desiring to give to the United States a strong proof of his friendship, doth hereby cede to the said United States, in the name of the French Republic, for ever and in full sovereignty, the said territory, with all its rights and appurtenances, as fully and in the same manner as they had been acquired by the French Republic in virtue of the . . . treaty concluded with his Catholic Majesty [Charles IV of Spain]." This clause referred to the Treaty of San Ildephonso of October 1, 1800, whereby Spain had agreed to retrocede Louisiana to France six months after ratification of the document.[35]

Other provisions of the French-American treaty stipulated that the inhabitants of Louisiana would be accorded equal rights under the Union and would "be maintained and protected in the free enjoyment of their liberty, property, and the religion which they profess."[36] Spanish or French ships carrying native goods would not have to pay any import duties at New Orleans for twelve years, and thereafter France and Spain would be granted most-favored-nation status. Finally, any treaties between Spain and the Indian tribes of Louisiana were to be honored until superceded by treaties with the United States, and the Paris treaty was to be ratified jointly with the two conventions within six months.[37] Spoliation claims were not to exceed $3,750,000.[38]

Two months after the treaty was signed in Paris, the Boston *Independent Chronicle* broke the staggering news to Americans on June 30, 1803, under the headline, "LOUISIANA CEDED TO THE UNITED STATES!" The Republican newspaper commented, "Thus our former anticipations have not only been realized, but exceeded; and thus the wise, seasonable and politic negotiation of the President, approved and confirmed by Congress, has gloriously terminated to the immortal honor of the friends of peace and good government, and to the utter disappointment of the factious and turbulent throughout the Union." The *Chronicle* concluded, "We shall now only say, that we hope this highly brilliant event will contribute to unite the candid and honest of every party, in an increasing confidence in the wisdom of that administration, whose greatest pleasure centers in the unbiased and enlightened, of every description; and in the peace, liberty and safety of this favored country."[39]

On July 4, 1803, the news reached Washington, D.C. The *National Intelligencer* announced calmly, "The Executive have received official information that a Treaty was signed on the 30th of April, between the Ministers Plenipotentiary and Extraordinary of the United States and the Minister plenipotentiary of the French government, by which the United States have obtained the full right to and sovereignty over New Orleans, and the whole of Louisiana, as Spain possessed the same."[40]

The Philadelphia *Aurora* heralded the event on July 7, 1803, and citizens throughout the country soon learned of the Louisiana Purchase as local newspapers everywhere were informed of the event by the three leading Republican newspapers in the United States—the Boston *Independent Chronicle*, the *National Intelligencer*, and the Philadelphia *Aurora*. The Federalist press, on the other hand, immediately set up a clamor because details of the acquisition of Louisiana were kept secret by the Senate. This secrecy was the first bone of contention.

The Philadelphia *Aurora* pointed out that the treaty could not be published until the Senate so authorized or had acted on it; that the treaty was not binding on the United States until ratified; and that the House of Representatives also had to consider the measure since it involved the expenditure of money. Hence, the *Aurora* stated, "upon the whole the public are already informed to the full extent which is authorized by the constitution; that is, that the *negotiation set on foot by our executive has been successful.*" Was this not sufficient cause for rejoicing? "That the objects for which a war was so violently advocated have been obtained without bloodshed or the creation of an enemy. That the free and perpetual sovereignty of all the Mississippi has been obtained to us, with all the natural and incidental advantages which were held forth as just motives for a war."[41]

Criticism of the Louisiana treaty was especially virulent in Federalist New England, a section that feared the loss of political power as new states were created out of the western territory. Federalist denunciation of this implication of the treaty was triggered immediately in Congress and in the Federalist press. As the Boston *Independent Chronicle* noted:

> Nothing will please the *Essex Junto*—One while New-Orleans was so important, it was declared that we ought to go to war to obtain it. Now this is accomplished, and a great deal more, without fighting; yet these uneasy creatures are still displeased. What will satisfy them? Nothing short of an alliance with crazy *John Bull.* How must the President smile at the absurd paragraphs in the tory papers on his conduct! They want war, he wishes peace; and it lies with the people to approve or disapprove his policy. If the vote should be taken, this day [July 4, 1803], we believe the Junto would be left in a *contemptible minority.*[42]

The *Chronicle* declared later that war with France or Spain would have cost the United States one hundred thousand lives and fifty million dollars. "But now we have obtained [Louisiana] by an amicable Negotiation, this immense and opulent Territory is nothing more to them [the Federalists] than a *'whistle!'* Fifteen thousand Kentuckians were to be armed to invade it, but as Monroe and Livingston have obtained the acquisition without the 'loan of a pistol,' the Tories are dissatisfied!!—A hopeful set truly!!!"[43]

As criticism mounted, arguments advanced by the Federalists against the treaty began to take on a systematic form. Most of the various lines of reasoning taken by Federalist editors against the approval of the Louisiana treaty were contained in the first editorial notice taken of the transaction in the Boston *Columbian Centinel,* a letter by "Fabricus" published on July 13, 1803. The writer condemned the territory gained as "a great waste, a wilderness unpeopled with any beings except wolves and wandering Indians," which "may be cut up into States without number, but each with *two votes in the Senate.* A President may be thus made for the people without their being at the trouble to choose him. A federative system without energy; and with no other bond of union than *Virginia*

—imperial *Virginia,* arbitress of the whole ... *Virginia* will wield that influence and be confirmed in her claim of dominion over the rest of the states." Louisiana may be bought, but for what purpose? "We are to give money of which we have too little for land of which we already have too much." The very vastness of the acquisition would destroy the balance in the Union because "this unexplored empire, of the size of four or five European kingdoms will destroy *that*—will drain our people away from the pursuit of a better husbandry, and from manufactures and commerce." The writer asked, "Can an Empire so unwieldy, so nearly uncivilized, that will for a century or two require such heavy charge, and contribute so little towards defraying any part of it, will it be, can it be subject to *one* Government? ... Does it not threaten to sever, and if not to sever to subjugate the Union?" Finally, the residents of "these new mountaineer states" would, like all westerners before them, "claim power and resist taxes."[44]

The Philadelphia *Aurora* explained, "The policy of our possession does not so much arise from a *want of land,* as from a prudential and early precaution to guard against dangerous or perfidious neighbors."[45] The *National Intelligencer* added, with a great deal of optimism, that the Louisiana Purchase "has removed forever a fertile source of factious intrigue and malignant opposition to the best of governments!"[46] The *National Intelligencer* summed up for the defense:

> By the cession of Louisiana, we shall preserve peace, and acquire a territory of great extent, fertility, and local importance. However great the latter object may be, the former is of inestimable value, and it is principally in relation to it that the importance of the cession is to be estimated. A nation, whose population is doubled in twenty-four years, whose resources increase with still greater rapidity, and which enjoys a free government, only requires peace to elevate her in a few years above the storms which with so little intermission, agitate the European world.[47]

But the torrent of criticism was in no way stemmed. As the Boston *Independent Chronicle* said on July 14, 1803: "The cession of *Louisiana* to the United States, by the French Government, has not lessened the malignity of *opposition;* but on the contrary, federalism, if possible, is this moment more rancorous than ever. The more perfectly successful, & the more eminently beneficial to the country, the measures of the present administration are hourly becoming, the more virulent becomes the abuse and outrage which is daily displayed in the federal papers." Federalist writers were denouncing the Purchase as "the most visionary project that ever entered the most visionary head." Before they had demanded the acquisition of New Orleans, but now that Monroe's mission was successful, "from a Paradise *Louisiana* has degenerated to a desert. . . . "[48] Later, the Boston *Independent Chronicle* observed, "Another opportunity [the Louisiana Purchase] recurs for the enemies of the administration to sheathe the sword. Will they embrace it?"[49]

Decidedly not. The *National Intelligencer* deplored "the pitiful attempts, made in some of the federal prints, to derogate from the merit due to the President of the United States" for the acquisition of Louisiana. Before the purchase, these same writers had "ridiculed the idea of obtaining the cession of even New Orleans by pacific means as the wildest chimera of a moon struck brain." Now some of them were praising Livingston and Monroe to detract from the president's accomplishment. "Mr. Livingston's merit may have been great," said the *Intelligencer,* "but his merit consists, not in standing alone, but in carrying into effect the will of those he represented."[50] The Washington newspaper hastened to explain in its next issue that it did not intend to deny Livingston "the credit due to his diplomatic talents and to the attention and ability he has exerted in this negotiation." In one of its rare attempts at humor, the *Intelligencer* added: "The small wits of the day have jested at Mr. Livingston's deafness, and queried how he would figure in a cabinet interview with Bonaparte. They now find that he has at least had his eyes well open, and that he has carefully watched the moment of striking with most advantage to his country."[51]

On the other hand, the Boston *Columbian Centinel* viciously attacked both Livingston and Monroe. On August 10, 1803, the Federalist newspaper commented:

> Great pains have been taken to give a popular complexion to the purchase of Louisiana; and a contest is maintained by the respective friends of LIVINGSTON and MONROE for the exclusive honor of the transaction.—Whoever has read the Memorial of the former and the famous BOOK of the latter will see that France has no reason to complain of either of them.—Both have discovered a zeal to serve her in her conflict with England which could hardly be exceeded if we were a colony of France and those men our agents at the Directorial and Consular Court.[52]

In the verbal battle for the acquisition of Louisiana, the greatest skirmish occurred on the matter of cost—exorbitant, in the Federalist newspapers; trifling, in the Republican journals. The Boston *Columbian Centinel* noted on July 20, 1803:

> It has not transpired at what price the United States has purchased *Louisiana.* It rises daily.—One of the *New-York* papers states it at *Fifteen Millions* of dollars; and this is confirmed by a letter from the Spanish consul at *New-York.* One who professes to know some of the secrets of the cabinet, and who is a warm democrat, has put it at 40,000,000 dollars; and declares there are three hundred speculators who stand ready to give Eighty millions of dollars for the unlocated lands. But we consider all these statements as the wild progeny of conjecture.[53]

"It is quite certain, however," the *Centinel* continued later, "that the payment of fifteen millions of Dollars to France for the restoration of our rights will not be

thought wise by the American People, when they have had time to consider it;—
they will easily perceive that FRANCE COULD NOT KEEP NEW-ORLEANS and must
have been glad to cede it to the U.S. that it might not fall into the hands of the
English;—they will see that THE ADDITION OF LOUISIANA IS ONLY A PRETENCE
FOR DRAWING AN IMMENSE SUM OF MONEY FROM US which can only be viewed
as a contribution to support a power [France] already too great for the safety and
liberty of the civilized world."[54] John Bach McMaster admirably summarized the
Federalist objections to the price for Louisiana by compiling the illustrative
devices used to emphasize the greatness of the sum in the Federalist newspapers:

> Weigh it, and there will be four hundred and thirty-three tons of solid silver.
> Load it into wagons, and there will be eight hundred and sixty-six of them.
> Place the wagons in a line, giving two rods to each, and they will cover a dis-
> tance of five and one third miles. Hire a laborer to shovel it into the carts, and,
> though he load sixteen each day, he will not finish the work in two months.
> Stack it up dollar on dollar, and, supposing nine to make an inch, the pile will
> be more than three miles high. It would load twenty-five sloops; it would pay
> an army of twenty-five years; it would, divided among the population of the
> country, give three dollars for each man, woman, and child. All the gold and all
> the silver coin in the Union would, if collected, fall vastly short of such a sum.[55]

The Philadelphia *Aurora* immediately attacked such dazzling arguments.
Actually, the Republican newspaper stated, "the *democratic* government has obtained a territory as large as France, for the amount of one years public expenditure under the any thing or nothing administration."[56] The *National Intelligencer*
recalled that Federalist newspapers once had said "that too great a price could
not be given for New-Orleans, and one print has informed us that rather than
not acquire Louisiana, fifty millions ought to be given, and that even that sum,
large as it is, would be a cheap purchase."[57]

To combat the Federalist charge of extravagance in paying so much for the
Louisiana Purchase, the *National Intelligencer* continually stressed the fact that
the transaction had been accomplished without war and without bloodshed.
Here was "the acquisition of a vast territory without the effusion of a drop of
blood," something which could not have been gained "by arraying the largest
army, incurring the most lavish expenses, and by the prodigal waste of human
life."[58] In early 1804 the *Intelligencer* declared, "Never have mankind contemplated so vast and important an accession of empire by means so pacific and
just, and never, perhaps, has there been a change of government so agreeable to
the subjects of it."[59] When commenting on a victory celebration in Washington,
the newspaper added:

> The reduction of a petty fortress which has cost the lives of thousands; the
> conquest of a town, in which the widow, the orphan, and the helpless virgin

have had ample cause to heap curses on the heads of the conquerors, have too often furnished occasion for joy and festivity. But what must have been the sensations of those who were now assembled, when they have reflected, that without exciting the anguish of one heart, they had extended the blessings of liberty to an hundred thousand beings who were added to the population of their country; and by means unstained with the blood of a single victim, they had acquired a new world, and had laid the foundation for the happiness of millions yet unborn![60]

Meanwhile, ratification of the Louisiana treaty was proceeding on both sides of the Atlantic. It was learned in Washington on August 19, 1803, that Napoleon had ratified the agreement—as expected—on May 22, 1803.[61] President Jefferson, overcoming his constitutional scruples, called a special session of Congress for October 17, 1803, to meet the six-month deadline for ratification. On the second day of the debate in the Senate, the treaty was approved by a vote of 24–7.[62] Shortly afterward, the House of Representatives gave its affirmative by a party vote of 90–25, successfully concluding the biggest real-estate deal in history.[63] The United States had doubled its original territory, and—although the exact boundaries of the acquisition would not be known for years—had obtained about nine hundred thousand square miles of some of the most fertile land in the world. The Louisiana Purchase was greater in extent than the nations of Great Britain, Germany, France, Spain, Portugal, and Italy combined.[64]

The American press was having a difficult time keeping up with this rapid chain of events. It was not until January 27, 1804, that the *National Intelligencer* received and printed the treaty transferring Louisiana from Spain to France, long after that once hotly debated issue had become a dead letter.[65]

Meanwhile, the actual transfer of the territory was underway. France had dispatched Pierre Clement Laussat as a civil agent to Louisiana to prepare the way for General Claude Perrin Victor and a military force, which was to assume control of the area from Spain. Laussat arrived at New Orleans on March 26, 1803, not knowing that within a few days his mission would be extended to the formality of handing the received territory over to the United States. The Marquis Sebastian de Caso Calvo de la Puerta y Farrill arrived from Havana on April 10 and with Governor Juan Miguel Salcedo delivered the province to France on November 30, 1803.[66] Military forces of the United States under the command of General James Wilkinson had advanced to Point Marigny a few miles from New Orleans by December 17, and three days later marched into the city to receive the territory.[67] At eleven o'clock on the morning of December 30, the citizens of New Orleans assembled in the Place d'Armes to witness the solemn transfer;[68] as the Tricolor was slowly hauled down, the Stars and Stripes rose in its place. So ended three centuries of "over-feeble and badly organized colonization" by France in the New World.[69] Some of the inhabitants present at the ceremony had seen Louisiana transferred from one hand to another six times during their lifetimes, including its placement in private hands by Louis XIV. Laussat left New Orleans on April 21, 1804, with Louisiana in the hands of U.S. Governor William C. C. Clairborne. On departure, the Frenchman said, "It is a hard thing for me, having once known this land, to part from it."[70]

Thus, the acquisition of Louisiana became an accomplished fact, despite the doubts by President Jefferson and some Federalists over the constitutionality of the event. The *New-York Evening Post* reported on December 31, 1803: "A gentleman, who was present in the House of Representatives at the debate on the treaty, yesterday informed the editor that he heard both Mr. Gallatin, the Secretary of the Treasury and Mr. Lincoln, the Attorney General, say, that without question the third article of the treaty incorporating Louisiana into the Union, was not warranted by the constitution: but they thought the constitution might be amended as to cure this objection."[71] President Jefferson twice proposed such an amendment to his cabinet, but few Republicans felt that the fait accompli needed to be justified. Joseph H. Nicholson adopted the viewpoint that the power to make treaties and declare war granted by the Constitution offered sufficient constitutional grounds for the Louisiana Purchase. After all, territory could be acquired only by treaty or conquest, and Chief Justice John Marshall vindicated this opinion in his decision in the *American Insurance Co. v. Canter* in 1828.[72]

On the ratification of the Louisiana treaty in both houses of Congress and the formal transfer of the territory, jubilant Republicans celebrated in the national capital. On January 30, 1804, several congressmen sponsored a ball in Georgetown that proved to be the great social event of the season, attracting five hundred ladies and gentlemen. The walls of the assembly room were decorated with festoons of laurel, and at one end was placed a transparent portrait of the president, surrounded by several military banners. As the *National Intelligencer* described the scene, "All the windows of the House were illuminated, and from its high situation, at the angle of one of the principal streets, the extent of its front, and the reflection of the snow, the effect and brilliancy of the illumination, were great, and extended to a considerable distance." The *Intelligencer* delighted in praising the republican lack of ornamentation on this occasion:

> The plain unembellished walls of our rooms, the want of that splendor, and of that admiration which painting, and gilding, & all the artful scenery of architecture can produce, and the still plainer quality of our manners, may, perhaps, to a foreign eye, and to foreign habits, place the grade of such a public festival far below the spectacles that celebrate the achievements of Warriors, or the peace that only suspends the career of destruction—But when humanity rejoices in the extension of the empire of freedom, and of peace, the superficial effects of the arts of the painter, and of the gilder, vanish before the splendor of the event, and put place and form out of consideration.[73]

On the occasion of a celebration at Stelle's Hotel in Washington, an ode, "translated from the Latin, by one of the company, and adapted to the occasion, was sung by several voices accompanied with instrumental music." The last of four stanzas follows:

PAX BELLO POTIOR.

To Jefferson, belov'd of Heav'n,
May golden Peace be ever given,
And when Death at last shall come,
To lay him in the silent tomb,
May weeping Angels gather near,
And Laurels strew around his bier,
And waft him, on the wings of Love,
To everlasting Peace above.[74]

If the president were in attendance, he must have stirred uncomfortably on realizing that only his own demise could furnish the poet with material of suitable grandeur for the occasion.

Of all the newspapers that commented on the Louisiana Purchase, the editorial record of the *New-York Evening Post* offers the most interesting case study. It alone of the Federalist journals defended the acquisition as a positive good to the country. William Coleman, on learning of the treaty on July 5, 1803, brought his Federalist newspaper into the Republican camp, by stating forthrightly: "At length the business of New-Orleans has terminated favorably to this country. Instead of being obliged to rely any longer on the force of treaties, for a place of deposit, the jurisdiction of the territory is now transferred to our hands and in future the navigation of the Mississippi will be ours unmolested. This, it will be allowed is an important acquisition; not, indeed, as territory, but as being essential to the peace and prosperity of our Western country, and as opening a free and valuable market to our commercial states."[75]

When Spain threatened to refuse to recognize the cession of Louisiana to the United States from France, as a violation of her agreement with France, the *New-York Evening Post* also stood squarely behind the Jefferson administration: "If . . . a war should ensue, as there must if Spain is just to herself—the blood be on the heads of those who have resorted to arms to enforce injustice."[76]

Although the *New-York Evening Post* sided with the Republicans on the issue of the Louisiana Purchase, the newspaper could not help making comparisons between its position on the Louisiana treaty and that of the Republican newspapers on the Jay Treaty:

We have not, indeed, commissioned any demagogue to get together a rabble of the lowest of the populace in every sea port in the Union, and demand of them to vote that the treaty contains commercial stipulations ruinous to our interest. We have had no citizens to mount a bench in the midst of a frantic crowd, and move to *"kick the treaty to Hell."* We have not had a thousand forms of objections prepared beforehand, and sent round the country to appear as original in all the newspapers. We have not hired blackguards to assail with brickbats in the streets any man who dare speak his mind; nor have we procured one of the L—— to march to the battery with a mob at his heels and burn the treaty, together with the negotiator in effigy.[77]

While the *New-York Evening Post* approved the Louisiana Purchase because of its effect on American foreign relations, it ridiculed the intrinsic merits of the area acquired, and here the gifted pen of William Coleman came into full play. With humorous satire, the *Post* lampooned the "Louisiana Tract" submitted by President Jefferson to Congress—a collection of fact and fancy about the great unknown region. The New York newspaper considered the tract "a tinsel attempt to flourish and embroider at the expense of good sense, if not of truth and sincerity." The *Post* continued:

In his [Jefferson's] description of Upper Louisiana, he soberly informs Congress that the land on the borders of the Mississippi yields *"an abundance of all the necessaries of life and almost spontaneously."* Now surely this is a very extraordinary license of expression, unless indeed Mr. Jefferson really means to be understood as saying, that not only *salt,* but bread and meat, and some other necessaries grow "of their own accord," in this vast garden of Eden; where, according to him, man is exempt from the denunciation of *eating his bread in the sweat of his face.* He next informs Congress that "that part of Upper Louisiana, which borders on North Mexico, is one immense prairie (he would not say *meadow* for the world) it produces nothing but grass; it is filled with buffalo, deer and other kind of game; the land is represented as *too rich* for the growth of forest trees." We have always understood that the richer the land the larger the forest trees, and we have heard of land being too poor to bear timber at all, but this is the first time we have heard of its being too rich for that purpose.[78]

Jefferson, according to the *New-York Evening Post,* had soberly informed Congress that upper Louisiana contained a mountain 180 miles long and 45 miles wide, composed of *"solid* ROCK SALT." This statement was a ready-made opening for William Coleman:

Methinks such a great, huge mountain of solid, shining salt, must make a dreadful glare in a clear sun-shiny day, especially just after a rain. . . . We think that it would have been no more than fair in the traveller who informed Mr. Jefferson of this territory of solid salt, to have added, that some leagues to the westward of it there was an immense lake of molasses, and that between this lake and the mountain of salt, there was an extensive vale of hasty pudding, stretching as far as the eye could reach, and kept in a state of comfortable eatability by the warmth of the sun's rays (a capital place, this for fatting hogs [and] into which the natives, being all Patagonians, waded knee deep, whenever they were hungry, and helped themselves to salt with one hand to season their pudding & molasses with the other to give it a relish.)[79]

Curiously, on the same day that this famous item appeared in the *New-York Evening Post,* the *National Intelligencer* was solemnly informing its readers: "We learn that the President of the United States has received from Louisiana, specimens of SALT, taken from the extensive mountain of that substance, and of *Plaster of Paris,* of which article there are said to exist great masses in Louisiana."[80]

The national capital got its first look at the inhabitants of the newly acquired territory when a deputation of Osage warriors and chiefs visited President Jefferson on July 10, 1804.[81] The *National Intelligencer* noted that "their stature is from six feet, to six feet three inches. They have two boys with them, who promise to rival the men in size. Their complexion is light, and their countenances are indicative of less ferocity and more intelligence than the writer . . . has observed in *any people.*" The editor concluded that "Buffon can produce no fat Englishman or meagre Frenchman superior to these people."[82] As a fitting climax before leaving Washington, the Osage chiefs performed a war dance in the Capitol, "accompanied by the Italian band."[83]

A year and a half later, another group of Indians "from the waters of the Missouri, and those from the Cherokee country" visited Washington, where they went to the Capitol to pay their respects "to their Fathers, the Representatives of the People."[84] This delegation of awestruck Indians visited the frigate *Adams* early in January 1806, accompanied by President Jefferson and the secretaries of the navy and of war. Said the *National Intelligencer:* "A short time after [they were conducted on board] a salute was fired from the frigate. They were then shown the different parts of the vessel, and the military apparatus. They were highly pleased with this mark of attention, and made their acknowledgments to this effect to the President. They evinced little, if any emotion, at the spectacle of the firing."[85]

While all this was going on in Washington, Meriwether Lewis and William Clark, younger brother of George Rogers Clark, pushed deep into Louisiana territory on a presidential mission to see exactly what the country had acquired. With his small band of twenty-one men,[86] Captain Lewis left St. Louis in May 1804 and reached the shores of the Pacific on November 15, 1805. On August 16, 1805, the *National Intelligencer* had announced: "We learn that a part of the collection of the curiosities collected by Captain Lewis on the Missouri, has reached Baltimore. Among these are a living animal, called the wild dog of the Prairie, and one magpie. Four magpies were sent but one of them destroyed the other three."[87] And finally on December 31, 1806, the *Intelligencer* could announce with "high satisfaction" the return of Captain Lewis to Washington, D.C., adding that "few expeditions have been conducted with more patience, perseverance, or success. . . . "[88]

At "an elegant dinner" given Captain Lewis by the citizens of Washington, John Beckley recited "the following elegant and glowing stanzas" from the pen of Joel Barlow. These are two of the nine stanzas:

ON THE DISCOVERIES OF CAPTAIN LEWIS.
Columbus! not so shall thy boundless domain
Defraud thy brave sons of their right:
Streams, midlands and shorelands illude [*sic*] us in vain,
We shall drag their dark regions to light.
With the same soaring genius thy Lewis ascends,
And, seizing the car of the sun,
O'er the sky-propping hills and high waters he bends.
And gives the proud earth a new zone.[89]

"A new zone!" These three words expressed the sense of wonder and amazement felt by many Americans on the acquisition and exploration of the Louisiana Purchase. What lay beyond the Mississippi? The *New-York Evening Post* could laugh at Mr. Jefferson's "mountain of salt," and the *National Intelligencer* could and did discuss seriously such matters as a prairie dog rattling around in its cage in the President's Mansion, and a magpie that naughtily destroyed its three mates. The image of Louisiana as presented in the newspapers of the time glittered with many facets: Indians who did not flinch when naval guns were discharged, fine strapping Indians who brought to mind Jefferson's old controversy with the French naturalist Buffon; quiet river deeps in the morning mist; mountains of mighty grandeur which were to inspire a century of western artists from Albert Bierstadt to George Catlin, and rough settlements spearheading their way into the wilderness.

Federalist criticism of the Louisiana Purchase did not cease with the expeditions of Lewis and Clark, or that of Zebulon Pike, despite the wondrous vistas unfolding in the West. As late as February 19, 1805, the *Richmond Enquirer* commented, "The Federal prints have not yet ceased to anathematize this measure; perhaps the most important, which has occurred under the present administration."[90] The opposition Federalist press was tenacious, but it was not able to tarnish the luster of the event. The Louisiana Purchase acquired an aura that has not yet dissipated; it evoked a feeling of pride and a sentiment of nationality that stirred the invalid of the East as well as the young and sturdy who followed the trails westward. And yet at the time, no one realized the true significance of this vast acquisition. The fact that France was eliminated once and for all from the North American continent seemed the important thing, not the seemingly limitless stretches of rolling prairie that later, under the plow, revealed the rich black soil of America's corn belt, nor the ore-laden shafts of the Rockies, nor the grasslands of the West beckoning later hordes of emigrants from Europe. The press came together on the Louisiana Purchase more solidly than on any issue since the Stamp Act of 1765. Thomas Ritchie of the *Richmond Enquirer* led the bandwagon, declaring "the acquisition of Louisiana will . . . form the most important epoch of Mr. Jefferson's administration."[91] It was an event easily translatable into vast popular approval, and one that even the waning Federalists could not ignore.

SEVEN

Duel at Weehawken

When we say that HAMILTON IS DEAD! We can add nothing
to the cause of grief—When we remember how he lived!
We can add nothing to the lustre of his fame.

—Philadelphia *Register,* republished in the
New-York Evening Post, July 19, 1804

. . . we are not bound to endure an annoyance the most disgraceful, or attacks
upon the virtuous living through a constrained charity for the useless dead.

—Philadelphia *Aurora,* July 30, 1804

At seven o'clock on the morning of July 11, 1804, the wooded heights of Weehawken, New Jersey, echoed with the crack of two pistol shots that reverberated
through the pages of American history. One bullet spent itself in the air after
ripping leaves from a low-hanging tree branch, but the other lodged in the spine
of America's most distinguished Federalist, Alexander Hamilton. As the opposing second, William P. Van Ness, shielded the face of Aaron Burr with an
umbrella, Dr. David Hosack rushed to the side of the stricken Hamilton, supported in the arms of his second, Nathaniel Pendleton. Hamilton mustered the
strength to say, "This is a mortal wound, Doctor," and then lapsed into temporary unconsciousness.[1] He died thirty-one hours later in the home of William
Bayard in Greenwich Village; Aaron Burr lived thirty-two years after the duel,
but his political career died on the sun-flooded heights of Weehawken.

Americans everywhere mourned the premature death of Alexander Hamilton at the age of forty-eight with a lavish sentiment that transcended political
differences. No event had touched the young nation with deeper grief since the
death of George Washington five years earlier. With very few exceptions, newspapers throughout the country lamented the loss of Hamilton, while several
Republican editors seized on the occasion to discredit Burr, whom the party had
discarded on February 25, 1804, by selecting the six-term governor of New York,
George Clinton, as Jefferson's running mate in the election of 1804. Ahead for

Aaron Burr lay his ill-fated western conspiracy, acquittal in three courts-martial and a trial for treason, years of exile and anguish. Ahead for the Federalist Party lay futile schemes for dismembering the Union, unsuccessful attempts to recoup its fortunes, and political oblivion.

The sudden death of Alexander Hamilton at the hand of Aaron Burr thus marked a tragic dividing line in the political history of the young Republic. In the words of Henry Adams, "The death of Hamilton and the Vice President's flight, with their accessories of summer-morning sunlight on rocky and wooded heights, tranquil river, and distant city, and behind all, their dark background of moral gloom, double treason, and political despair, still stands as the most dramatic moment in the early politics of the Union."[2] Fortunately for the Jefferson administration, however, the fugitive Burr was viewed by an incensed public on his individual merits and not as the vice president elected with Thomas Jefferson.

The star-crossed careers that met in tragic collision at Weehawken had much in common. Both Hamilton and Burr had been child prodigies. Hamilton's newspaper description of a hurricane that swept St. Croix in the West Indies brought him to public attention at the age of fifteen, and Burr entered the sophomore class at the College of New Jersey at the age of thirteen, graduating with distinction three years later. In the American Revolution, Hamilton became a captain commanding a battery of artillery at nineteen, and Burr was a major at twenty. At different times each man served General Washington—Burr in the New York campaign of 1776 before being transferred to the command of General Israel Putnam, and Hamilton as secretary and aide-de-camp to Washington after March 1, 1777. After a disagreement with the patriot commander-in-chief, Hamilton headed an infantry regiment in Lafayette's corps and later directed a brilliant attack on one of the two main British redoubts at Yorktown. Burr was named lieutenant-colonel of the Continental line in July 1777 and assigned to a regiment stationed in Orange County, New York; he narrowly escaped being implicated in the "Conway Cabal" before illness forced him to resign from the army in March 1779.[3]

After the Revolution both young men turned to law careers, and each made a reputation for himself in this field. Burr took up the study of law with an old college friend, William Paterson, at Raritan, New Jersey, and later continued his studies at Haverstraw, New York. In 1782 he was licensed as an attorney and counselor at law after two years of study. Hamilton was licensed after five months of study with Robert Troup at Albany, New York.

Both men moved to New York to practice their profession after the evacuation of the British in 1783; by then each of them was married. Burr had married the widow of a British officer, Mrs. Theodosia (Bartow) Prevost, ten years his senior, assuming the responsibility for five stepchildren and later for his own daughter, Theodosia. In late 1780 Hamilton had married Elizabeth, the second daughter of General Philip Schuyler, head of a wealthy and politically influential

New York clan. The Hamiltons' first child, Philip, was born on January 22, 1782, and they later had five other children.

Politics also claimed the interest of each man. Hamilton entered the Continental Congress in November 1782 but retired in 1783 to practice law in his New York office at 58 Wall Street. In 1787 support from the New York business community won him a seat in the New York legislature, where he was selected as a delegate to the Constitutional Convention. His work in that historic body has been judged "not of the first importance,"[4] his longest stay in Philadelphia being May 27 and June 29, but his role in securing adoption of the Constitution in New York was of paramount significance. Together with James Madison and John Jay he wrote the series of *Federalist* papers that appeared in the New York *Independent Journal* for seven months after the first number on October 27, 1787. Moreover, Hamilton played a decisive role in the New York ratifying convention that met in June 1788 in Poughkeepsie, where his forensic skill won him the later encomium that "in parliamentary battle he was to have no real equal until the senatorial giants of the generation of Webster and Clay appeared."[5] Hamilton sat again in the Continental Congress in February 1788, and after the new government under the Constitution was organized in April 1789 he was commissioned secretary of the treasury on September 11, 1789. Clearly, the next few years until his retirement from Washington's cabinet on January 31, 1795, marked the flood tide of Hamilton's career. Brilliant, energetic, capable, and determined, he fought for his financial program, which was to provide a stable economic basis for the new government, establishing the funding of state debts, chartering a national bank, imposing excise and import duties, and encouraging manufactures.

Aaron Burr had drifted into politics at a somewhat later point in his career. Although he opposed the election of Governor George Clinton in 1789, he was appointed attorney-general and served in the U.S. Senate from 1791 to 1797. His long-standing animosity with Alexander Hamilton dates from his selection as senator from New York in 1791 over Hamilton's father in law, General Philip Schuyler. Burr received one electoral vote in 1793 and thirty in 1797; he was twice mentioned as gubernatorial material for New York during his term in the Senate, but his campaign never got underway in either instance. Defeated in his bid for a second term in the Senate, he was elected to the New York Assembly in April 1797 but defeated again two years later for having pushed a bill to aid the Holland Land Company, in which he had a financial interest. Burr then developed the nation's first political machine in the St. Tammany's Society of New York, which roundly defeated the Hamilton forces in the state and national elections of 1800. At the close of his frustrating term as vice president, Burr was nominated for the governorship of New York by his friends in the state legislature on February 18, 1804. Hamilton opposed him vehemently during the campaign, which Burr lost by a majority of eight thousand votes—the most crushing defeat in New York politics to that time.[6]

Always ready to take up his pen to oppose Burr's political ambitions, Hamilton had written and spoken reckless words about his rival during the gubernatorial campaign. Even Allan McLane Hamilton, the renowned Federalist's grandson, wrote long after the event: "In political antagonism the worst offence was given, for Hamilton's attacks had been unremitting and bitter, and though undertaken because he believed the welfare of the nation demanded the defeat of Burr, he could expect no other ending than that which followed."[7] In a letter later printed in the Albany *Register* Dr. Charles D. Cooper wrote, "Gen. Hamilton . . . has come out decidedly against Burr; indeed when he was here he spoke of him as a dangerous man and ought not to be trusted." To another correspondent, Cooper wrote, "I could detail to you a still more despicable opinion which General Hamilton had expressed of Mr. Burr."[8]

Once these letters had appeared in print, James Cheetham enquired in the New York *American Citizen,* "Is the vice-president sunk so low as to submit to be insulted by General Hamilton?"[9] The honor of both gentlemen as well as their political futures were at stake. Correspondence between Burr and Hamilton, and between their seconds, William P. Van Ness and Nathaniel Pendleton, dragged on from June 18 to June 27, 1804, when the challenge to a duel was finally given and accepted.[10]

Thus the scene was set for the violent climax to a personal and political feud that had smoldered since 1791 and had become more intense with the passage of time. William Graham Sumner wrote, "From 1800 to 1804 the causes which were to bring about a collision between Hamilton and Burr marched on with the precision of a classical tragedy."[11]

As he stated in one of his last letters, Alexander Hamilton abhorred the practice of dueling.[12] The death of his oldest son, Philip, in 1801 at the age of twenty in a duel at Weehawken with George Eacker, a partisan follower of Burr, haunted Hamilton in the few days of respite before the duel with Burr, which was set for July 11, 1804.[13] Hamilton had once challenged James Monroe to a duel, but the incident was peacefully settled, while Burr had fought duels with John Church and Samuel Bradhurst.[14] Only seven days before the duel, Hamilton and Burr faced each other across the dinner table of the Society of the Cincinnati on the Fourth of July. Burr was pensive; Hamilton, feverishly gay, singing the old military song "How Stands the Glass Around?" supposed to have been written by General James Wolfe the night before his death on the Plains of Abraham.[15]

The duel on the heights of Weehawken a week after the Cincinnati dinner was later described by William Coleman, editor of Hamilton's *New-York Evening Post,* in these words:

> It was nearly seven in the morning when the boat which carried General Hamilton, his friend Mr. Pendleton, and the Surgeon mutually agreed on, Doctor Hosack, reached that part of the Jersey shore called the *Weahawk.*

There they found Mr. Burr and his friend Mr. Van Ness, who, as I am told, had been employed since their arrival, with coats off, in clearing away the bushes, limbs of trees, etc., so as to make a fair opening. The parties in a few moments were at their allotted situations. When Mr. Pendleton gave the word, Mr. Burr raised his arm slowly, deliberately took his aim, and fired. His ball entered General Hamilton's right side. As soon as the bullet struck him, he raised himself involuntarily on his toes, turned a little to the left (at which moment his pistol went off), and fell upon his face. Mr. Pendleton immediately called out for Dr. Hosack, who, in running to the spot, had to pass Mr. Van Ness and Col. Burr; but Van Ness had the cool precaution to cover his principal with an umbrella, so that Dr. Hosack should not be able to swear that he saw him on the field.[16]

After Hamilton's death thirty-one hours later, the newspapers of the nation broke into a solemn dirge of mourning when they learned of the sad event. By the deadly aim of Aaron Burr, Alexander Hamilton was guaranteed popular immortality. In the words of Nathan Schachner: "A few days before the fatal duel, Alexander Hamilton was merely a well-known lawyer, the leader of a moribund party whose members by a large majority considered him a useless encumbrance rather than an asset. The day following, he was translated into herohood and apotheosized. There was some partisan purpose in the exalting, but there was also a sudden knowledge that a great man had passed away."[17]

Appropriately enough, it was the *New-York Evening Post* that announced the sorrowful news to an unsuspecting nation:

> With emotions that we have not a hand to inscribe, have we to announce the death of ALEXANDER HAMILTON. He was cut off in the 48th year of his age, in the full vigor of his faculties and in the midst of all his usefulness. We have not the firmness to depict this melancholy, heart-rending event. Now—when death has extinguished all party animosity, the gloom that pervades every bosom, bear irresistible testimony of the esteem and respect all maintained for him, of the love all bore him; and assure us that an impression has been made by his loss which no time can efface. It becomes us not to enter into particulars; we have no doubt, that, in compliance with the universal anxiety of the inhabitants, a statement will soon be exhibited to them containing all the circumstances necessary to enable them to form a just opinion of this tragic scene.[18]

This heavily black-bordered issue of the *Post* also included a letter by the Reverend Bishop Benjamin Moore describing Hamilton's last agonized hours, written with the thought "it would be grateful to my fellow citizens, would provide against misrepresentation, and perhaps, be conducive to the advancement of Religion. . . ."[19] The *New-York Evening Post* retained its heavy black borders and inverted column rules from July 13 to July 21, 1804—a period of typographic mourning unprecedented in the history of American journalism.

The Philadelphia *Aurora* was also one of the first newspapers to announce Hamilton's death. Two days after the duel, the Republican newspaper headlined its information *"Very Distressing!"* and printed an extract from a letter written by a New York Federalist: "The greatest man in America has this morning fallen in a duel!—GENERAL HAMILTON!—yes—HAMILTON!—the pride of every true American is, by this time no more! . . . The agitation which this affair has produced in this city, is indescribably great. The cause of the duel is not yet known." The *Aurora*'s only comment was, "It is with infinite regret that we have received the [above] melancholy information."[20]

The *New-York Evening Post* released the details of the duel on July 15, 1804, printing an account furnished by the seconds, but Hamilton's newspaper was scooped on the biggest story of his life by the New York *Morning Chronicle,* edited by Dr. Peter Irving, which rushed the details of the duel into print on the morning of the same day. On July 14 the Philadelphia *Aurora* noted, "The intrigue of 1801 is the true origin of the duel (particulars at large hereafter)," but in a spirit of largesse rare to William Duane, the newspaper added:

> We have received four more letters, nearly of the same tenor; their publication we deem inexpedient, under the impression, that it would be ungenerous to triumph over even the most inveterate enemy in his fall. On a future day, when the feelings of an afflicted family, cannot interfere with the solemn obligations of public interest, if those interests should require it, we shall not hesitate to enter into a review of the political character and conduct of the man. It would be barbarous at this time, to attempt to impede the current of grief, which very naturally overwhelms the friends and adherents of the unfortunate man, for whom we should have been more disposed to wish an honorable, long life and a milder passage from this to a better world.[21]

Duane's barbed gesture toward a temporary political truce during the period of mourning was vigorously denounced by the Federalist New York *Gazette,* which called the above *"a diabolical paragraph* . . . as malicious and hellish, as perhaps ever was penned!"[22] The Philadelphia editor countered this criticism by reminding his readers of the Federalist reaction to the deaths of General S. T. Mason of Philadelphia and Samuel Adams. With a good deal of justice, Duane added: "we will merely observe that Mr. Hamilton's situation as leader of the federal party was too prominent, and his principles and efforts of too strong a character to render it correct or expedient to observe *eternal* silence. . . . Mr. Hamilton was a federalist, and the whole nation is desired to mourn; and no doubt whoever does not turn hypocrite and mourn, must be guilty of a very heinous offence! . . . let us not be forced to touch again upon this inexhaustible subject."[23] But the squabble between the two newspapers continued, and on July 23 Duane wrote with apparent exasperation: "The Royal Gazette of N. York continues to *sport* with the forbearance which has been shown, in the case of Gen.

Hamilton; Lions do not prey upon dead carcasses; but . . . we are not obliged by any law moral or just to suffer imposture to supercede truth."[24]

The news of Hamilton's death reached Boston and Washington, D.C., on July 18 and Richmond on July 21. With characteristic restraint, Samuel Harrison Smith of the *National Intelligencer* noted simply, "The mournful death of *General Hamilton* has excited at New York the most lively sorrow. All descriptions of citizens united in manifesting their respect for his memory."[25] The newspaper offered a two-column description of the funeral procession and oration and then withheld any further comment on the incident. The Boston *Columbian Centinel* announced the event with heavy black borders and a small illustration of a coffin.[26] On July 21 the *Centinel* published the correspondence preceding the duel, under a headline set in Gothic type, "PAINFULLY INTERESTING." Shortly afterward appeared a small advertisement, bordered in black: "*Appropriate Mourning.* In consequence of the late afflicting event of the death, of the much lamented General *Hamilton*, TUCKER & THAYER will sell their black ITALIAN CRAPE, at the reduced price of one dollar per yard 4–4 wide:—God takes the *Good,* too good on earth to stay, / And leaves the *Bad,* too bad to take away!"[27]

While sentiment was selling black crape in Boston, the *Richmond Enquirer* would not be hypocritical:

> While we lament the departure of such splendid talents, lost forever to his country, let us not cease to forget that these talents had long before his death, been appropriated to the support of an erroneous system. Death may cancel our resentment against the man, but our disapprobation of his political conduct cannot expire. To admire some of his illustrious qualities, will be our duty & our delight. But to deny that this man had eminent failings, would be the most obvious inconsistency: & to suffer his name to be brought up hereafter as the pretext and justification of improper measures, would be an act of injustice to our country. . . . [28]

The *Richmond Enquirer* also thought that Federalist reaction to Hamilton's death was entirely out of proportion to the nature of the event: "Gen. Hamilton is no more; but the consequences of his death will not probably be so considerable, as our imagination is ready to conceive. His party have certainly lost a great, an influential man. But the energy of his party will soon supply his place."[29]

Last of the newspapers under consideration to announce the death of Alexander Hamilton was the Boston *Independent Chronicle,* which presented details of the duel and commented on the event on July 23, 1804:

> Though this event may be deplored, they [Republicans] must not be intemperate in their expressions of lamentation—if we are not generous in the direction of the noble-passions, friendship may degenerate into folly—*pity* into weakness,

and resentment become *injurious* to justice. When the partial fervour of the moment has subsided, we shall endeavor to present the public with such a brief commentary upon the life and political character of Gen. HAMILTON, as may be proper for a *Philanthropist* to write, and a *Republican* to peruse.[30]

Meanwhile, newspapers everywhere injected their editorial comments into descriptions of the funeral held in New York on Saturday, July 14, 1804. It was an occasion unparalleled in somber pageantry and sorrowful indulgence. A meeting of New York merchants and other citizens at the Tontine Coffee House on the evening of July 12, 1804, had resolved that business be suspended on the day of the funeral, July 14; that mourners assemble at the house of Mr. Church in Robinson Street at ten o'clock in the morning to form the funeral procession; and that owners or masters of vessels in the harbor be requested to strike their colors at half-mast for the occasion.[31] The Common Council of the City of New York authorized the closing of shops for the day to "entertain the most unfeigned sorrow and regret for the death of their fellow citizen, ALEXANDER HAMILTON, and with a view to pay a suitable respect to his past life and future memory, and to afford the most unequivocal testimony of the great loss which, in the opinion of the Common Council, not only this City but the state of New-York, and the United States have sustained by the death of this great and good man. . . . "[32] The council also suspended a regulation forbidding the tolling of city church bells for funerals and agreed to attend the rites as a group. New York lawyers met at Lovett's Hotel on July 13 and resolved to wear crape mourning bands six weeks for "the brightest ornament of their profession."[33]

On the morning of July 14 muffled church bells tolled from six to seven o'clock in the morning as the city bade farewell to its illustrious son. Minute guns were fired from the forts and armed vessels lying in the harbor until the corpse was buried. The funeral procession, led by militia units and the Society of the Cincinnati, marched with measured tread through the silent streets. As the New York *Gazette* described the scene: "The sides of the streets were crowded and the windows were filled with spectators, and many climbed up into trees and got on the top of houses. Not a smile was visible and hardly a whisper was to be heard, but tears were seen rolling down the cheeks of the affected multitude."[34]

In front of Trinity Church the procession halted, and on an improvised platform Gouverneur Morris delivered a funeral oration, his words unheard by the far reaches of the crowd. James Cheetham, editor of the New York *American Citizen,* was beside himself when he tried to render an account of the setting:

> The scene was impressive; and what added unspeakably to its solemnity, was the mournful group of tender boys, the sons, the once hopes and joys of the deceased, who, with tears gushing from their eyes, sat upon the stage, at the feet of the orator, bewailing the loss of their parent! It was too much; the sternest powers, the bloodiest villain, could not resist the melting scene. I wish I could

go on and describe the sensations I felt and those which were manifest on every countenance.[35]

The orator himself entertained somewhat different sentiments as he faced the grieving multitude. Gouverneur Morris wrote later in his diary, "How easy would it have been to make them, for a moment, absolutely mad!" He was also intent on the words he was about to speak, for delivering a funeral oration for Alexander Hamilton had its pitfalls. Morris noted later:

> To a man who could feebly command all his powers this subject is difficult. The first point of his biography is that he was a stranger of illegitimate birth; some mode must be contrived to pass over this handsomely. He was indiscreet, vain, and opinionated; these things must be told, or the character will be incomplete, and yet they must be told in such manner as not to destroy the interest. He was in principle opposed to republican and attached to monarchical government, and then his opinions were generally known and have been long and loudly proclaimed. His share in forming our Constitution must be mentioned, and his unfavorable opinion cannot therefore be concealed. The most important part of his life was his administration of the finances. The system he proposed was in one respect radically wrong; moreover, it has been the subject of some just and unjust criticism. . . . I must not, either, dwell on his domestic life; he has long since foolishly published the avowal of conjugal infidelity.[36]

In short, Morris had come to bury Hamilton, not to praise him.

From seven to eight in the evening the bells again tolled, but with nightfall an undoubtedly welcome silence fell upon the city—the guns had been fired, the bells tolled, the words spoken, the gestures made, the body interred. Alexander Hamilton was dead, and on the morning of July 15 the city resumed its normal life. For weeks William Coleman, grief-stricken editor of the *New-York Evening Post,* was to insist that a heavy pall of gloom still gripped the city, but Coleman saw the world through the eyes of a man deeply attached to Hamilton. For weeks he continued to fan the dying embers of grief for his departed friend. On July 15 the *Post* published fifteen letters arranging the duel along with Hamilton's will and addressed a few words "TO THE AMERICAN PUBLIC":

> The shocking catastrophe which has recently occurred, terminating the life of ALEXANDER HAMILTON, and which has spread a gloom over our city that will not be speedily dissipated, demands that the circumstances which led to it, or were intimately connected with it, should not be concealed from the world. When they shall be truly and fairly discovered, however some may question the soundness of his judgment on this occasion, all must be ready to do justice to the purity of his views, and the nobleness of his nature.[37]

In Philadelphia, William Duane's *Aurora* echoed the events of the funeral rites for Hamilton. On July 16 the Republican newspaper noted with considerable reserve, "In this city, among the general's friends, there were shown on Saturday many testimonials of sincere grief, and we make no doubt that by hundreds his death is most sincerely and deeply deplored."[38] The citizens of Philadelphia, Southwark, and the Northern Liberties adopted resolutions commemorating the occurrence, along with members of the bar and law students of Philadelphia. Sunday, July 15, was designated a day of prayer in the churches of the city; muffled bells tolled throughout the day, and flags were flown at half-mast in the harbor. The citizens of Philadelphia also resolved "That the clergymen of the several denominations be requested to expatiate, on the same day [July 15], upon the irreligious and pernicious tendency of a custom [dueling] which has deprived our country of one of her best and most invaluable citizens, and has proved so fatally destructive to the happiness of his family."[39]

On July 17, 1804, the *New-York Evening Post* began a long series of comments extracted from newspapers in the city and throughout the nation. The editor stated, "As we presume many of our readers will be desirous of seeing in what manner the several morning papers speak of the melancholy subject which engrosses this city, we present our readers with what each of them have said of it."[40] To the New York *Gazette* Alexander Hamilton was "the enlightened statesman, the skillful lawyer, the eloquent orator, the disinterested patriot, and the honest man." With little variation, such encomiums would be reproduced throughout the Federalist press. The death of Hamilton, said the New York *Gazette,* "renewed their [the citizens'] grief for the death of Washington, to see his friend and councellor cut off in the highest vigor of his faculties, and the United States deprived of their great earthly stay." So perished America's "first and most beloved citizen."[41]

Other comments were equally unrestrained. The New York *Mercantile Advertiser* was gratified that at the last rites, "The military made a mournful appearance and the funeral was highly deep and interesting."[42] The New York *Daily Advertiser* added, "We never witnessed, in this country or in Europe, on any similar occasion, so generally a sorrow, such an universal regret, or a ceremonial more awful and impressive."[43]

The New York *Morning Chronicle,* founded by Nathaniel Paulding and Peter Irving on October 1, 1802, leaped to the defense of its patron, Aaron Burr. "We have . . . the most satisfactory assurances," the newspaper stated, "that when a fair and candid statement is laid before the public, the conduct of Col. Burr will be justified by every disinterested and unprejudiced man, who considers the honor of a gentleman under the protection of his own arm."[44] But the *Morning Chronicle* was not able to convince an incensed public that Burr, whose political fortunes the newspaper was established to further, acted within his prerogatives as a gentleman in slaying Alexander Hamilton. The *Chronicle* waned after Hamilton's death and expired in the summer of 1805, when it was absorbed by the *Poughkeepsie Journal.*[45]

On July 18, 1804, the *New-York Evening Post* continued its dirge for Hamilton: "With melancholy satisfaction, we perceive that the public sorrow for the death of General Hamilton, is not confined to this city or state. The following extracts from the Philadelphia papers show the impression his loss has made in that capitol."[46] Highlighted was a quotation from the Philadelphia *Political Register:*

> After WASHINGTON, (who alone surpassed him)—After the first of Men and greatest of Heroes, who has rivalled HAMILTON in usefulness to our country?—in attachment to its interest?—in unceasing labour, in the exertion of the most splendid talents for its welfare? The generous and gallant SOLDIER, the wise and virtuous STATESMAN, the eloquent and accomplished ORATOR, the ardent and magnanimous PATRIOT, has fallen the victim of unyielding honor and inflexible integrity. His memory is embalmed in the esteem and affection of his contemporaries, and will be consecrated by the gratitude of his country to future ages.[47]

The first poem on the event, "Lines on the Death of General Hamilton," appeared in the *New-York Evening Post* on July 19, 1804:

> In yonder tomb, beneath the valley clod,
> Lies, shut from day, "the noblest work of God."
> A man upon whose high, distinguished head,
> Heav'n had the choicest of its blessings shed—
> Whose giant-mind no equal had on earth.
> Except the peerless splendor of its worth—
> Worth which, too sure, must be deplor'd in vain,
> For never shall we "look upon his like again."[48]

In the same issue, the *Post* resumed its roundup of editorial opinion concerning Hamilton's death, noting, "Of all the distant papers which have spoken of the recent melancholy event, we particularly notice the Philadelphia Register. The pieces which have appeared in this paper, both from the pen of the editor, and of his correspondents, are distinguished for their elegance, pathos, and discrimination." The Philadelphia *Register* had stated:

> The liberal and patriotic Ministerialist [Republican], with what ardor and violence he may have opposed the Founder of Federal politics, while living, is yet grieved, sincerely grieved, that our nation should be deprived of powers which conferred honor upon man. And the Federalist who has long listened with wonder and delight to the just precepts of political science, which have issued from his lips—who has surrendered to his wisdom and integrity the post of his Protector, and most influential of his advisers, is overpowered with anguish for his friend—and sinks into despondence for his country.[49]

No praise was too lavish for the *Register:* "If the pathetic voice of Cicero were to speak, even from the gloom of the tomb, it could open no new source of regret, it could raise no new emotion of sorrow."[50]

Likewise, the Philadelphia *Port Folio,* edited by Joseph Dennie, gave free rein to its emotions in "an elegant strain of lamentation," capped with a Biblical quotation: "KNOW YE NOT THAT THERE IS A GREAT MAN FALLEN, THIS DAY IN ISRAEL?"[51] William Coleman was highly pleased, noting, "All the federal papers at Philadelphia, (with the exception of one just received) have spoken of the catastrophe in a manner which does high credit to the literary accomplishments of the gentlemen of that city."[52] Said the *American Daily Advertiser:* "Our HAMILTON, alas! is no more. HAMILTON! the pride and ornament of his country, now sleeps in the tomb."[53] The *Gazette of the United States* commented:

> When a great man falls, his nation mourns. When a great man and a political father falls, in the midst of his days: in his full strength; in the very vigour of his age; at the noontide of his usefulness, his bereaved nation suffers deep affliction. When such a man falls, aside from the ordinary course of nature; cut off by the hand of violence; and sent suddenly and prematurely to be numbered with the silent dead; his fall is yet more deeply and peculiarly bewailed.—Such a man has fallen in our nation—Such a man, such a father was Alexander Hamilton; and in such a manner has he fallen. . . . [54]

The *New-York Evening Post* waxed poetic in the seemingly never-ending torrent of praise for the dead Hamilton. The first three stanzas of "Verses on the Death of General Hamilton" are as follows:

> Soldiers of Freedom! veil your eyes,
> For low in dust your leader lies:
> No more his gleaming steel he draws,
> The foremost in his country's cause.

> Patriots! who in the rolls of fame,
> Have nobly earn'd a glorious name:
> With melting grief your loss deplore—
> The Second Washington's no more!

> Ye Children of Columbia! weep—
> Your Statesman's lock'd in death's long sleep;
> And, till the course of time has roll'd,
> His like you never shall behold.[55]

Another poem, "The Grave of Hamilton," almost a column long, was republished in the *Post* from the New York *American Citizen.* "An Irregular Ode" closed with the lines:

High o'er the scene the curling cloud aspires,
Fraught with a nation's fervid sighs
The mighty incense seeks the skies,
And Heav'n approves the scene—for HAMILTON expires![56]

All this outpouring was much too much for the Boston *Independent Chronicle,* which condemned Federalist observances of Hamilton's death as "this pagan toil for an Apotheosis!"[57] It was probably Benjamin Austin Jr. who observed in the *Chronicle* "that the public obsequies of this day would have been '*More honore'd in the breach, than th' observance.'*" The writer objected to an eulogium then being planned by James Otis for these reasons: "First, because it may be detrimental to popular morals to deliver a methodical, and in all probability, an elegant apology for the practice of duelling, by praising the unfortunate gentleman who has fallen in the barbarous act. Secondly, because the permission to deliver such an Eulogy, in the interior of a Christian church, consecrated to holy ordinances, may be contemplated with horror, as a profane intrusion before the Almighty, and as an indelible stain upon the hallowed character of his temple!" The *Chronicle* vigorously denounced the "overstrained ceremony" and "party pageantry" indulged in by "the *Royal Faction* in the United States" to commemorate Hamilton's death.[58]

The Republican editor who seemed to mind Federalist excesses least was the socially-conscious Thomas Ritchie of the *Richmond Enquirer.* Describing the funeral rites for Hamilton, the editor concluded, "We have no observations to add—This scene was enough to melt a monument of marble."[59] But to Abijah Adams of the Boston *Independent Chronicle,* the scene was enough to turn one's stomach. On July 26, 1804, about three hundred Bostonians and a hundred and fifty persons from neighboring towns marched in a procession to hear the eulogy by James Otis, while a bell tolled and a militia unit of thirty men led the vanguard. This occasion prompted Adams to disregard the maxim about "treading lightly on the ashes of the dead" to observe:

Did he [Hamilton] distinguish himself as a politician? He was in the cradle when Hancock, Adams, Franklin, Rutledge, Randolph, Lee, with many others, laid the foundation principles of our freedom, and many of those men went down to the grave in peace, without eulogy or crape. Was he very eminent in his profession, as a lawyer.—We have buried Worthington, Hawley, Sargeant, Lowel, Bradbury, Sprague, Sumner, and many others, without crape, processions, or eulogies.[60]

The Boston *Independent Chronicle* was also repelled that such a demonstration was made for a man who "fell, shocking idea! on the sod wet with the blood of his son, who fell in a duel two years ago!"[61]

Other Republican papers in Massachusetts followed the lead of the *Chronicle* in condemning the excessive displays of sentiment. The Norwich *Republican* argued that right-thinking citizens should not eulogize the bloody results of a duel, which was both immoral and illegal. Would the elaborate obsequies "serve as a *memento,* to warn others against the detestable practice of duelling?" the newspaper enquired. And should these remarks "be viewed as *brutal* or *savage,* it will be of no consequence to us—Posterity will decide rightly on the subject, and to their verdict we commit the issue of the case."[62]

The Boston *Columbian Centinel* promptly replied to such statements, whether originating in the *Independent Chronicle* or republished there. The Federalist newspaper decried the *"gross and unfeeling illiberalities"* of such *"malignantly pointed* remarks" as those contained in the *Chronicle* article, and concluded its answer with a brief verse:

> Why Scribbler, turn thy busy senseless head,
> To slur the living, and adjudge the dead?
> Know, worthless man, thy folly sneers in vain,
> Nor need thy arts, a Prophet's skill explain;
> HAMILTON alive, beyond thy slander stood,
> And *dead* contemns the *rancor of thy blood.*[63]

The Boston *Independent Chronicle* replied the next day: "The *Calumniating Centinel,* a paper long pre-eminent in saucy folly, and which may be considered as the AORTA of Columbian monarchy, conveying the heart's blood of the *Royal Faction* of New-England . . ." could libel the *Chronicle* writer to its heart's content, but the newspaper would continue to uphold Republican simplicity in the matter of funeral arrangements, and especially that of Alexander Hamilton.[64]

One Republican editor joined the Federalist bandwagon with wholehearted enthusiasm, seizing the occasion of Hamilton's death to publicize his break with the party of Thomas Jefferson. This man was James Cheetham, an English radical who had fled to America after the Manchester riots and who had bought the New York *Argus* from Thomas Greenleaf in 1800. Cheetham rechristened his journal the New York *American Citizen,* which until 1804 served both Jefferson and the Clinton faction of the state Republican Party. One of the more persistent attackers of Hamilton during his lifetime, Cheetham performed a journalistic somersault on the Federalist's death. William Coleman of the *New-York Evening Post* was surprised and delighted to find the *American Citizen* heaping praise upon the dead Hamilton. "To the honour of Mr. Cheetham," the *Post* stated, "be it mentioned, that notwithstanding his political rancour, he has announced this sad catastrophe in the following handsome and respectful manner—Death has sealed the eloquent lips of GENERAL HAMILTON! He died yesterday about two o'clock. As soon as our feelings will permit we shall notice this deplorable event —this national loss."[65]

Cheetham was as good as his word, and the *New-York Evening Post* tried to make the Republican editor's conversion appear as representative of the entire Republican press. Wrote William Coleman:

> Amidst the repeated demonstrations of sorrow, produced by the late mournful catastrophe, there is a soothing, melancholy pleasure, in observing that even those who most strongly oppose his [Hamilton's] political opinions, whilst living, are found uniting with his friends, in one common sentiment of esteem for his private worth, gratitude for his public services, and admiration of his exalted talents. Among the many instances of this sort which we have seen, there is none that bears more honorable testimony to the merits of the departed Soldier and Statesman, than the following editorial article from the American Citizen of this morning. It discovers a spirit of justice and feeling, which does the highest credit to the writer. If the same liberal discrimination was indulged towards the living, how much would the animosity of party spirit be diminished![66]

Cheetham had written, "To a *few* of those with whom I think and act in whatever relates to the administration of the State and General Governments, it may seem extraordinary that I, who while the General lived to give comfort to his family, and splendor to his nation, was opposed to him on *some* political points, should, when laid in the cold and silent tomb, become a guardian of his fame, a vindicator of his wrongs." Cheetham glowed with "becoming pride" as he said that he would "disclaim and renounce that illiberality which will not award to illustrious merit its just due." Certainly, he had disagreed with Hamilton on some political issues, and he still disagreed, "but, alas! he [Hamilton] is dead and I cannot pursue him to the grave for *opinions* HONESTLY entertained, calmly and dignifiedly asserted, luminously and instructively enforced, and conveyed to the public with all the elegance of a scholar, and enriched with all the erudition of a distinguished jurist." All great men had a few private vices.

> But were I asked whether General Hamilton had *vices* in the face of the world, in the presence of God I would answer, NO. Like all men he sometimes *erred,* but I cannot admit that even his *errors* were those of the *heart.* He was human, and therefore not perfect. But if we correctly judge of human perfection by *purity of heart*[,] by *rectitude of intention* I hesitate not to say that, in my opinion, General Hamilton was most perfect.[67]

"Perhaps to him," added Cheetham, "more than to any other man, we are indebted for the excellent constitution under which we live." Cheetham called the *Federalist* series "the *ablest political papers in the world*" and the heart of Alexander Hamilton "the seat of every manly virtue."[68]

In the doleful clamor that greeted Hamilton's death, the fate of Burr was momentarily forgotten. Not until about the beginning of August did newspapers begin commenting on the vice president's role in the affair. After recapitulating the details of the duel, the *New-York Evening Post* declared: "We therefore do not scruple to pronounce that ALEXANDER HAMILTON *was wilfully and maliciously* MURDERED *by the hand of* AARON BURR, *Vice President of the United States.* He is now an exile from the State; but wheresoever he flies, unless he can escape from himself, *the voice of a brother's blood will cry aloud to the Almighty from the ground.*"[69]

A New York coroner's inquest found "That *Aaron Burr Esq.* Vice President of the United States, was *guilty* of the MURDER of ALEXANDER HAMILTON—and that William P. Van Ness, Esq. Attorney at law, and Nathaniel Pendleton, Esq. Counsellor at law, were accessaries," the *National Intelligencer* reported.[70] A grand jury in New Jersey, where the shooting actually took place, reached a similar verdict. Thus the vice president of the United States became a fugitive from justice. Burr slipped out of New York at night by way of a barge to Perth Amboy, from which he made his way on to Philadelphia and points south.[71]

Commented the Trenton, New Jersey, *Federalist:* "How degrading to the majesty of our government that its second officer should thus be under the real or fancied necessity of travelling with studied privacy, through bye-roads, and in unusual vehicles. It becomes the man, however, who has extinguished the bright constellation of genius and worth, himself to walk in darkness and obscurity. . . . The honour of New-Jersey demands that its shores should no longer be made places of butchery for the inhabitants of New-York and Pennsylvania."[72]

Except for the New York *Morning Chronicle,* no newspaper dared to come to the defense of Aaron Burr. The *Newport* (Rhode Island) *Mercury* found that "by a perusal of all the communications on this subject [the Hamilton-Burr duel], it will very evidently appear, that there existed, in the mind of Col. Burr, a pre-determined hostility and inveteracy of design, which no language could assuage—no honourable concession could appease."[73] In the New York *American Citizen,* Cheetham viewed the death of Hamilton "as the inevitable and deplorable effect of a *long meditated and predetermined system of hostility on the part of Mr. Burr and his confidential advisers.*" To Cheetham, Burr was "the plotting, mischievous citizen, whose bloody hand, guided by cool malignancy, terminated his [Hamilton's] existence," and the Code Duello could not excuse him.[74] Cheetham also published a story blaming Hamilton's death on a New York "Society of Duelists," an association of "cold-blooded and systematic stabbers" of which Aaron Burr was a prominent member.[75]

The duel at Weehawken was still discussed in the newspapers long after the immediate circumstances and the shock of Hamilton's death had receded into the background, as an argument to enforce the abolition of dueling. The *New-York Evening Post* was publishing comments from other newspapers on this topic as late as September 1804, almost two months after the duel. The newspaper explained that the Hamilton-Burr duel was "a subject which ought to be occasionally presented to the minds of the community, till an impression shall have been made on all classes of society—an impression deep and lasting, against the horrible custom which has been attended with such awful consequences to this country."[76]

But as for the specific details of the duel at Weehawken and the expressions of mourning for the death of Hamilton, the newspaper audience soon became sated with this somber fare. Enough was enough. For weeks it seemed that William Coleman of the *New-York Evening Post* had become obsessed with the topic and would never relinquish it. Finally, on August 20, 1804, the New York editor announced in the columns of his newspaper:

> I now return to those customary editorial duties which have been, for more than a month, suspended to give place to the most awful and afflicting subject that ever occupied my mind and weighed down my heart.—It was my intention to have closed all discussion of the melancholy event, by an attempt to exhibit the character of him whom I can never cease to mourn as the best of friends, and the greatest and most virtuous of men; but that ground has been so much preoccupied, that the design, though in great part actually executed, is for the present deferred. And unless it should be rendered necessary, by attacks or remarks from a certain quarter, I shall not again be disposed to bring the affair into the papers.[77]

At last it seemed that Alexander Hamilton would finally be laid to rest.

But not so. The temptation to republish eulogies from other newspapers proved too much for Coleman, and he devoted the Saturday editions of his newspaper to the topic for two weeks in late August and early September, 1804. He prefaced the first such edition of "TESTIMONY OF RESPECT" with these words:

> Although we have quitted the melancholy subject which has so long cast a gloom over our columns, yet we have thought it would afford a melancholy satisfaction to those who love the memory of Hamilton, to see the manner in which he is spoken of in various parts of the United States, since his death. We therefore have concluded to devote some part of our Saturdays papers to this purpose. This will account for the complexion of this evening's paper.[78]

And so the matter rested. A subscription was raised by New York Federalists for the widow and children of Hamilton, and in due time Aaron Burr returned to Washington, where he presided at the impeachment trial of Judge Samuel Chase. Burr's public appearance in the Senate of the United States drew a few scattered sniper's shots from the *New-York Evening Post* but stirred no excitement elsewhere. The duel on the heights of Weehawken had passed into history.

Aaron Burr never once questioned his own conduct in the affair, and men of honor agreed that he had acted within his rights. After all, Burr thought that Hamilton should have been grateful. "I made him a great man," Burr is supposed to have said.[79] It will never be known whether Hamilton really intended to withhold his fire, as he said before and after the duel, but a twentieth-first-century psychiatrist might make a good case that Alexander Hamilton wished for death. He might have satisfied Burr in the early exchange of correspondence without compromising his own honor, but he failed to do so. And when his second, Nathaniel Pendleton, won the drawing of lots for choice of position, Hamilton chose to stand facing the bright July morning sun.

The well-placed bullet at Weehawken ended Hamilton's life and began his legend. With great assistance from the newspapers of the period, the Hamilton-Burr duel became firmly fastened on the public mind and even entered the realm of ballad and folklore. During his lifetime, Burr saw some doggerel scrawled under an exhibit of the duel in a traveling show of wax figures:

> O Burr, O Burr, what hast thou done?
> Thou hast shooted dead great Hamilton.
> You hid behind a bunch of thistle,
> And shooted him dead with a great hoss pistol.[80]

Alexander Hamilton always had a keen flair for the dramatic gesture, and in this respect his life ended on an appropriate note. The tragic climax of a feverishly busy public career served to underscore the accomplishments of that career, so today praise of Hamilton has become extravagant indeed. Arthur H. Vandenberg considered him "The Greatest American," maintaining, "Never in human contribution to republican institutions and the destinies of progressive, autonomous freedom, had one man done so much in so few years."[81]

In conclusion, one may say that the Federalist press was as influential in establishing the popular reputation of Alexander Hamilton as it was in destroying that of Thomas Paine. The fancied evil of Paine's later career erased the "good" that went before, while Hamilton's martyred ending cast the man's less desirable characteristics into obscurity. So the Federalist press would have it, and newspapers such as the *New-York Evening Post* were remarkably successful in effecting this aim, whether consciously striving for it or not.

Republican newspapers fought to hold the line against the unbounded eulogies for Hamilton, the unceasing praise that threatened to obscure the achievements of Jefferson's administration and revivify the Federalist Party. As in the case with Thomas Paine, however, they largely failed in their purpose. However restrained their language in urging separate consideration for the man and his political philosophy, anything negative they published was probably considered ungracious if not vicious, for the American people would not see their newfound hero desecrated. The Philadelphia *Aurora* and the Boston *Independent Chronicle* took the lead in demanding moderation in the unseemly praise heaped upon the dead Hamilton, and these two newspapers were supported in the South by the *Richmond Enquirer.* Once again, however, the *National Intelligencer* refused to enter the debate.

The event of Hamilton's death marked the defection of James Cheetham of the New York *American Citizen* from the ranks of Republican editors, and he was regarded a traitor for the benevolent views he expressed toward Hamilton. In the eyes of the Boston *Independent Chronicle,* Cheetham "out Herod[s] Herod," weeping for the dead Federalist "with more profusion than the very intimates of the General's bosom!"[82] So Cheetham joined the ranks of the opposition and at the same time became a bitter enemy of Thomas Paine during the remaining years of Paine's lifetime. James Thomson Callender deserted the Republican cause in 1802, James Cheetham in 1804. The party could not withstand many such desertions by editors from within its ranks.

As in the controversy that raged around Paine's return, the flurry of Federalist sympathy awakened by Hamilton's death did not seem to harm the Jefferson administration. Indeed, it had a positive effect in that it removed Aaron Burr once and for all from the public councils—except for his brief remaining tenure as president of the Senate—an event probably pleasing to Jefferson. Yet it caused Jefferson trouble later, for the duel with Hamilton sent Burr into his wild-eyed schemes for a western empire. This highly complex escapade stripped Burr of whatever public respect he continued to enjoy after the "interview at Weehawken."

The western conspiracy finally persuaded the *National Intelligencer* to say a few words on the subject of Aaron Burr, which the newspaper did in late 1807:

> On Sunday last AARON BURR passed through George Town and this City for Baltimore. For our own part, we confess, it would be most agreeable to our feelings to let this wandering spirit, move to and fro without notice, were it not for the duty of keeping a vigilant eye on those who, having distinguished themselves by their abortive efforts to destroy every thing that is dear and sacred, may, from despair, be impelled, if possible, to deeds of greater darkness. We congratulate the city of Washington, that it does not contain this man, whose purpose was, it is said, to take up his residence here.[83]

Thus, three years after the duel with Alexander Hamilton, Aaron Burr was persona non grata in the national capital, where he once served as vice president. Burr went to his death in 1836 still maintaining his loyal and patriotic intentions, but few heeded his words. Meanwhile, the Philadelphia *Aurora* and other Republican newspapers called for the same honest response to Alexander Hamilton dead as living.

EIGHT

Assault on the Judiciary

The simple truth is, Mr. Jefferson has been determined
from the first to have a judiciary, as well as a legislature,
that would second the views of the executive.

—*New-York Evening Post,* January 13, 1804.

If the twelve Apostles, with the Angel Gabriel at their head, were to form a court
in this country, for the trial of Judge [Samuel] Chase, or any other federal
culprit, we firmly believe that the editor of the [Boston *Columbian*] *Centinel,* or
some his "Washington correspondents" would doubt the impartiality
and question the judgment of even this holy tribunal.

—Boston *Independent Chronicle,* January 17, 1805

No domestic problem during the administration of Thomas Jefferson proved more difficult or vexing than how to combat the Federalist-controlled judiciary. When Jefferson took office in 1801 there was not a single Republican judge sitting in a federal court in the country.[1] The Republicans eliminated the sixteen Federalist circuit judges appointed under the judiciary act of February 13, 1801, by repealing that measure—an action which, in the opinion of Henry Adams, "did more to define the character of the government than any other single event in Jefferson's first administration, except the purchase of Louisiana."[2] But how could the Jefferson forces obtain a voice in the decisions of the Supreme Court, where the strongly Federalist chief justice, John Marshall—technically one of John Adams's "midnight appointments"—was settling down for what in all likelihood would be a long tenure? Here the Republicans were not so successful, for the impeachment trial of Justice Samuel Chase proved disastrous. In the judgment of Henry Adams, "The failure of Chase's impeachment was a blow to the Republican party from which it never wholly recovered."[3] Whether the administration appointed Republican judges at lower levels or attempted to remove a Federalist justice from the highest court in the land, the Republican assault on the judiciary kept the newspapers in a turmoil. Supposedly the judiciary was the weakest of the three branches of government, but under the Jeffersonian attack it proved to be the toughest.

The opening skirmish of the assault centered on efforts to repeal the Federalist judiciary act of 1801, adopted less than a month before Jefferson assumed office. Odious to the Republicans of 1801, this measure has since won considerable praise from legal historians. Albert J. Beveridge, the biographer of John Marshall, has called it "one of the best considered and ablest measures ever devised by that constructive [Federalist] party."[4] A more realistic appraisal has been offered by Felix Frankfurter and James M. Landis, who wrote, "Jobbery it was, but by no means the design only of hungry politicians, or the effort of a party to entrench itself on the bench after the country had sent it into the wilderness. . . . This measure combined thoughtful concern for the federal judiciary with selfish concern for the Federalist party."[5] Republicans of the time objected to the Federalist judiciary act of 1801 because it provided for sixteen circuit-court judges, and these new positions were uniformly filled with Federalists by John Adams's celebrated "midnight appointments"—federal officers appointed after December 12, 1800, when the electoral returns from South Carolina indicated that Adams and many other Federalists would soon be leaving office. Local Republicans also feared that the newly created circuit courts would eventually usurp the judicial machinery of the individual states.

Yet the Federalist judiciary reorganization adopted on February 13, 1801, must not be viewed as a purely partisan measure. As Max Farrand has pointed out, "the judiciary act of 1801 was not adopted solely because the recent presidential election had gone against the Federalists."[6] Demands for judicial reform had been voiced ever since the adoption of the original judiciary act of September 24, 1789. This measure had provided that two Supreme Court justices must hold circuit courts in each of the three circuits—Eastern, Middle, and Southern —at an intermediate judicial level between the seventeen federal district courts and the Supreme Court. Complaints by circuit-riding justices were many because of the primitive means of transportation and because a justice on the bench of the Supreme Court might be called on to rule on a case that he had previously decided in a circuit court. As early as 1790, Attorney-General Edmund Randolph condemned the practice. Some relief was provided by the act of March 2, 1793, which stipulated that one Supreme Court justice sitting with a district judge was sufficient to hear circuit-court cases, but the basic awkwardness of the original system remained.[7]

Nor was the Federalist reform bill of February 13, 1801, a last-minute thought on the part of an outgoing administration. In his speech opening the first session of the Sixth Congress in 1799, President John Adams had insisted on such "a revision and amendment" of the federal judiciary system as "indispensably necessary."[8] A bill proposing the establishment of twenty-nine revamped federal judicial districts was reported by a committee of the House of Representatives on March 11, 1800—long before Jefferson's election—and its provisions later became the foundation of the act finally passed early in 1801.[9] Thus, the measure called for the appointment of sixteen new circuit-court judges.[10]

The Republican-dominated Seventh Congress lost little time in stalking its quarry, the Federalist judiciary act of 1801, known derisively to them as "Old Jude."[11] Senator John Breckinridge of Kentucky introduced a motion for repeal on January 6, 1802, touching off a stringent debate two days later that continued intermittently until February 3. The struggle revolved around the constitutional issue of whether Congress had the right to abolish as well as to create inferior courts, in view of the injunction that judges were not to be removed during "good behavior." Federalists argued that to abolish the newly created circuit courts would infringe on the constitutional rights of the incumbent judges by removing them from office without cause, while Republicans considered this argument absurd in that the judges could not continue to hold offices when those offices had been abolished. Moreover, Republicans contended that the judiciary act of 1801 would cost the federal government an additional $137,500 a year. (The actual increased expenses were under $50,000.) They also denounced the appointment of three representatives and one senator named to fill vacancies in the district courts after four district judges were elevated to the new circuit-court positions.[12]

Republicans carried the day by repealing the disputed act in the Senate on February 3, 1802, by the close vote of 16–15, followed by similar action in the House of Representatives on March 3, 1802, by a vote of 59–32.[13] But the Federalists won their case in the verdict of history even though they had lost "their last great fight."[14] Although circuit duty remained the burden of Supreme Court justices until 1869,[15] never again after the repeal of 1802 did Congress interfere with the tenure of existing judges when altering the court system.[16]

Republican newspapers did not care for posterity, however; halfway through the Senate debate on the repeal measure, the *National Intelligencer* noted that the upper chamber seemed to be deciding "that it is *expedient* to repeal the act of the last Session, and have by implication also decided the constitutional power of the legislature to vacate all judicial appointments made under that part of the constitution, that authorizes the erection of inferior tribunals." This expected decision, continued the *National Intelligencer*, "will be a memorable one, as well from the importance of the point decided, as from the cool, dignified, and enlightened deliberation by which it was reached."[17] In reporting the passage of the repeal measure by the Senate, the *National Intelligencer* commented:

> This act will not fail to be recorded among the most memorable events of the present period. It preeminently marks the triumph of republican principles. It demonstrates the inflexible determination of those who now hold the reins of authority, to adhere in power to the same principles, avowed by them when out of power. Their theory was a good one; but their practice is better. Economy in

the public expenditure, distrust of extravagant executive patronage, a dread of whatever tends to the unnecessary aggrandizement of the powers of the general government, constitute a few of the features of the repealing act; and they are features which, it is not hesitated to say, will recommend it to national approbation.[18]

Later, when the bill passed the House of Representatives on March 3, 1802, "by a majority unprecedented since the existence of party," the *National Intelligencer* breathed an editorial sigh of relief. "Hereafter we may indulge the pleasing hope that the streams of justice, polluted by party prejudice or passion, will flow pure," the newspaper stated. "Judges, created for political purposes, and for the worst of purposes under a republican government, for the purpose of opposing the national will, from this day cease to exist."[19]

Meanwhile, the Federalist press was by no means silent on this issue. The *New-England Palladium* published at Boston denounced the Republican maneuver vigorously, saying, "A precipitate repeal of this law, upon the grounds of its mutability, at this period of its operation, and for such reasons as have been brought forward, can be nothing else than a wanton, if not a perfidious abuse of power, as well as a dereliction of those generous, honorable sentiments, which give security and confidence, where laws are inefficient." Arguments favoring repeal advanced by the Republicans were "exactly adapted to the sort of minds which most philosophers have displayed, when it pleases God, in his wrath, that they shall exercise power." In short, to repeal the Federalist judiciary act of 1801 "breaks down almost the only barrier against licentiousness and party tyranny," the *Palladium* concluded.[20]

A speech by Alexander Hamilton before a meeting of the New York bar opposing repeal of the act elicited much comment in the Republican press. Hamilton declared that if the repeal bill were passed, "the constitution was but a shadow, and we should be ere long divided into separate confederacies, turning our arms against each other." In the opinion of the great Federalist leader, "Between a government of laws administered by an independent judiciary, or a despotism supported by an army, there is no medium. If we relinquish one, we must submit to the other."[21]

Before the repeal measure was even introduced into Congress, the *Gazette of the United States* asserted:

It was, clearly, the design of the framers of the constitution, and of the respective state conventions which ratified it, that such should be the stability of our judiciary, that it should never be affected by the changes and revolutions to which, from the nature of the government, the other departments would be subject. . . . It will it be deemed safe for Congress, at every change in the administration, to overturn the established systems, and attempt to hurl from their seats, Judges upon whose independence and uprightness, the preservation of our government, and the security of our rights and liberties absolutely and wholly depend?[22]

The *Gazette of the United States* insisted that the Republican attempt to repeal the law was not for the purpose of judicial reform; rather, "it must be for the mere purpose of displacing judges, who have not been active in promoting the views and designs of the ruling party, and to place in office, men who have sacrificed the interest of the country for the hopes of personal honour and private emolument." Besides, why such precipitate action in repealing a law which had only been in operation one year? "It, certainly, has not been so long in operation, that we can determine, that all its contemplated advantages, over the old one, will not be fully realized."[23] But the arguments of the Philadelphia Federalist newspaper were in vain, and on January 23, 1802, it headlined an item of "important and unwelcome intelligence," "JUDICIARY LOST!"[24]

No one in Philadelphia was more antagonistic to courts in general than William Duane, fiery editor of the *Aurora,* who threw all the resources of his newspaper into the struggle for repeal. After the federal judiciary were returned to its pre-1801 standing, Duane observed, the courts "will still remain as independent of the executive, as could be wished by themselves, or their warmest friends; but, as it ought to be in a republic, they will not be altogether independent of the sovereign people, or their representatives." Duane emphasized the desirability of a restricted judiciary:

> it would be a monstrous incongruity in a republic where the first magistrate and all the legislative body are dependent on the people, to see the judges placed above all power—for the moment they found themselves out of the reach of the people, they would also place themselves beyond the law, and being the constitutional expounders thereof, it would be bent and twisted into any form which might best suit their purposes—how far this has been attempted already, when they thought themselves firm on the saddle, is best known to those who attended in the courts during the trials of Cooper and others.[25]

"Cato," writing in the *Aurora,* wanted only to restore matters to "the moderate principles which subsisted in the administration of Washington." The writer asserted, "It has been proved that the Judiciary system, as it then stood, was equal to all the purposes of distributive justice, and yet some who pretend to be republicans, are not satisfied to return to the old system, but must have more than enough. . . . How many years will it take to eradicate the seeds of discord sown in the days of John Adams?"[26]

The Philadelphia *Aurora* also charged that the constitutional scruples avowed by the Federalists formed merely a smokescreen to conceal their real desire of keeping the sixteen Federalist circuit-court judges in office as a judicial check on the Republican administration.[27]

The Federalist judiciary act of 1801 expired on July 1, 1802, amid acclaim from the Republican press and whimpers from the Federalist newspapers. As the *National Intelligencer* commented, "Some of the federal prints have gone into *mourning* for the judiciary act of the expiring administration, which drew its last breath on the first day of July. And well may THEY mourn. They have lost a friend in need; the only friend left them amidst their misfortunes. . . . If, however, mourning is considered as an evidence of contrition and self-humiliation for our manifold sins, we cannot too highly appreciate the pious act, nor recommend it too strongly to the general observance of our federal friends."[28] It was evident that Samuel Harrison Smith was beginning to learn how to play the game of editing a partisan newspaper.

Next came the more difficult challenge of breaking the solid Federalist front of the Supreme Court. Three years passed before the attempt to convict Justice Samuel Chase of "high crimes and misdemeanors" came to its unsuccessful conclusion. To challenge the official conduct of a justice of the highest court in the land was no light matter, and congressional Republican leaders hesitated for a considerable length of time before undertaking the step. Even then, the affair was bungled from start to finish, and the incident mangled the political reputations of all those intimately connected with it. President Jefferson wisely maintained a hands-off policy, letting the brunt of the failure fall on the key manager of the impeachment proceedings, Representative John Randolph of Virginia, whose political leadership was seriously impaired by the failure to remove Justice Chase. "A worse champion than Randolph for a difficult cause could not be imagined," wrote Henry Adams.[29] The Virginian's erratic brilliance was well enough adapted to push the impeachment measure through the House of Representatives, but as leader of the prosecution in the trial before the Senate, John Randolph met disaster. The job was so badly bungled that no Supreme Court justice has been impeached and tried from that day to this.[30]

The assault on the Supreme Court actually commenced with the repeal of the Federalist judiciary act of 1801, for the repeal measure stipulated that the Supreme Court would not meet again until February 1803—providing a cooling-off period of more than a year so that the Supreme Court could not avail itself of the radical new doctrine embodied in the preliminary *Marbury v. Madison* decision to declare the repeal law unconstitutional. In the meantime, Republicans cast around for a likely Federalist judge on whom to try the impeachment remedy. A suitable candidate soon appeared in the person of John Pickering, district judge of New Hampshire, who according to informants was accustomed to appear on the bench drunk and to indulge in profanity. By a vote of 45–8, the House of Representatives sent Joseph Nicholson and John Randolph to the bar of the Senate on March 3, 1803, to deliver notice of the lower chamber's impeachment of Judge Pickering. Tried during the next session of the Senate, the New Hampshire judge failed to appear when called on March 2, 1804, but his son

Jacob Pickering presented evidence that clearly showed that Judge Pickering had been insane for two years before the time the alleged offenses occurred and had remained so ever since. This unexpected development threw the Republican prosecutors into a quandary and the Senate into confusion. Clearly, a madman could not be allowed to continue sitting in a federal courtroom and yet the fact of insanity precluded his being convicted of wilful "high crimes or misdemeanors." To avoid this thorny legal tangle, a subterfuge was adopted requiring the senators to vote yea or nay only on the question whether Pickering was guilty "as charged," not whether he was "guilty" or "not guilty" of high crimes and misdemeanors. This maneuver so confused matters that in a Senate of thirty-four members only twenty-six dared to vote on the question. By a vote of 19–7 Judge Pickering was declared "guilty as charged." As Henry Adams has so clearly pointed out:

> So confused, contradictory, and irregular were these proceedings that Pickering's trial was never considered a sound precedent. That an insane man could be guilty of crime, and could be punished on *ex parte* evidence, without a hearing, with not even an attorney to act in his behalf, seemed such a perversion of justice that the precedent fell dead on the spot.[31]

Yet, perplexing as it had been, the impeachment trial of John Pickering established another immediate precedent for Republicans desirous of purging the Federalist judiciary. After all, a Federalist district judge was eliminated by the proceedings, so administration leaders in Congress turned in pursuit of higher game. The resolution ordering the impeachment of Justice Samuel Chase was introduced into the House of Representatives on March 6, 1804—when the Senate trial of Pickering was in its fifth day—and exactly one hour after the conviction of Judge Pickering in the Senate on March 12, 1803, the House of Representatives without debate voted the impeachment of Justice Samuel Chase along party lines, 73–32.[32]

Republicans were riding the tiger's back and in time would find themselves inside. In the judgment of Richard B. Lillich, a New York lawyer, "The annals of American legal history contain no trial with greater political overtones and constitutional ramifications [than] the Chase affair . . . [which] rendered impeachment as a political weapon forever impractical."[33] But to understand the Chase trial, one must first understand the man who stubbornly pushed his judicial career to the brink of disaster and yet averted disgrace, the "hanging judge" of Baltimore, Maryland—Justice Samuel Chase.

Chase was a great deal more than the impartial and somewhat anonymous figure behind a federal-court bench; he was a highly colorful individual whose political career had been turbulent and provocative. In the words of Frederick T. Hill, "It was not in his judicial capacity alone that Samuel Chase had earned his reputation. For years he had been known as a pugnacious lawyer and politician who sought quarrels and delighted in them. Indeed, his entire career had been marked by such intemperance of word and action that he seemed 'to move perpetually with a mob at his heels,' which sometimes pursued but quite often followed him."[34]

Samuel Chase (1741–1811) was born in Somerset County, Maryland, son of the rector of St. Paul's Church in Baltimore. He began the study of law in 1759 in the offices of Hammond & Hall in Annapolis and was admitted to practice in the mayor's court in 1761 and in chancery and certain of the county courts in 1763. Chase was a member of the Maryland Assembly from 1764 to 1784. At the time of the Revolution, vigorously opposing the royal governor of the colony, he was a member of the Maryland Committee of Correspondence in 1774, and he also served as a delegate to both Continental Congresses, where he was an influential member of various committees, including the one that recommended rejection of the British peace proposals of 1778. Chase accompanied Benjamin Franklin and Charles Carroll of Carrollton on the unsuccessful mission to secure the alliance of Canada in the spring of 1776, but Chase's reputation fell under a cloud when he attempted to corner the flour market with others on the approach of the French fleet at the end of 1778. He sued for relief from bankruptcy in 1789 and in this manner withdrew from two business partnerships. In 1785 he attended the trade convention at Mount Vernon that drafted the compact between Virginia and Maryland regulating navigation of the Potomac, but by the time the new federal government was launched in 1789 he was best remembered as a signer of the Declaration of Independence.[35] As "Caution" writing in the *Maryland Journal,* he opposed the adoption of the Constitution with great fervor,[36] and he was one of eleven members of the Maryland ratifying convention who cast negative votes. Edward S. Corwin has written, "Just why Chase turned Federalist is something of a mystery, especially in view of his strong anti British prejudice which he voiced as late as 1793."[37] But as the national political parties took shape, Samuel Chase was definitely in the Federalist camp. President Washington considered appointing him attorney-general but on January 26, 1796, nominated him to the Supreme Court. The nomination was unanimously ratified in the Senate on the following day.

"Chase's performance on the Supreme bench was the most notable of any previous to Marshall," Corwin has observed. "His opinion in *Ware v. Hylton* remains to this day the most impressive assertion of the supremacy of national treaties over state laws."[38] Yet Justice Chase was viewed somewhat differently by his political adversaries. As Henry Adams has written:

> If one judge in the United States should have known the peril in which the judiciary stood, it was Justice Samuel Chase of Maryland, who had done more than all the other judges to exasperate the democratic majority. His overbearing manners had twice driven from his court the most eminent counsel of the

circuit; he had left the bench without a quorum in order that he might make political speeches for his party; and his contempt for the popular will was loudly expressed.[39]

Chase was notorious for his partisan handling of the treason trial of John Fries and the sedition trial of James Thomson Callender, both conducted in 1800, and on May 2, 1803, barely two months after Marshall's decision in the Marbury case, Justice Chase unburdened himself to a Baltimore grand jury on the evils of democratic government, with pointed references to Jefferson's administration. "The late alteration of the Federal judiciary . . . and the further alteration that is contemplated in our State judiciary (if adopted) will in my judgment take away all security for property and personal liberty," said Justice Chase. "The independence of the national judiciary is already shaken to its foundation, and the virtue of the people alone can restore it. . . . Our republican Constitution will sink into a mobocracy,—the worst of all possible governments."[40]

Less than two weeks later President Jefferson wrote to Joseph Nicholson recommending Chase's impeachment, and after almost a year of deliberation the House complied on March 12, 1804. In the eight articles of impeachment, Chase was charged with: (1) prejudicing the jury in the John Fries treason trial in Philadelphia, April-May 1800, by addressing the jury on points of law before Fries's counsel was heard in his defense and refusing to let Fries's lawyers address the jury on matters of law as well as fact; (2) not excusing John Basset as a member of the jury called to hear the sedition trial of James Thomson Callender in Richmond in May 1800, even though Basset wished to be released from jury duty because he had already made up his mind on the case; (3) refusing to admit the evidence of John Taylor in the Callender trial because Taylor "could not prove the truth of the whole of one of the charges, contained in the indictment, although the said charge embraced more than one fact"; (4) requiring Callender's counsel to submit questions to Taylor in written form to the bench first; refusing to postpone the trial despite an affidavit proving the absence of material witnesses; "use of unusual, rude, and contemptuous expressions toward the prisoner's counsel"; "repeated and vexatious interruptions of the said counsel," and "indecent solicitude" manifested by Chase for Callender's conviction; (5) refusing to allow Callender's release on bail, even though he was not charged with a capital offence; (6) trying Callender in the same session that he was presented and indicted, contrary to the common law of Virginia, which the circuit judge was bound to respect according to the judiciary act of 1789; (7) refusing to release a grand jury at Newcastle, Delaware, in June 1800 at which time Chase "descend[ed] from the dignity of a judge and stoop[ed] to the level of an informer" by haranguing the grand jury on the "seditious" activities of the editor of the Newcastle *Mirror of the Times and General Advertiser;* and (8) degrading his office by "an intemperate and inflammatory political harangue" to the

Baltimore grand jury in May 1803.[41] The eighth article was the real grounds for impeachment, and the House document charged Chase with being "highly indecent, extra-judicial, and tending to prostitute the high judicial character with which he was invested, to the low purpose of an electioneering partisan."[42] The vote on the various articles of impeachment revealed the partisan nature of the action:[43]

Article 1	83 (for)	34 (against)
2	83	35
3	84	34
4	84	34
5	72	45
6	73	42
7	73	42
8	73	42

The impeachment trial of Justice Samuel Chase opened on January 3, 1805, although it did not actually get underway until a month later. The scene in the Senate chamber was adorned with colorful trappings, as if a medieval joust and not a solemn trial were about to commence. The thirty-four senators sat in two rows of benches—seats and fronts covered with crimson cloth—facing the accused and the galleries. A temporary elevated gallery with three rows of seats covered with green cloth was erected for women spectators, and the boxes facing the bar of the Senate containing the managers of the prosecution on the left and the accused with his counsel on the right were draped with blue cloth. The three rows of benches on the floor, likewise bedecked in green cloth, were occupied by members of the House of Representatives and the Supreme Court, with a special box arranged for foreign ministers and visitors from the executive branch.[44] As Henry Adams has pointed out, barely ten years had passed since the House of Lords had rendered judgment in the impeachment of Warren Hastings, "and men's minds were still full of associations with Westminster Hall."[45]

A ripple of excitement passed through the crowded Senate chamber when Aaron Burr walked in on the opening day of the trial to preside as president of the Senate. Burr was still under two state indictments for the murder of Alexander Hamilton, and his calm appearance prompted whispered comments throughout the chamber. When the sergeant at arms presented an armchair for Justice Chase, Burr was reported to have waved him away, saying, "let the Judge take care to find a seat for himself." William Plumer, Federalist senator from New Hampshire, noted later, "Mr. Burr in a very cold formal insolent manner [said] he presumed the Court would not object to his taking a seat."[46]

The trial of Justice Samuel Chase turned on the interpretation of the constitutional provision (Article III, Section 4) that impeachment could be rendered for "high crimes and misdemeanors." The brilliant phalanx of Federalist lawyers defending Chase—Luther Martin, Charles Lee, Robert Goodloe Harper, Joseph Hopkinson, and Philip Barton Key—argued forcefully that any grounds for impeachment must be for indictable offenses. Otherwise, the Constitution would be violated in another provision (Article III, Section 1) that judges could not be removed during "good behavior." The Republican managers of the prosecution—John Randolph, George Washington Campbell, Joseph Nicholson, Caesar Rodney, Peter Early, Christopher Clarke, and John Boyle—contended that a less strict interpretation of the phrase "high crimes and misdemeanors" was manifestly necessary to remove incompetent or partisan judges who had committed no indictable offense. The situation was further complicated by Article 5 of the impeachment document, which alleged no evil intent and in effect made mere error of judgment an impeachable offense. In the opinion of Richard B. Lillich, "conviction of Chase on this count would have put the courts at the mercy of Congress."[47]

Chase's answer to the charges against him was read on February 4, 1805. The Supreme Court justice explained his conduct on the first seven counts and denied the eighth charge absolutely and entirely. After all, district judges had acquiesced in each of Chase's questioned rulings, and no action had been taken against these men.[48] Randolph read the House's replication on February 9, 1805, opening the case for the prosecution. In the next four days, eighteen witnesses were called to support the impeachment charges, and the defense cross-examined only six of them. Robert Goodloe Harper opened for the defense on February 15, producing thirty-one witnesses in four days, bringing to a close the nine days of testimony. Eight days of summation began on February 20, during which the prosecution's case was demolished by Chase's gifted counsel. One of the highlights of the trial was Luther Martin's address to the court, which began, "I see two honourable members of this court, who were with me in the convention, in 1787." Joseph Hopkinson said, "we appear for an ancient and infirm man, whose better days have been worn out in the service of that country which now degrades him, and who has nothing to promise you for an honorable acquittal but the approbation of your own consciences."[49]

For the prosecution Caesar Rodney stated, "From a view of the constitution, it must appear that this mode of prosecution was instituted more to restore the purity of the office than to punish the officer."[50] Summing up, John Randolph added:

> We demand not that an independent judge shall be removed from office.
> There are independent judges on the bench, whose dismissal we do not seek.
> We only ask that a man, who is unworthy of the high judicial station which he
> fills, should be dismissed from the service of his country at the age of seventy
> years. A man who has marked his whole character with oppression, and been
> constantly employed in preaching politics and construing treason.[51]

At 12:30 P.M. on March 1, 1805, the senators were polled on each of the eight articles whether Justice Samuel Chase was guilty or not guilty. Twenty-three votes were necessary for conviction, but nineteen—on the eighth article concerning Chase's charge to the Baltimore grand jury in 1803—were the most the Republicans could muster. Nearly one-fourth of the Republican senators deserted the party on the vote, six voting "not guilty" on all eight articles. Not a single senator voted "guilty" on the fifth article, which charged a simple error in judgment.[52] John Randolph stalked angrily from the Senate chamber to the House, where he immediately introduced a resolution for submitting to the states an amendment to the Constitution: "The judges of the Supreme and all other courts of the United States shall be removed by the President on the joint address of both Houses of Congress." And Joseph Nicholson moved still another amendment—that the legislature of any state might, whenever it thought proper, recall a senator and vacate his seat.[53] So ended the impeachment trial of Justice Samuel Chase, which, "it is generally agreed . . . probably saved Marshall [and] is therefore of fundamental importance in our constitutional history."[54]

Press reaction to the impeachment proceedings in the House of Representatives and to the trial in the Senate was heated from the beginning. A few days after Justice Chase made his controversial remarks to the Baltimore grand jury on May 2, 1803, the *National Intelligencer* condemned the charge as "the most extraordinary that the violence of federalism has yet produced, and exhibits humiliating evidence of the unfortunate effects of disappointed ambition."[55]

The most spirited defense of the federal judiciary during this phase of the assault was conducted by the *New-York Evening Post*, which commented soon after the motion of impeachment was introduced into the House of Representatives:

At length Mr. Jefferson's leading democrat in the House of Representatives [John Randolph] has begun an attack on one of the Judges of the Supreme Court [Samuel Chase]. Having got rid of all the circuit judges, they now have advanced a step higher.—Judge Chase, it seems, has made it his practice in his charges to several Grand Juries, to take these occasions to inculcate sound and of course anti-Jeffersonian principles among the people. This has given great offence at Washington. At first their editors misrepresented his sentiments and circulated the wicked misrepresentations through all their papers in the union, and when he on one occasion furnished a federal paper with his charge itself as delivered, the Jefferson editors carefully abstained from republishing it or retracting any thing they had said. It was hoped he might in this way be brought into a sufficient degree of unpopularity as a judge to facilitate the ultimate measure now resorted to of *impeachment*. Let the people look carefully at these things and ponder on them deliberately, seriously, solemnly. They know not yet what a scene they are to be called upon to witness, nor how soon.[56]

Soon after the above comment, the *New-York Evening Post* advised its readers, "let us not be deceived, justice is not the object [of the Chase impeachment], party rage is still unsatisfied, our Courts are filled by Federal judges; here is the mighty crime, here the high misdemeanor." Justice Chase was the first sacrificial offering, for "the bench in short is to be cleared of its present incumbents, no matter by what means, and filled with men subservient to the views of the powers that be, no matter altho' at the expense of all that renders a court of justice respectable." The *Post* concluded, "Unless, therefore, this measure is viewed in its proper light, and draws down upon its advocates the indignation of the country, it does not require the gift of prophecy to fortell, that the period is not very remote, when all for which a WASHINGTON fought and devoted his life, shall cease to have existence."[57]

As to the charge against Chase for his remarks to the Baltimore grand jury, the *New-York Evening Post* declared: "If to have expressed an abstract opinion upon government is so heinous an offence as to subject Judges to a solemn prosecution, what ought to be thought of Mr. Justice Livingston, Mr. Justice Thompson, and Mr. Justice Spencer, who have so far forgotten the respect due to their judicial characters, as to sign an electioneering address? They have thus publicly declared themselves party men; they have enlisted their passions in a party contest; and become the active instruments of a party."[58]

Meanwhile, the *National Intelligencer* carefully avoided comment on the impeachment proceedings until April 4, 1804, when the newspaper stated: "It was not our intention to make any remarks on the grounds of the impeachment of Judge Chase. That measure, in its initiation, having been amply and ably investigated on the floor of congress, and the debate, on that occasion, having been given to the public, our opinion was, that a newspaper discussion, previous to the trial by the constitutional tribunal, would be unnecessary, and premature, and might in its operation, be injurious, particularly to the accused." The *National Intelligencer* added that it was hoped "that the republican prints of the country would not provoke a conflict of prejudice and passion, which might tend, in some measure, to wrest the solemn measure of an impeachment from that dispassionate investigation which its importance eminently demands." Yet the resolution to refrain from comment was shattered by Justice Chase himself:

> He, who of the whole community, ought to have maintained the dignified attitude of composure, and should have been the last to excite the public feeling, has come forward in a manner, unprecedented, with an address to the people, connected with a request "to the Editors of *all* the newspapers in the United States, to insert his letter and memorial, and the articles of impeachment reported by the committee." To decline publishing these productions, would be denounced as partial or pusillanimous. They are therefore subjoined, excepting the articles of impeachment, already inserted in the National Intelligencer.

Having given them, we shall add some remarks, still avoiding, as much as possible, any implication of the grounds of impeachment, & confining ourselves to the extraordinary strictures of the judge upon the conduct of the House of Representatives in their collective capacity, and of several individuals of that body in the discharge of delegated powers.[59]

Justice Chase's letter, printed in the *National Intelligencer* with the above preface, requested newspaper editors throughout the land to print his memorial to the House of Representatives in answer to the articles of impeachment, "as they contain the most aggravated and inflamed construction, which it was possible for passion and party spirit to put on the ex-parte evidence, whereon the vote of impeachment was founded, [and] they will become a very powerful engine in the hands of calumniators and party zealots, for heightening to the utmost the prejudices and odium which all the former proceedings in this case are so well calculated to excite." Thus, Samuel Chase made his plea "to the world and to posterity, against the injustices and illegality of the proceedings in this case, and as a solemn protest against the principles on which they are founded."[60]

In his memorial to the House of Representatives, Chase requested that Congress not adjourn until the articles of impeachment had been drawn up so that he would have time to form a defense, "to vindicate that innocence, for which he solemnly appeals to the Almighty Searcher of hearts, to the testimony of his own conscience, to his country, and to an impartial posterity." Chase denounced the method of voting for the impeachment because all charges were lumped together, whereas there may not have been majority votes on each of the charges if considered separately. "Your memorialist," the judge concluded, "trembles for the honor of his country, and for the success of republican government in this her last and fairest experiment, much more than for his own safety, when he reflects on the excesses that under such a cloak may be committed."[61]

The *National Intelligencer*'s comment on Chase's "long and inflammatory remarks" was brief and to the point: "We disclaim all appeal to Heaven, to the almighty searcher of hearts, and to the dread tribunal of another world. We address ourselves exclusively and confidently to the honest judgment of upright men. It is through them that Deity proclaims his will, and with their suffrages in our favor we dread nothing."[62]

Meanwhile, the *New-York Evening Post* kept up its running attack on the impeachment proceedings as the opening of the trial neared. The Federalist newspaper declared that the forthcoming trial "involves in its issue the fate of the Judicial Branch of the government, and ought to excite the most earnest solicitude of the whole American people"[63] and fervently denounced the individual charges against Justice Chase.

Perhaps goaded by the Federalist defense, Thomas Ritchie of the *Richmond Enquirer* tried the impeachment charges against Justice Chase in the columns of his Republican newspaper before the case even reached the Senate. On December 15, 1804, the *Enquirer* commented:

> It is perhaps aggravating too highly the offences of Judge Chase, to compare him, as some have done, to the infamous Jeffries of England. But if the articles of impeachment which are laid against him be really founded in truth, *his* offences are not easily to be vindicated, or soon to be forgotten. If he was really the political persecutor which these articles represent him to be, I do not hesitate to say, that Judge Chase is no longer worthy of being the organ of a limited constitution, or the judge of a free people.[64]

Ritchie maintained that in selecting a jury for the Callender trial, Justice Chase had instructed the federal marshal not to include any Republican veniremen on the panel. "It is a fact well known to every man who knew the names and characters of the Jurors, that no one sat on that trial, who was not at that time the political opponent of J. T. Callender," the *Richmond Enquirer* charged, adding the comment:

> When a judge descends to so minute a development of qualifications, he may be properly suspected of employing an extra official authority, and of employing that authority not for the purpose of obtaining an impartial, but a packed and prejudiced jury.—That Judge Chase *did* exercise *such* an authority in the empannelling of a Jury for the trial of Callender, is *not* among the charges which are alleged against him by the articles of impeachment: This fact must have either escaped the researches or the memory of the select committee of Enquiry. But that such was the fact; that Judge Chase *did* exercise such an usurped influence in the empannelling of a jury, is supported by testimony too respectable to be denied, and too pointed to be refuted in its inference.

After making these charges, the *Enquirer* primly observed, "How far these charges are supported by truth, and whether the dismissal of the judge shall constitute the punishment of his offences; it is the province of an official investigation to ascertain and unfold."[65]

A week later, long after the damage to Justice Chase had already been done, Ritchie withdrew these charges, observing lamely, "Judge Chase, standing at this time before the bar of his country to answer the articles of impeachment which have been already collected and arraigned against him, has certainly a claim upon the impartial and forbearing judgment of his opponents."[66]

The *New-York Evening Post*, however, was not going to let the Richmond editor off so easily for such a flagrant violation of newspaper ethics—even for that time—"Never, perhaps, was there a more unjust and injurious attack made on innocence and integrity," the *Post* declared, "and never were more extra-ordinary and outrageous measures resorted to for the purpose of carrying it through." The newspaper added:

The venal presses of administration, with scandalous & unexampled effrontery, were all opened against the accused, and their attacks continued pending the whole course of the trial. We in particular took notice of the Virginia paper, called the *Richmond Enquirer*. This insidious paper, assisted by labours of your Edmund Randolph, your Hays, your Masons and others of the same stamp, soon after the trial commenced, advanced a new accusation against Judge Chase, respecting his conduct at the trial of Callender and charged him with an indirect attempt to pack the jury; deeply lamenting that this had not been made an article in the impeachment. In the next number the writer forsooth was very sorry he had been so hasty and indiscreet and had committed such an impropriety, for really it had not occurred to him, he swore in faith it had not, that to advance additional accusations against a man pending his trial, was rather unfair and improper. This was precisely the hypocrisy and the cunning of Anthony.[67]

The *New-York Evening Post* also carried a letter from a correspondent reporting on the Pennsylvania impeachments at Lancaster, which concluded, "*there are too many blocks waiting for Judiciary wigs.*" William Coleman added, "I wonder now if there is not a *block* at Washington waiting for Judge Chase's *wig*? What say you Mr. manager N——n? Do you know any *block* it would fit?"[68] The newspaper of the late Alexander Hamilton was also upset when Aaron Burr appeared in Washington to preside over Chase's trial. The *Post* caustically observed, "We were always sure that Burr would be *in at the death.*"[69] The Trenton, New Jersey, *Federalist* also had a few words to say on this matter: "*The World upside down; or, the trial of Judge Chase.* Formerly, says the Boston Palladium, it was the practice in Courts of Justice to arraign the *murderer* before the *Judge*, but *now* we behold the *Judge* arraigned before the *murderer*. Mr. Burr sits as President of the High Court of Impeachment on the trial of *Judge Chase.*"[70]

On the other hand, the *Richmond Enquirer* was horrified that Justice Chase should continue sitting on the Supreme Court "at the very time, when [he] was brought before the great tribunal of his country on a charge of violating its laws. . . ."[71] But the Federalist press continued to lacerate Aaron Burr. "It is indeed altogether a very curious and wretched spectacle," said the *New-York Evening Post*, "but when we said *criminal* tribunal [in a preceding paragraph], the seriousness of the subject did not admit any idea like the levity of a pun, nor do we thus intend an illusion to the *blood* stained Fugitive that presides, or any of his associates that may pollute or prostitute the judgment seat."[72] And the New York *Political Register* exclaimed, "how disgraceful is it, to the character of the nation, that in the highest court of judicature known to our constitution, the word MURDER cannot be pronounced before the *presiding judge*, without exciting universal surprise and observation?"[73]

Despite what Federalist newspapers thought about the presiding officer, Aaron Burr, the *National Intelligencer* insisted that Samuel Chase had received "a full, patient, and deliberate hearing." The newspaper added, "During the whole progress of the trial a degree of order and decorum has been preserved, which reflects high honor on the Senate of the United States, and the individual who presides over their deliberations."[74]

The Boston *Columbian Centinel* thought that Chase, not Burr, was star of the show because "the more his character is scrutinized the brighter it appears." The Boston *Federalist* newspaper also declared, "There was perhaps never more glaring proof of a malicious, revengeful prosecution. But still I think the chance for acquittal or condemnation about equal."[75] This report, written from Washington on February 19, 1805, revealed that the outcome of the trial was far from certain to the most partial observers.

Finally, on March 4, 1805, the *National Intelligencer* announced, "JUDGMENT PRONOUNCED ON THE IMPEACHMENT AGAINST SAMUEL CHASE," giving a table of the individual votes but offering not one word of comment. For several days the Republican newspapers under consideration remained silent on the topic. The Philadelphia *Aurora*, which had remained unusually virtuous in refraining from commenting on the trial while it was in progress, praised Burr's conduct as "very dignified and manly," but said nothing of the acquittal.[76] But the *Richmond Enquirer* was not so restrained: "True, S.C. has been acquitted by the constitutional majority; true, there were not *two-thirds* of the Senate willing to find him guilty: but it is true, also, that there was an actual majority against him on three of the articles. . . . The innocence of the judge therefore finds its refuge, not in the decision of common sense, but in the mercy of our constitution. To me, therefore, who estimates truth by probability, Mr. Chase must appear virtually condemned. . . ."[77]

After announcing the acquittal on March 5, 1805, the *New-York Evening Post*, jubilantly commented the next day, "Upon this event we felicitate the country, that there is still in our senate sufficient virtue to dictate a decision in conformity with law and equity, though opposed by the loud and malignant clamours of vindictive and unprincipled disorganisers, both in and out of congress."[78] The New York *Political Register* headlined its account of Chase's vindication, "ACQUITTED. . . . *LAUS DEO.*"[79]

Doing its best to salvage something from the fiasco, the *National Intelligencer* rushed its two-volume edition of an account of the Chase trial into print, stating, "We are the more solicitous to do this, that there may be laid before the public a correct statement of this important trial, which, viewed in its various aspects, merits and will reward as great attention, as any event which has occurred in the United States."[80]

The event of Chase's acquittal also had a deeper significance. "For the first time since his appointment, John Marshall was secure as the head of the Supreme Bench," Albert J. Beveridge has written.[81] John Quincy Adams was convinced that Jefferson intended to sweep the Supreme Court clean of Federalist judges if the attack on Chase proved successful, and rumor went so far as to indicate that the president had Judge Spencer Roane of Virginia in mind as Marshall's successor.[82] Yet Jefferson's attitude toward the judiciary has sometimes been exaggerated. As Charles A. Beard has pointed out:

> The great authority of Jefferson is often used by the opponents of judicial control; and it is true that, after his party was in command of the legislative and executive branches of the government, he frequently attacked judicial "usurpation" with great vehemence. The Federalists were in possession of the Supreme Court for some time after his inauguration. Jefferson was not a member of the convention that drafted the Constitution nor of the Virginia convention that ratified it. There is, however, absolutely no question that at the time the Constitution was formed he favored some kind of direct control.[83]

In conclusion, press support for the Jeffersonian assault on the judiciary was influential in getting the country to accept the unprecedented repeal of the Federalist judiciary act of 1801, but Republican newspapers were unable to sway either the Senate or the public toward the conviction of Justice Samuel Chase. After all, the Maryland judge was a signer of the Declaration of Independence, and few outside of political circles remembered Chase's high-handed conduct in the trials of Fries and Callender. On the surface, the conviction failed because too many charges—all but one of which were four years old—were dragged into the indictment, because the prosecution was inept and the defense superb, and because Samuel Chase had the full support of the Federalist Party. The theory of impeachment urged by the Republican managers of the prosecution was inconsistent and self-contradictory, and the extreme position taken by Giles and Nicholson "was certainly far too extreme for a court manned predominantly by lawyers who perhaps envisaged themselves upon the bench someday."[84] Moreover, the Republican-dominated Senate voted in a creditable demonstration of fairness in what was obviously a partisan action.

Yet beneath the surface, the failure to convict Justice Chase was largely a failure to convince public opinion that he should be convicted. In the judgment of William Plumer, Federalist senator from New Hampshire, "The removal of Judge Chase was deemed an imprudent measure—public opinion so far as it could be collected was decidedly opposed to the measure."[85] And as the *New-York Evening Post* concluded, with more than a modicum of truth:

> in the selection of Judge Chase for their first victim, they [the Republicans] most egregiously mistook their man. They relied on his want, as they supposed, of personal popularity. But he rose in his might; with abilities of the first order, he repelled their unjust charges, and in such a manner that he has erected a monument to his fame beyond the reach of time or accident to impair. His triumph over his and our enemies, affords a proud day for the cause of Federalism.

Even more telling in the newspapers of the time, the Republicans lost an ill-conceived and poorly executed political venture. William Coleman of the *New-York Evening Post* summed up the Federalist opposition: "Jefferson had from the first to have a judiciary, as well as a legislature that would second the views of the executives."[86]

The results of the attempt to remove Justice Samuel Chase from the Supreme Court of the United States became apparent in the years succeeding the ill-fated Republican effort to redress the political balance. Federal judges refrained from active participation in politics, and their courtroom manners were seen to improve remarkably. And threats to impeach Supreme Court justices were heard no more.

NINE

The Embargo and Commercial Warfare, 1807–1809

Under such circumstances the best to be done is what has been done;
a dignified retirement within ourselves; a watchful preservation
of our resources; and a demonstration to the world, that we possess a virtue
and a patriotism which can take any shape that will best suit the occasion.

—*National Intelligencer,* December 23, 1807

. . . it requires all the confidence,—all the faith, of which a stupid
party bigotry is capable to approve of this terrible desolation [the Embargo].—
The justification of this dreadful butchery of the political body, requires indeed the
sacrifice of all the pride, and all the liberty, and all the good sense of the nation.

—*New-York Evening Post,* February 2, 1808

"Never before have the American prints been overwhelmed with such a flood of momentous intelligence," declared the *National Intelligencer* on December 23, 1805. Great Britain and France were once again at each other's throats, and the shadow of Napoleon fell starkly across all of Europe. Once again America's shipping was endangered, her seamen molested, her honor flaunted. Once again the United States was forced into the impotent stance of neutrality while the massive armed camp of Europe, seething with intrigue and sullen with despair, carried its internecine warfare to the high seas. "Events, of the most astonishing nature," the *National Intelligencer* continued, "succeed each other with a rapidity unprecedented; events on which the fate of empires, and, we might almost say, the destiny of the whole world hang."

As Doron S. Ben-Atar has summed up the international situation, "In 1807, with Europe torn by seemingly endless conflict, Jefferson gambled that American commerce could be used as an instrument for forcing the belligerent nations to do America justice and to respect the republic's honor."[1]

The commerce of the United States was soon involved in the resumption of the European wars in 1803, after the short-lived Peace of Amiens. In 1805 Great Britain seized and condemned the American ship *Essex,* engaged in trade with the French West Indies, and in 1806 Monroe reported that more than 120 American vessels had been taken by the British. On April 18, 1806, Congress clamped nonimportation bans on many articles previously imported from England. By May 16 the British blockade of the European coast extended from the Elbe to Brest, provoking Napoleon to issue his Berlin Decree of November 21, 1806, which denounced "the injustice and the barbarism of the English maritime laws" and placed a paper blockade around the British isles.[2] In turn, Great Britain issued the Order in Council of January 7, 1807, prohibiting any vessel from trading with any port of France or her allies, and the Order in Council of November 11, blockading all ports in Europe from which the British flag was excluded. Napoleon replied with the Milan Decree of December 17, 1807, which made any ship searched by the British enemy property. The effects of these measures on American interests bore most heavily on the mercantile class of New England, which formed the backbone of the Federalist Party, and under the pressure of the crisis that political group seemed to be gaining in strength. The *National Intelligencer* asserted on May 9, 1806: "For a considerable time past, federalism has slumbered, until the unsuspicious had begun to cherish the hope of the speedy arrival of those halcyon days, when harmony and brotherly love should universally prevail. But it is only necessary to look back on the circumstances which have occurred for a few months past, and to fix an attention upon those which are now passing before us, to be convinced, to use a memorable federal phrase, that the tiger has only crouched that he may the more fatally spring on his prey."[3]

Burton Spivak has put all the pieces together in this tangled international scene:

> When it became increasingly difficult to distinguish French from British high-
> handedness, when an intimidating fear of European madness overwhelmed
> the liberating fear of English malice, an instinct to withdraw overwhelmed a
> desire to fight. From this powerful urge to remain safe in the New World, to
> keep American ships and sailors—the nation really—out of "harm's way,"
> Jefferson's Embargo was born.[4]

At the same time, the prestige of Jefferson's administration fell to an all-time low because of the depredations on American shipping. Abuse in the Federalist newspapers was unleashed full force against the president and his "do-nothing" administration. One Federalist editor lashed Jefferson for submitting to impressment and confiscations while at the same time welcoming European immigrants to American shores:

Without the wisdom or spirit, and certainly without the necessity of the original founders of Rome for doing so, he [Jefferson] has like them opened an asylum for all the VAGABONDS, TRAITORS, and VILLAINS vomited forth from Europe, thereby to establish his kingdom. *The picture only wants a rape to complete it, and make it companion to the Roman. But it is to be hoped that however neck-bending the American men may be, the American ladies will set their faces against SABINE women, and that our modern Romulus will be, like him of old, soon* TRANSLATED TO THE GODS, *with the* GOOD WILL OF THE SENATE.[5]

After the passage of the nonimportation act directed against Great Britain, the *National Intelligencer* commented: "The crisis in our affairs has been met with a proper temper and an honorable decision. There is no American, who has not felt the indignity offered to his country, and who has not boldly avowed his preference of war to abject submission. . . . It remains, perhaps, for us to demonstrate this fact to an unbelieving world."[6]

But the unbelieving European world continued to deny any neutral shipping rights to the United States. Impressment of American seamen for duty on British vessels had been an issue that had plagued the Jefferson administration from its inception; in fact, it was this troublesome issue that had first caused William Duane of the Philadelphia *Aurora* to criticize the new administration.[7] The Republican *Aurora* was generally loyal to Jefferson, and its charges of governmental inaction on the matter of impressment indicated that this emotional issue was incendiary enough to transcend party loyalty—especially after the notorious *Chesapeake* incident of June 27, 1807, when the British warship *Leopard,* intent on recovering four English sailors, opened fire on the American naval vessel, killing three and wounding eighteen American seamen. After the efforts of William Pinckney failed to conclude a satisfactory treaty with Great Britain, the United States undertook retaliatory action by proclaiming a general embargo on December 22, 1807.

The Embargo was an attempt to find an alternative to war by commercial coercion; in sweeping terms, it froze all American shipping and closed all American ports, except for controlled trading along the coast. The statute placed all seagoing commerce "under the immediate direction of the President of the United States," and all forthcoming regulations were to be enforced by navy and revenue cutters. Coastal trade was allowed when the shipmaster gave a bond double the amount of the value of his merchandise, to be repaid when the vessel unloaded at another American port. Foreign ships in American harbors at the time of the passage of the Embargo were to be allowed to depart.[8] One historian has called the Embargo "a sublime experiment carried out under impossible conditions."[9] The contemporary *New-York Evening Post* called it, "this horrible act of National suicide."[10]

The administration defended its measure as an unpleasant but absolutely necessary alternative to war. Unfortunately, however, Americans were not and had never been averse to war when the national honor was at stake; they would have responded with characteristic vigor to a call to arms but were bewildered by an appeal for economic self-sacrifice. A few days before the Embargo was enacted, "Americanus" in the Boston *Independent Chronicle* declared, "A state of war will always be deprecated by all wise and good men; but when it becomes unavoidable, a patriotic mind will cheerfully submit to all its calamities, rather than see the rights of his country wantonly violated."[11]

The *National Intelligencer* sought to direct such nationalistic fervor into more constructive channels. In preparing the nation for the Embargo, the administration's newspaper stated on December 25, 1807:

> A crisis has arrived, that calls for some decided step. The national spirit is up. That spirit is invaluable. In case of a war it is to lead us to conquest. By the vigor with which it shall wield the physical force of the country, it is to inspire us with unshaken confidence in our strength, and to appall our enemy. . . . The people having shown their spirit, the season has arrived for the government to sustain, second and direct it. . . . The crisis not requiring war, still hoping, if not expecting peace, an embargo is the next best measure for maintaining the national tone. It will arm the nation. It will do more. It will arm the Executive government. It is an unequivocal, and efficient expression of confidence in the Executive; and gives the President a new weapon of negotiation—we say *weapon* of negotiation, for, in the present state of the world, even negotiation has ceased to be pacific.[12]

Any concept of freedom of the seas or the rights of neutral nations had disappeared from the world. "Thus the ocean presents a field only where no harvest is to be reaped but that of danger, of spoliation and of disgrace," the *Intelligencer* asserted. The newspaper pleaded for all Americans to submit "patiently and proudly . . . to every inconvenience which such a measure necessarily carries with it,"[13] and expressed the belief that the Embargo would be "a popular measure with all classes." The editor maintained, "We are certain that the farmer, the planter and the mechanic will approve it from the security it offers to the public interests; and if the merchants be as honest and enlightened, as we trust they are, they will perceive the indissoluble connection between their solid and permanent prosperity and the general welfare."[14]

No other measure of Jefferson's entire administration received such elaborate advance publicity or such careful and detailed explanation in the columns of the *National Intelligencer*, as Samuel Harrison Smith tried valiantly to meet objections before they arose, and no other measure was so roundly denounced in the pages of the Boston *Columbian Centinel* and the *New-York Evening Post*.

The Embargo was announced in Boston on December 30, 1807, by the *Columbian Centinel*, which could not decide whether the measure was aimed at the British (Ambassador George Henry Rose was scheduled to land soon) or against France. "The accounts from Washington are multitudinous and contradictory," the Federalist newspaper complained. A letter from Washington, dated December 29, 1807, stated: "We are full of fearful apprehensions, that the Executive is resolved to hurry the United States into War; and that there is a majority in both houses ready to vote his will. The *Peace* party is however on the increase; and I have some hopes mixed with those fears, that before the appeal is made to the sword, returning reason will avert hostilities."[15]

The *New-York Evening Post*, consulting its copy of the "Extra paper" issued by the *National Intelligencer* on December 22, 1807, announced the news in New York three days later. "It appears the great and important secret is at length disclosed," the *Post* said. "Congress have declared an embargo. The act goes into immediate operation, and is without limit in respect to time."[16] Previously passed by the Senate, the Embargo was adopted by the House of Representatives on December 22, 1807, by a vote of 62–44. On December 29, the *Post* published a letter from a Washington correspondent which stated: "On Monday the house was 12 hours in constant session [the last of three days of debate]. During all that time not a single friend of the bill rose to vindicate the measure. Whenever an opponent closed his speech, loud calls for the question were vociferated from every part of the house; when they were speaking there was such noise and confusion, such talking, and coughing, and hemming, that little or nothing could be heard. In this manner was the debate conducted upon a measure of as much importance as any that has engaged the attention of congress since the organization of the government."[17]

Announcing the Embargo on December 26, 1807, the *New-York Evening Post* commented: "At the present moment of uncertainty, apprehension, dismay and distress, every one is running eagerly to his neighbour to inquire after information. The measure at last adopted by the Government, of an EMBARGO, brings with it immediate bankruptcy to the merchant, and of course less of employ and want of bread to some thousands of the labouring poor of this city." Still, the *Post* tried to be fair, admitting that it might be possible "that the administration may have sufficient or at least plausible reasons for keeping the people so much in the dark as to the particular and express object of this important measure." Yet an examination of the individual votes in Congress revealed that "all the talents, the patriotism, the sterling integrity of the House [are] on one side and against this measure, and on the other the mere force of voting figures." The first circumstance concerning the adoption of the Embargo that caught the *Post*'s editorial eye was one sentence in President Jefferson's message to Congress recommending the measure: "I ask a return of the letters of Messrs. Armstrong and Champagny, which it would be improper to make public." This provoked a long series of editorial comments demanding that public measures be publicly known.[18] But for the time the *New-York Evening Post* was willing to meet the administration halfway: "Make us once sensible that the Administration have acted or mean to act an honourable and independent part, and it shall find us among the most ready and zealous, if not the most able of its supporters, in any controversy with any nation."[19]

As one of the more sophisticated of the Federalist newspapers, the *New-York Evening Post* realized that the nature of the crisis was too urgent to permit the usual partisan bickering. On December 28, 1807, the *Post* republished in full the explanations of the Embargo that had appeared in the *National Intelligencer* on December 23 and 25, 1807. These items were prefaced with the comment, "While the public mind is so much agitated by this extraordinary measure, it would almost seem little less than a want of duty in us not to permit it to occupy the principal part of our paper."[20] The *Gazette of the United States* likewise adopted a cautious attitude on first announcing the Embargo on December 24, 1807. "Whether the policy which dictated this law, be wise or foolish, I presume not to determine," wrote Enos Bronson. "It is now a law of the land: it must be obeyed, and complaint or resistance will be vain."[21]

Everyone agreed that it would take some time for the effects of the legislative experiment to be determined. As the *Gazette of the United States* pointed out, "It will take at least three months for information of the law to be transmitted to Europe, for it to produce its effect there, and for us to receive notice of it; so that the most sanguine friends of the embargo cannot entertain the idea of its being removed in less than three months at soonest."[22]

By December 29, 1807, the attitude of the *New-York Evening Post* was formulated: it would oppose the Embargo with all the resources at its command. The previous conciliatory tone of the newspaper was dropped as the *Post* personalized its attack: "As the Administration paper informs us that it was emphatically the PRESIDENT's *measure,* we beg leave to ask the President's friends, if they suppose the people will continue to *idolize* him when they find themselves without food or clothing, and that he persists in concealing himself and his measures in the impenetrable secrecy which he is now pleased to observe; especially, when they recollect that he has formerly been one of the loudest to exclaim—*no secrets in a republic?*"[23] Comment on this statement by the Philadelphia *Aurora* was brief and to the point: "Why is the N.Y. Eve. Post like a man with disordered bowels? —because he engenders *foul reports.*"[24]

The international conditions that prompted the Embargo revived the old dichotomy in American politics between French and English sympathies, and this question was the first issue in the great debate. As the Philadelphia *Aurora* stated in a poem six days after the measure was adopted:

HEAR THEM!

This embargo has put party men in a pother;
"'Tis for France!" says the one—"this for England,"
says t'other;
A third, rather dryly exclaims—'tis in troth [truth]
An act of hostility made against both;
While a fourth says—"this measure of prudence will save
"From the eagle and lion the little we have."[25]

The Washington correspondent of the *Gazette of the United States* reported that the minority in the congressional debate on the Embargo had "denounced it as a measure that originated in mandates from France. I am assured that most if not all of those who opposed it expressed their entire belief that it proceeded from Bonaparte and was intended to co-operate with his scheme of destroying British commerce."[26] And there was no doubt where the New York *American Citizen*, edited by James Cheetham, stood on this matter:

Napoleon, the inexorable tyrant of Europe, he who in society has confounded the moral and political relations of man to man blasted with his pestilential breath the germinations of republicanism in Europe—rivetted anew upon the poor and the oppressed the ignoble and galling chains of slavery, and destroyed even hope itself of a better state of things in that unfortunate portion of the globe; this man, this great enemy of freedom, not content with lording it over all continental Europe, has stretched forth his strong and bloody arm across the Atlantic, and *menaced* us with WAR, unless we comply with his insolent demands to *shut* our ports against the commerce of England! Such are the intimations which are privately given of the contents of Messrs. Armstrong and Champagny's letters, which it would be improper to make public, but upon which the embargo is bottomed.[27]

This frenzied response by a former Republican editor revealed how completely he had broken with Jefferson's administration—a break that first became apparent on the death of Alexander Hamilton. Cheetham's fiery reaction was probably also influenced by the personal feud he was conducting at this time with his former friend, Thomas Paine. The reply to Cheetham's tirade by the Philadelphia *Aurora* was once again brief: "Why does the *N.Y. Eve. Post* recommend the stupid productions of the *American Citizen* to the public attention?—from a fondness to *Cheet'em*"[28]

Whether the Embargo was more pro-French than anti-British was a theme that constantly recurred during discussion of the measure in the nation's newspapers, Federalist and Republican. It is revealing to follow this line of argument throughout the period before considering other aspects of the reaction by the press. On January 25, 1808, the *New-York Evening Post* republished an extract from the New York *Morning Chronicle,* called "the *Jeffersonian* print of this city" and the "New-York *Aurora*" by the *Evening Post,* which "made no scruple to avow, that [the Embargo] is against England and not against France." The *Morning Chronicle* had stated:

> *The conduct of Britain* has driven us to our last and only expedient, an Embargo, which the British apologist so unfeignedly laments, because he is conscious it is a measure that will *bring the nose of England to the grindstone,* and make the British ministry sensible of their injustice towards this country. . . . As a proof of what we could do, Congress placed an embargo on our ports. Should it affect England more than France, let her look to it, for *she was the cause, and not France.*[29]

The *Richmond Enquirer,* a Republican newspaper edited by Thomas Ritchie, was considerably more objective in assigning blame for the instigators of the Embargo. "It were sincerely to be wished," said the *Enquirer,* "that G. Britain was alone in these aggressions. But such has been the contest of herself and her enemy, that much of what related to maritime aggressions applies also to France."[30]

The *New-York Evening Post* led the pack of Federalist newspapers that castigated the Embargo as a measure expressly dictated by France. "Mr. Jefferson, from a servile dread of Napoleon," the *Post* commented, "not only obstinately persists in refusing to settle our differences with England, but even, like a mere PREFECT obeying the orders of his master, seems determined on going to actual war with that bulwark of our country—that only remaining hope of nations; and, of course, to form an alliance with France. . . . "[31]

But the servile or pro-French attitude on the part of the administration was fast losing support, the New York *Commercial Advertiser* maintained: "They [the people] are quitting with precipitation the whitened sepulchre of all-unhinging democracy, that slaughter-house of true liberty, inhabited only by the blood-stained ghosts of Robespierre, Marat, &c. to enter once again into the temple of truth, candor and federalism, where the paternal shade of Washington, with anxious solicitude, beckons their approach, and with characteristic benignity welcomes their return to their father's mansion, from which in an *evil hour* they had strayed!!!"[32] The *National Intelligencer* republished this item under the headline "INSANITY . . . *Mad, madder than the maddest of March hares!*"[33]

The *National Intelligencer* found a veritable epidemic of mental derangement raging throughout the Federalist press. Week after week, the *National Intelligencer* culled choice items from the opposition newspapers and placed them under a standing headline of "INSANITY!" The Boston *Repertory* was adjudged insane for declaring, "Mr. Jefferson is endeavoring to prepare the public mind for war with England, by every charge against that nation, that his VIRGINIAN

HATRED of commerce, of his French hatred of England can suggest, and by excusing every encroachment of France on our honor and independence."[34] The Baltimore *North-American* was insane (a charitable view, the *Intelligencer* noted) for saying, "The belief that Messrs. Jefferson and Madison are really *naturalized as French citizens,* gains ground."[35] And the *Washington Federalist* joined the list of journalistic invalids by referring to Great Britain as *"the first nation that ever existed on this globe."*[36]

Meanwhile, the *New-York Evening Post* was deriding what it considered "republicanism with a vengeance" or the return of the Jeffersonians to their former attachment to France and antagonism toward England. The Embargo, said the *Post,* "from an *impartial* measure of precaution 'to preserve our essential resources' . . . has taken a hostile attitude against England alone, and like every other War, by calling forth the unfriendly feelings of the nation against which it is particularly levelled, it must be of much longer duration than its blind advocates have any idea of."[37] Three days later, the *Post* again condemned "the blind partiality manifested by our present rulers towards France, and their deadly hatred for Great Britain." This hatred had become so virulent, the *Post* believed, "that an attempt will be made at the opening of Congress in November [1808] to plunge us with a war with Great-Britain. . . . "[38] In December 1808, "A Boston Yankee" contributed a poem to the *New-York Evening Post* that summed up that newspaper's stand on the issue of French influence:

> No *"British Orders are the Embargo's cause"*
> But love to FRANCE, and fear of *Bony's* paws.
> There do we find, (from that polluted source,
> Which blights and blasts all Europe in its course)
> There do we find, why ruin throngs our strands
> Why *Jacobin Embargoes curse our land.*[39]

As this systematic campaign of denunciation ran its course, the Republican newspapers appealed to the "patience and gallantry" of the American people to bear willingly the hardships of the Embargo for the national good. A typical appeal of this sort appeared in the *Richmond Enquirer* soon after passage of the Embargo:

> This measure emphatically addresses itself to the spirit and patriotism of the people. If *they* uphold it, the Embargo will continue to operate until it leads to the most salutary results. If they oppose it, if they murmur at it, if like children, they will not put up with a little temporary inconvenience for the sake of obtaining some great ultimate good; it is in vain that their government has taken this dignified stand. . . . No doubt it will give a temporary sock to the value of our produce, and if the merchants choose to encounter the obloquy of the speculation, it will raise the price of goods. But the honor of our country is

at stake. It is our firm belief too, that it will contribute to bring the European nations to a sense of justice.[40]

"An Appeal to the Well-Disposed Citizens" in the Boston *Independent Chronicle* reflected that Republican newspaper's first response to the restrictive commercial legislation. "It would be the greatest folly for the Americans to sport their property between the contending powers of Europe," the *Chronicle* stated. "We shall hear a great deal about the poor farmer, and the poor tradesman, on account of the embargo," the newspaper continued, "but the fact is . . . these noisy turbulent opposers, who write in the federal papers, are desperate speculators, who don't care whose property they hazard, if they can get a chance to help themselves." Those who cried loudest against the Embargo were *"nominal merchants"*—speculators in goods who risked nothing of their own. "If the REAL farmer, tradesman and merchant, will stand firm in prosecuting the Embargo and other measures of the government, the United States will see the effects of their *restrictive energies* in bringing the powers of Europe to a just settlement with this country," the *Chronicle* predicted. "The BRITISH FALCON knows this—and WE KNOW, 'by their roaring,' the government has 'hit them right.'"[41]

In the Middle Atlantic states, which would be hard hit because of their grain and meat exports, the Philadelphia *Aurora* adopted a tough attitude that seemed intent on coercion rather than persuasion:

> "He *who is not for us, is against us.*"—Such must be the creed of every American henceforth. It is not now a question of this man or that man, for this or that office. The question now—shall we continue to be a *free, sovereign,* and independent nation, as the immortal Congress of 1776 proclaimed us to be, and as eight years of sanguinary contest proved us to be worthy of sustaining. This is not time for the cavils of silly men, any more than for the audacious villainy of the knavish—the spirit of manhood disdains to trifle with the one, or to submit in silent connivance to the other. The *country* now calls for the extinctions of faction—and for the direction of all the energies of the noble soul, against the oppressor. There is no intermediate course between *public patriotism* and *perfidy.*[42]

These positive appeals had no effect whatsoever on the policy of the *New-York Evening Post,* which continued to denounce the *"Dambargo."*[43] The *National Intelligencer* had referred to the measure as "a weapon of negotiation." But, asked the *Evening Post,* "whoever, before this period of *philosophy,* ever thought of employing a weapon, which, for every stroke aimed at any adversary, inflicts a deep and deadly wound on the very hand that uses it?" Intended to deprive the British of needed goods, the Embargo would actually deprive the Americans of more-desperately needed markets, and the American carrying trade would also fall into the hands of the English. In several conundrums, the *Post* drove this point home: "Why is the Embargo like a pig in the water? Because it cuts its own throat."[44] And in another issue of the newspaper:

> Why is the Embargo like an old musket?
> Because old muskets so contrive it,
> As quite to miss the mark they aim at,
> And though well aim'd at duck or plover,
> Bear wide, and *kick their owner over*.[45]

The *Post* reported a speech by Governor James Sullivan of Massachusetts in which, "after some little writhing about for reasons to justify" the Embargo, the Republican executive said: "At this important crisis, . . . when our wisest and best men, (meaning Thomas Jefferson and others) cannot decide, *with satisfaction to themselves what measures to pursue;* we ought to be instructed, as a people, from this, not rashly to condemn the measure, or suddenly to censure our leaders for their decisions." Commented the *New-York Evening Post*, "we remember, when at school, to have been struck with the following remark of Lord Chesterfield's 'Wise men, when they do not see their way clear, always stop, till they do; fools and blockheads rush on, and blunder succeeds to blunder, till they are disgraced and probably ruined.'"[46]

Supplementary acts to the Embargo were adopted on January 9 and March 12, 1808. Meanwhile, copies of the British Orders in Council of January 7 and November 11, 1807, finally reached Washington, and the *National Intelligencer* used them for propaganda purposes. "They establish the wisdom of the Embargo beyond a shadow of doubt," the administration's newspaper said. "For so extensive and sweeping are many of their provisions, that it is almost impossible to perceive what commercial ruin might not have ensued from their enforcement, but for this measure [the Embargo]."[47] The *New-York Evening Post* replied caustically, "Our administration will, I suppose, now publish a fourth paper in defence of the *Embargo,* and prove beyond all doubt, that Mr. Jefferson did it to prevent our vessels from falling into the hands of the Algerines."[48]

Soon the Embargo ceased to provide opportunity for humorous comments, however, as its effects on the American economy began to be noticed. The town of Salem, Massachusetts, one of the most important commercial centers in the United States in 1808, suffered severely. In 1807 a total of 134 vessels had left Salem for overseas ports, but in 1808 not a single ship cleared the Salem harbor. A year later, 1,200 destitute persons were being fed at the Salem soup kitchen, and about one-fifth of the town's inhabitants had been reduced to beggary.[49] A difficult problem in every seaport town was caused by bands of unemployed sailors who roamed the streets and turned to crime. Others were joining the crews of foreign vessels that had been in American harbors when the Embargo was imposed. The *New-York Evening Post* reported on March 12, 1808, that "the British Packet sailed this forenoon, with her decks literally crowded with sailors going to another country to seek employment. It will be seen whenever the Embargo shall be raised, (but that is not to be expected from the *present* administration) there will not be found sailors enough left to man our vessels."[50]

Widespread distress in New England was reflected in the spring elections of 1808. In Hartford, Connecticut, which had been Republican for two years previously, the Federalist ticket won all the municipal offices "by a handsome majority," and in Portland, Maine, the Republican selectmen were replaced by Federalists by a majority vote of 172.[51] Fall elections in the interior towns of Connecticut also returned Federalists to office. A Connecticut correspondent wrote to the *New-York Evening Post*, "Jefferson's Embargo is an excellent mother, for she brings forth federal children in abundance." The *Post* commented, "We hope this kind mother will extend her maternal care over the Southern, as well as the Northern and Eastern states."[52] A rhymester in the *New-York Evening Post* underscored the election results when he wrote "A Short Address to Democrats, On the Happy Effects of the Embargo." New Englanders had gone to the polls after

> . . . having seen, in various views,
> My gentle friend and neighbour,
> The course our President pursues
> "To feed the mouth of labour."[53]

Beyond doubt the most vitriolic attack on President Jefferson in verse form came from the pen of thirteen-year-old William Cullen Bryant in a pamphlet published in Boston in 1808:

> Go, wretch, resign the presidential chair,
> Disclose thy secret measures foul or fair,
> Go, search, with curious eye, for horned frogs,
> Mongst the wild wastes of Louisianian bogs;
> Or where Ohio rolls his turbid stream,
> Dig for huge bones, thy glory and thy theme;
> Go scan, Philosophist; they ****** charms,
> And sink supinely in her sable arms;
> But quit to abler hands, the helm of state,
> Nor image ruin on thy country's fate![54]

Republican newspapers were hard pressed to devise new arguments for supporting the Embargo. The *Richmond Enquirer* reported that a speech of Henry Richard Vasam, Lord Holland, in the House of Lords, which had just reached the United States, revealed that "not less than *seventy-five* merchant vessels belonging to the subjects of the United States" had been seized and brought into British ports "in the course of *one fortnight,* even *before* the Orders in Council were *issued!!*"[55] The *National Intelligencer* declared, "It is impossible for a candid, unprejudiced mind to contemplate the miserable condition of most of the nations of Europe, and their vassal provinces, without feeling grateful for our exemption from the distresses inflicted upon them; and without acknowledging that the effects of the Embargo, itself the effect of foreign oppressions, are light as air, compared with them."[56] Had not the Federalists passed the hated excise law, asked the *Richmond Enquirer,* to meet an emergency? But the excise law "was only the creature of a visionary fear, the invasion of a French army; whereas the orders of council and the decree of Milan, were gigantic monsters of real flesh and blood."[57] Finally, the *National Intelligencer* was reduced to parading the endorsements of Revolutionary figures to drum up support for the Embargo. "There is nothing which more unequivocally tends to prove the wisdom of the Embargo than the almost universal approbation of all our great revolutionary characters," said the *Intelligencer.* "We find it supported by a Langdon, an Adams, a Gerry, a Thomson, a Jefferson, a Page, a Pinckney, and a host of other men whose patriotism in the worst of times was most signally exerted for the salvation of their country."[58]

The Republican press also emphasized the beneficial effect of the Embargo in encouraging domestic manufactures. "We rejoice to hear that the pulse of Virginia beats high in favor of manufactures," exclaimed the *National Intelligencer,* delighted to learn that Virginians were busily engaged in enterprises "to make us truly independent."[59] But, countered the *New-York Evening Post,* "We venture to say, that every manufactory in the U. States at this period, with our present population, our immense quantities of uncultivated land, and our high price of labour, will prove a sinking fund to those concerned."[60]

In the Federalist newspapers, Jefferson was depicted as a revengeful enemy of all commerce. "Thus Tommy destroys / A great part of our joys," wrote Henry Mellen of Dover, Delaware, in his well-known satire, "The Embargo." Two of the many stanzas represent political poetry at its best:

> Our great politicians,
> Those dealers in visions,
>   On *paper* to all lengths they dare go;
> But when call'd to decide,
> Like a *turtle* they hide,
>   In their own pretty *shell* the Embargo. . . .

> Our ships all in motion,
> Once whiten'd the ocean,
>   They sail'd and return'd with a cargo;
> Now doom'd to decay,
> They have fallen a prey
>   To Jefferson, worms, and Embargo.[61]

A more poignant protest against the president's anticommercial policy appeared as an advertisement inserted by one Abraham Brady in the *New-York Evening Post:*

> While I would heartily coincide in every measure adopted by our government for the general good, yet the present *embargo* has laid me under such embarrassments that I am unable to discharge my honest debts, and unless my creditors will give me some assurances that they will show me lenity, I must leave the city or subject myself to confinement, having been obliged to dispose of my goods. *Were it in my power I would pay all my just debts*—I would place my country in as respectable a situation as it was in the days of WASHINGTON—I would raise the *embargo*—I would negotiate treaties with the different nations, that these states might with safety wrest near a million of ships from the jaws of the WORMS, and once more enter on a commercial intercourse with all parts of the world.[62]

The *Washington Federalist* also viewed Jefferson as a long-established opponent of commerce, despite the exigencies of the international situation. "The fixed intention of the administration is to destroy commerce altogether," the *Federalist* declared, "and it will be persevered in until the people command it to be abandoned." The country was rapidly becoming a "mighty mass of ruin," merely to test "an experiment founded in folly and which must end in disgrace."[63] The Federalist *Boston Gazette* also hammered on this theme:

> Among our first and most important rights is the free use of the ocean, and of this WE WILL NOT be deprived, under the false pretence that the Leviathan will swallow us up. If when Congress meet they do not take off our chains, they will soon find but one sentiment pervades us from the Delaware to St. Croix. It will demand free commerce—No more Embargoes. If *Virginia* and her *satellites* choose, let them keep on a perpetual Embargo among themselves, we want it not, or if there be any among us who do, let those remove *beyond the Potomack.*[64]

The *National Intelligencer* replied angrily that there were no "Southern prejudices against commerce," despite the charges by these northern "disciples of Washington!"[65]

By the fall of 1808, Federalist editors were reaching for their most abusive epithets to blast the Embargo and anyone connected with it. A Federalist in New England was quoted as saying, *"I wish that Jefferson and Simon Snyder were both in hell and a clog of brimstone at each foot!!!"*[66] The *New-York Evening Post* cried that "no man can be safe in engaging in any undertaking whatever. Thus has all enterprise—nay, thus has the whole country been *palsied!* stiffened, by one dreadful electric shock from the Embargo."[67] On September 15, 1808, the *Evening Post* declared: "The leading merchants in the United States, federal and republican, condemn the Embargo. And who approves of it? Mr. Jefferson's office-holders, who enjoy good fat salaries."⁶⁸ When the president deigned to reply to the petitioners of Newburyport, the *Post* said:

Does Mr. Jefferson expect to put a stop to the Petitions from the Eastern States, praying a repeal of the Embargo laws, by his answer to the one from Newburyport? If he does, we think he will find himself mistaken. We hope to see the citizens in every town in the United States opposed to the Embargo, raise their voice, and call upon the Executive in energetic language to repeal it. Already have the inhabitants of Schenectady, in this state, voted in Town-Meeting to petition, and we trust the example will be followed throughout the state.⁶⁹

To dam the tidal wave of denunciation, the *Richmond Enquirer* pleaded for less emotionalism and more reason, for a more accurate perspective on past events. The *Enquirer* asserted:

> The repeal of the Embargo would still leave our commerce subject to a thousand restrictions, and our national *honor* an empty name; what discerning politician would ascribe our present inconveniences to the Embargo, and not to the Orders and Decrees of Europe?—That man must be actuated by sinister views, who ascribes them to the measures of the administration. War—Tribute, and the piracy of our vessels—or the Embargo, were the alternatives presented to us. War was an immense evil—Tribute was a greater—The Embargo was the only expedient for avoiding the disaster of War, and the disgrace of Tribute accompanied with the depredations of commerce.⁷⁰

The *Richmond Enquirer* further declared on November 11, 1808: "The affairs of this country have now approached a crisis which requires *all* the talents, and all the virtues of the assembled council of the nation. The world have never yet beheld so complete a prostration of all those laws which have been usually respected by civilized nations. History cannot furnish an instance, in which belligerent powers of equal influence have manifested so extravagant a desire to destroy the resources of each other, or so little regard for the rights of neutrals."⁷¹

Throughout the last twelve months of the Embargo's duration, one of the major topics of discussion in the newspapers was speculation as to how long the legislation would remain in force. Even in the middle of the summer of 1808 there was still no real indication of what effect the Embargo might be having on the European belligerents. As the *National Intelligencer* remarked on June 27, 1808: "The period is probably *not distant,* when we shall be enabled to form some judgment of the effect produced on the disposition of foreign governments by the Embargo. . . . Congress rose on the 26th of April, [1808] and information of this event with news of enforcing acts may be expected to have reached England about the 1st of June. Allowing a fortnight for deliberation, and six weeks for a passage across the ocean, we may calculate upon obtaining some interesting information about the beginning of August."⁷² The long delays in transatlantic communication contributed a great deal to the jittery war of nerves provoked by the Embargo.

How long would the controversial measure be in effect? On July 29, 1808, the *New-York Evening Post* referred to an article in the *Washington Federalist* saying, "Mr. Jefferson has repeatedly declared his opinion, that a perseverance in the embargo was our wisest policy, and that he had resolved on recommending it to congress, at the opening of the next session, to continue it *nine months longer.*"[73] Later, on September 9, 1808, the *Post* commented under the headline "THE CURTAIN RISES!": "Not a Farmer, nor Merchant, nor Mechanic, nor Seaman, nor Ship-owner, unless he had the *ear* of the President—not an American citizen has been permitted to know any thing on this point [probable duration of the Embargo] to guide his calculations."[74] The *Post* continued: "The people have been amused and trifled with most shamefully. One day a Democratic print encourages them to hope the Embargo will be raised, then again it is doubtful, and thus tossed about between hope and despair, no one has known what to think, to hope, or to fear."[75]

At the beginning of 1809, it appeared fairly certain that the Embargo must be raised within a few months. A letter from Washington, dated January 6, 1809, and appearing in the *Richmond Enquirer,* stated: "This vote settles for the present & indeed for this session, the repeal of the Embargo. A very decided majority of the republican party are in favor of its continuance until the latter end of May or first of June. . . . "[76] On February 10, 1809, the *Richmond Enquirer* reported that at a caucus of Republicans of both houses of Congress held on February 6, it was decided that the Embargo should be raised on March 4—giving the new president, James Madison, a free hand in the matter, but replacing it with a nonintercourse measure directed specifically at England and France. "Admitting this to be a *fact,*" the *Enquirer* said, "this is a course that I could no where consent to . . . I cannot . . . but condemn a proposition which, whilst it proposes to gain time, loses it; and which, whilst it proposes to be neither submission nor war, must eventuate demonstrably in one or the other."[77]

Meanwhile, the "Force Act" of January 1809 provided new fuel for the Federalist opposition newspapers. The *New-York Evening Post* was horrified at the amount of discretionary power granted to the president by this measure, which "makes such extraordinary provision for placing various species of armed force at the disposal of the President, in contempt of the civil magistracy of the country, that no reflecting freeman should be surprised to find the abhorrence of the act increasing and extending in proportion as it is examined and understood."[78]

"The city is in a buzz about the Embargo being taken off the 4th of March," the *New-York Evening Post* reported on February 6, 1809. In the same issue of the Federalist newspaper appeared an essay on "an interesting question now in agitation—namely *how far resistance to the general government may be justified as* LAWFUL?"[79] As talk of repealing the Embargo mounted, William Duane in

Philadelphia was angry and bewildered. In a long letter to a friend, the editor of the *Aurora* unburdened himself:

> What infatuation has seized the majority of the House of Representatives? Are they determined to prostrate the nation and the government at the feet of a despicable faction, and to fix forever the subjection of this nation to the pestilential influence of Great Britain[?] My very dear Sir, if the Senate has not virtue and intelligence enough to avert the prospect in which the other house has been proceeding, self government is abandoned and foreign corruption thro' a desperate faction as completely ruler as the court of St. James rules the chapel of St. Stephen.[80]

The Boston *Independent Chronicle* of February 27, 1809, contained a letter from an unidentified "member of Congress" dated February 18, which stated, "the bill respecting Non Intercourse is still under discussion. We have taken but one vote this day, which was on striking out that part of the bill which makes the repeal of the Embargo partial. The proposition was lost by 4 votes only, 53 to 57."[81] The *National Intelligencer* broke the news on March 3, 1809, by announcing simply, "The President of the United States on the 1st. inst. approved and signed the 'Act to interdict the commercial intercourse between the United States and Great Britain and France, and their dependencies; and for other purposes.'"[82]

President James Madison's inaugural speech, printed by the *National Intelligencer* in an extra edition on March 4, 1809, and comment on the incoming and outgoing administrations delayed any further comment on the Non-Intercourse Act in the *National Intelligencer* until March 22, 1809.

The Philadelphia *Aurora* received the news glumly. "The embargo ceased on Wednesday," the Republican newspaper noted, "but we already find few, very few, willing to take the embargo off themselves."[83] On the day of Madison's inauguration, the *Aurora* blasted the repeal of the Embargo in no uncertain terms:

> The *embargo* laws have been repealed; the voice of faction, and foreign corruption, have combined to raise a clamour; the representatives of the American people listened to that clamour, and to appease it, have removed the *embargo* which was the ostensible cause of the clamour. . . . Look at the occasion in whatever way you please—the *worst of all social calamities*, WAR, is the very best alternative that can be discerned as probable or possible; this worst calamity is then our best prospect![84]

Most Republican newspapers allowed the repeal of the Embargo to pass by with little or no comment, but the Philadelphia *Aurora* could not contain its rage. In William Duane's view, fifteen of seventeen states had supported the Embargo, and a minority of 23 out of 140 in Congress had brought about the repeal. Seven-tenths of the people of Massachusetts had supported the measure of the

Embargo, he claimed. "In Europe alone 88 million people [are] on our side against at most 12 millions. With right, power, justice, the world on our side, the republican party give way—the *minority* triumph, the *majority succumb.* Can any thing but *madness* account for these things? We are on the eve of a convulsion."[85]

The news reached Boston several days after Madison was inaugurated. The Boston *Columbian Centinel* said only, "THE EMBARGO! Positively to be partially raised on Wednesday next,"[86] and its Republican opponent, the Boston *Independent Chronicle,* headlined its announcement "EMBARGO REPEALED!" The *Chronicle* also mustered a little enthusiasm for the Non-Intercourse Act, but not much: "The present one is like every other great national measure, in some degree a system of accommodation, and though it may not exactly suit the views of every one, may perhaps afford as general satisfaction as any other course which in the peculiar circumstances of the country and of the world could have obtained."[87] Later, the *Chronicle* made one final statement on behalf of the Embargo:

> Notwithstanding all the federal declamations against the embargo, it is very apparent that the federalists are unwilling to have it repealed. The reader's own observation will convince him of this fact. We shall soon hear the repealing law, on some pretext or other, represented by them to be worse than the embargo itself. No matter what the existing measure of the general government is, it is to be opposed and run down as the worst of all that could be. This is the present organized system of opposition. From such conduct, people disposed to be contented and quiet, ought to learn a useful lesson of instruction, as to the views of the *Essex Junto, that grand Jacobin Society of New-England.*[88]

Federalists were by no means pleased with the Non-Intercourse Act, which took the edge off their celebrations on the repeal of the Embargo. As "Firm and Steady" remarked in the Boston *Columbian Centinel:* "But this system [the Non-Intercourse Act] is a cunning calculation, to enable [the] administration to avail itself of circumstances." To this writer, it was motivated by a "spirit of inveterate hatred and animosity" and was designed to influence the spring elections in New England. It would also serve as a straw man, inviting captures of American ships by British war vessels, thereby furnishing a pretext for a full-fledged renewal of the Embargo itself.[89] The *Columbian Centinel* pointed an editorial finger of shame at those New England Federalists—John Adams, John Quincy Adams, William Gray, and others—who had supported the Embargo, "which its authors are obliged to abandon with shame; without effecting a single object for which they pretend it was imposed! Alas! to what pitiable depths will not party spirit, and party despair descend!"[90]

The *New-York Evening Post* also balked at the Non-Intercourse Act. Wrote William Coleman: "A great part of the people still think the odious embargo is to come off the 15th inst. [March 1809]. Nothing is farther from the truth.

Instead of its coming off, it is to be enforced with additional rigour. The act which I now intend to examine [Non-Intercourse Act] is the most contemptible piece of knavery that ever an administration dared to attempt upon a people. It not only is a deception as to our hopes respecting the embargo, but the object it ultimately aims at, is nothing less than *to involve this country in a war with Great Britain.*[91] Almost anything that happened in Congress seemed to William Coleman certain to bring down the wrath of Great Britain.

Thus, after fewer than fifteen months, Jefferson's grand experiment in commercial warfare came to an inglorious end. James Madison was installed in the President's Mansion; ships cleared harbors for destinations other than Great Britain and France; and Thomas Jefferson quietly left Washington for Monticello on March 11, 1809, seeking respite from the storms of calumny and denunciation that had raged over his head for many months past.[92] One historian, Louis Martin Sears, has called the Embargo "the practical culmination of Jeffersonian pacifism" and a "warfare of self-denial."[93] Republican newspapers of the time emphasized these aspects of the measure, but too often they lamely concluded that the Embargo was the "only expedient," the "next-best" alternative to war itself. The idealism that motivated the measure never fired the public imagination, and this failure must be charged to Republican editors. Underneath their lukewarm support for the Embargo, these editors secretly disliked the measure perhaps as much as their Federalist opponents. America in the years between 1807 and 1809 was not a pacific nation, and the success of the Embargo called for a broader view than the aggressive young country could come up with so soon after establishing its independence against the combined land and naval might of Great Britain.

Perhaps the Embargo entailed too heavy a burden to ask any people to carry: it was all sacrifice and no glory. And it cost the United States a great deal of money. But the Embargo also had its positive effects. The demand for American manufactured goods increased; capital was transferred from shipping to industry; a greater labor force was available, and new factories sprang up across the country—especially in the Middle Atlantic states. On the other hand, commerce was prostrated and agriculture severely injured. Not to be forgotten was the fact that war with Great Britain was postponed for about five years (War of 1812), at which time the United States was in a much stronger position.

It was impossible in March 1809 to assess the results of the Embargo policy, and few newspapers attempted to do so. Republican journals seemed relieved that they could drop the subject, while Federalist papers turned their same arguments against the Non-Intercourse Act. William Duane regretted the passing of the Embargo repeal as a matter of party pride, but one has the impression that no editor—Republican or Federalist—really considered the Embargo in any way successful by 1809. It was too passive a remedy for an energetic young nation; it was a measure that called forth apology but not enthusiasm; it was, in short, "the *terrapin* system" that the *New-York Evening Post* labeled it.[94] Americans did not like to retreat into the shell of their own resources, and they would not accept a role of abnegation.

In retrospect, the Embargo was without doubt the most unpopular measure of Jefferson's administration and the low-water mark of his personal prestige. As Burton Spivak has noted, "The embargo years showed him [Jefferson], finally, retreating to the safety and purity of an idealized and largely imaginary American economy grounded in native production, internal trade, domestic purchasing power, and republican labor."[95] It was an action that recommended inaction, but the problem of aggressions on American shipping had to be met somehow. In the crisis President Jefferson did not hesitate to risk his popularity and his administration's record on a measure never before tried, if it might promote the national welfare. The Republican newspapers of the time failed to recognize the inherent daring of the president's stand, but the London *Morning Post* in a poem titled "Mr. President Jefferson's Last Speech" paid tribute to the president's courage:

> If I have, in my lofty sphere,
>   Your judgment e'er misled,
> I trust this error will appear
>   To issue from my *head.*
> For I must say in my own praise,
>   Ere from this Chair I part,
> That if my *understanding* strays
>   None can impeach my *heart.*[96]

When the Embargo went into effect in 1807, Samuel Harris Smith of the *National Intelligencer* had sought to shield Jefferson from the storm of controversy about to break, but his comments proved to be empty words:

Under such circumstances the best to be done is what has been done; a dignified retirement within ourselves; a watchful preservation of our resources; and a demonstration to the world, that we possess a virtue and a patriotism which can take any shape that will best suit the occasion.[97]

TEN

Jefferson and the Press

He comes, the Herald of a noisy world,
News from all nations, lumb'ring at his back.

—*Gazette of the United States,* February 23, 1801

One must take issue with Merrill D. Peterson, who in his sweeping biography of Thomas Jefferson states that the third president of the United States "had the good sense not to confuse newspaper opinion with public opinion."[1] Where, then, did people get the ideas on which their opinions were formed? Certainly not from their neighbors alone (although Jefferson valued talking with them) and not in the taverns and coffeehouses and markets if newspapers did not trigger discussion and argument. And probably not in the churches, which played an important role in the Revolutionary period, but Anglicans, Quakers, and others receded to a secondary role in this period. No, it was newspapers, from Boston to Richmond and beyond, that kept the political fires kindled in the new republic.

In his later years, however, Jefferson himself temporarily lost faith in the institution of newspapers available to all and serving a literate public—which he had championed so eloquently through the years. For a while, scathing indictments of the press flowed from Jefferson's pen after the attacks on his connections with Tom Paine, John Walker's wife, and Sally Hemings. Jefferson was always interested in the press, from 1791, when he was the moving force in the establishment of the *National Gazette* under Philip Freneau, to the time he collected eight thousand dollars from his Albemarle County neighbors near the end of his second term to keep the Philadelphia *Aurora* afloat.[2] Those who questioned the party loyalty of Jefferson to William Duane, editor of the *Aurora,* made the most of Duane's frequent difficulties with the law, charging he was in court more often as the defendant in libel cases rather than as a reporter covering court proceedings. They ridiculed this brash Irishman, not above an occasional street brawl, and yet he probably did more for the Republican cause, given the prevalent style of writing, than any of his contemporaries.

William Duane should be viewed through the prism of his times. For some, particularly in Pennsylvania politics, he was an embarrassment to the administration, described usually as "radical" or an "Irish firebrand." These detractors speculate that was why the *Aurora* was left behind when the capital moved from Philadelphia to Washington, D.C., in 1800, while the *National Intelligencer* was recruited as the semiofficial administration organ under the guidance of the erudite Samuel Harrison Smith. For others, this opinion is questionable. Why didn't Jefferson choose the daily *Aurora,* experienced in partisan warfare, as his spokesman, rather than the triweekly, newly founded *National Intelligencer* under Samuel Harrison Smith, who had no experience in newspapering? The *Intelligencer* printed mainly official announcements, appointments, and some national news couched in the mildest of terms. It seldom engaged in partisan conflicts.

After reading the files of both newspapers for this period (1801–9) and considering the correspondence between Jefferson and Duane,[3] one may conclude that Jefferson—unlike Alexander Hamilton—preferred to work behind the scenes rather than enter the "bear-garden" scene of early journalism. Actually, Jefferson relied on both newspapers in the battle for public opinion. The straightforward *National Intelligencer* served as window dressing in the capital, and the *Aurora* as unofficial partisan scrapper in Philadelphia. After all, Philadelphia was still the largest city in the United States, and perhaps Jefferson wanted the *Aurora* to remain at the nongovernmental center of things rather than follow him to Washington, D.C., which at the time was little more than a few buildings, muddy roads, and swampland.

There is no explicit evidence of such a formal arrangement in the letters between Jefferson and Duane (nor was there any written offer made to Samuel Harrison Smith), but perhaps there was a mutual understanding.

At least, with or without Jefferson's blessing, Duane and the *Aurora* became the leader of the Republican press. More items from the Philadelphia paper were republished from the *Aurora* in Republican newspapers up and down the land, than from any other newspaper, including the *National Intelligencer.* Jeffrey L. Pasley has noted, "Duane resolved early on in Jefferson's administration to pursue his own political course"[4] because he had been denied the national printing contracts by not moving to the capital. On the contrary, Duane remained loyal to Jefferson throughout his administration, even supporting him in the bitter Embargo crisis, and in his old age Duane briefly revived the *Aurora* to help Andrew Jackson, whom he regarded as the successor to Jefferson, in Jackson's clash with the Second Bank of the United States.[5] Dumas Malone noted that "Jefferson regarded him [Duane] as over-zealous but treated him with great respect and retained his confidence."[6]

Some friends undoubtedly were pained by Jefferson's disillusionment with the press in later life, expressed in his statement:

When I read the newspapers and see what a mass of falsehood and what an atom of truth they contain, I am mortified with the consideration that 90/100th of mankind pass through life imagining they have known what was going forward when they would have been nearer the truth had they heard nothing.[7]

Better known is the letter in which Jefferson unburdened himself about American journalism to a young man, John Norvell, who had written him for advice on starting a newspaper. The tenor of the times was indicated when the president of the United States sat down at his desk and wrote young Mr. Norvell a seven-page letter, which included the following:

It is a melancholy truth, that a suppression of the press could not more completely deprive the nation of its benefits, than is done by its abandoned prostitution to falsehood. Nothing can now be believed which is seen in a newspaper. Truth itself becomes suspicious by being put in that polluted vehicle.[8]

Jefferson liked to tell his friends that he read only one newspaper a day—Thomas Ritchie's *Richmond Enquirer*—and that only for the advertisements, but he also subscribed to the *National Intelligencer* and the Philadelphia *Aurora*, which bears out my thesis that these were the two leading Republican newspapers and spokesmen (each in its own way). In a letter of 1824 to Henry Lee, Jefferson revealed that occasionally, to encourage young printers, he would subscribe to their newspaper for one year, on condition of discontinuing it at the end of the year without further warning.[9] It should also be noted that Jefferson, a frugal man, registered in his account books that he spent one hundred dollars a year for newspaper subscriptions. Surely, with this outlay, he would have read them.

The question arises, then, if at any time in his career Jefferson was dissatisfied with newspaper political performance, why did he not write for the sheets himself? Alexander Hamilton did—vigorously and prolifically. Best known for his contributions to *The Federalist* series, the corpus of his occasional pieces probably will never be completely known because scholars do not have the keys to the Latin pen names he used. Also, of course, Hamilton founded the Federalist *New-York Evening Post* in 1801, anticipating the growth of that city, and several smaller newspapers.

Alexander Hamilton recognized the power of the press in the formation of public opinion, and for the most part he was willing to wield that power openly and unabashedly. Why then did the Federalists, who controlled three-quarters of the 235 newspapers in the young nation in 1800, fail to block Jefferson's election when they had been entrenched in power for twelve years?[10] In my opinion, although the Federalists had more wealth and therefore more newspapers, they were located in the cities (although still in their formative stages), away from the countryside and towns where the Jeffersonian concept of an agrarian democracy (called "mobocracy" by the Federalists) had greater appeal.

The Federalist papers simply did not speak to these people. Even Joseph Dennie's *Port Folio,* a magazine with high-toned literary and political articles, sometimes stooped to win readers (and voters), as in one paragraph that embraced the two major scandals of Jefferson's presidency: "The *circle* of our *felicities* is greatly enlarged by the indulgence of Sally, the sable, and the auspicious arrival of Tom Paine, the pious."[11]

What about Jefferson as a writer himself? He tended toward the elite but commanded a broad range. Words were almost sacred to him, as he once declared, "No republic is more real than that of letters."[12] It is estimated that Jefferson wrote eighteen thousand or nineteen thousand letters in his lifetime. Otherwise, views vary on Jefferson's writing style. One scholar makes this assessment:

> He [Jefferson] could conscript others to pseudonymous pamphleteering and newspaper writing and he could even speak past his correspondents to an interested posterity. . . . but he seems to have found it next to impossible to direct his writing squarely at the public."[13]

There are those who indeed find Jefferson writing for posterity rather than for John Norvell, the young man who wanted to know how to start a newspaper and instead got a disquisition on American journalism. We may not remember the correspondents of the past, but we have their prose. One tends to agree with Peter S. Onuf, who wrote, "As a writer, Jefferson was fluent in all these idioms. His words bridged the great divide between an enlightened, elitist 'republic of letters' and a new world of popular speech in a democratizing republican society."[14] Perhaps W. H. Auden should have the last word on this topic, "Time . . . worships language and everyone by whom it lives."

Jefferson was careful in his use of words, agonizing, for example, over his draft of the First Amendment, while James Madison was working on his. Here is their exchange, presenting both versions in their entirety:

> *Madison*—The people shall not be deprived or abridged of their right to speak, to write or otherwise to publish their sentiments, and the freedom of the press, the great bulwark of liberty, shall be inviolable.[15]

> *Jefferson*—The people shall not be deprived or abridged of their right to speak, to write or otherwise to publish anything [except] false facts affecting injurious the life, liberty, property, or reputation of others or affecting the peace of the confederacy with foreign nations.[16]

Madison's version was more succinct and therefore more flexible, and as such was the one that ultimately was adopted in substance. Jefferson, on the other hand, cluttered his version with caveats, raising libel to constitutional level, preserving the Lockean protection of property, and even including foreign affairs.

The result of the First Amendment as envisioned by Madison (ratified in 1791) stripped away the verbiage and left future generations open to interpret it to meet their needs while not infringing on the core genius of the Constitution itself. Actually, of course, freedom of religion was mentioned first in the First Amendment, followed in order by freedom of speech, press, assembly, and petition.

Later on, in 1823, Jefferson offered his advice on a French Constitution, noting that the guiding principles should include:

> Freedom of the press, subject only to liability for personal injuries. This formidable censor of the public functionaries, by arraigning them at the tribunal of public opinion, produces reform peaceably, which must otherwise be done by revolution. It is also the best instrument for enlightening the mind of man, and improving him as a rational, moral, and social being.[17]

In his first inaugural address, Jefferson was in a conciliatory mood, mentioning the phrase "freedom of the press" only once, perhaps to heal the wounds of the Alien and Sedition Laws (1798–1801), whose backlash some thought helped propel Jefferson into office. Once in the presidency, Jefferson did not clamp down on his opponents—leaving that on occasion up to the states. As he wrote Thomas McKean, governor of Pennsylvania, in 1803, "I have therefore long thought that a few [state] prosecutions [for seditious libel] of the most eminent offenders would have a wholesome effect in restoring the integrity of the presses."[18] He also wrote a letter to General Thaddeus Kosciusko expressing how the opposition press should be viewed:

> The people are nearly all united; their quantum leaders, infuriated with the sense of their impotence, will soon be seen or heard only in the newspapers, which serve as chimneys to carry off noxious vapors and smoke, and all is now tranquil, firm and well, as it should be.[19]

But the quintessential Jefferson on the press is a letter he wrote to Colonel Edward Carrington from Paris on January 16, 1787, parts of which are often quoted but frequently lifted out of context:

> The way to prevent these irregular interpositions of the people, is to give them full information of their affairs through the channel of the public papers, and to contrive that those papers should penetrate the whole mass of the people. The basis of our government being the opinion of the people, the very first object should be to keep that right; and were it left to me to decide whether we should have a government without newspapers, or newspapers without a government, I should not hesitate a moment to prefer the latter. But I should mean that every man should receive those papers, and be capable of reading them.[20]

Jefferson was not indulging in hyperbole in this letter, written two years before the French Revolution broke out. Not only should the people be informed to avoid "irregular interpositions," because a free press would allow them to air their grievances. Also, newspapers without government appealed to his ideal of an agrarian democracy peopled with farmers and mechanics (wage earners). Jefferson had some impressive intellectuals on his side, such as Samuel Johnson, who observed in the 1770s, "society is held together by communication and information."[21] Indeed, the standing masthead of Jefferson's semiofficial *National Intelligencer* proclaimed, "That Government Is Best Which Governs Least." But times were changing. By the end of Jefferson's second term, commerce was replacing agriculture; towns were becoming cities; and soon people would be calling his party "Democrats," previously a pejorative term.

Jefferson had clear sailing in his re-election bid of 1805, receiving 162 electoral votes against only 14 for the Federalist candidate, Charles C. Pinckney of South Carolina. (The Federalists fielded their last presidential candidate in the election of 1812.)

By 1805, much had happened to change Jefferson's attitude toward the press. Not only had James Thomson Callender of the Richmond *Recorder* spread in print the gossip (at that time) that Jefferson had fathered several children by his slave Sally Hemings, but also the vindictive incident Callender dug up (thirty-four years later) that in 1768 Jefferson had made "improper advances" to the wife of his neighbor John Walker, an incident Jefferson himself admitted. And Jefferson had been viciously attacked for offering to send a U.S. warship to bring home "the atheist" Tom Paine from revolutionary France.

In his second inaugural address of March 4, 1805, Jefferson addressed these scandals, however indirectly:

> During the course of [my first] administration, and in order to disturb it, the artillery of the press has been leveled against us, charged with whatsoever its licentiousness could devise or dare. These abuses of an institution [the press] so important to freedom and science are deeply to be regretted, inasmuch as they tend to lessen its usefulness and to sap its safety."[22]

Here was a new argument: that the press succumbing to abuses would be digging its own grave by losing its credibility and therefore its usefulness.

Jefferson was not impervious to the attacks bursting around him. He never answered such attacks publicly—and certainly not in the newspapers, knowing that such replies only compounded the injury. In a little-known letter to Francis Hopkinson in 1789, Jefferson declared he regretted having accepted the ambassadorship to France:

> My great wish is to go on in a strict but silent performance of my duty, to avoid attracting notice, and to keep my name out of newspapers, because I find the pain of a little censure, even when it is unfounded, is more acute than the pleasure of much praise.[23]

At times, Jefferson came down hard on the press, as when he placed state rights above civil liberties, as noted earlier in his exchange with Governor Thomas McKean in 1803. Leonard W. Levy, a sharp critic of Jefferson's record on civil liberties, wrote three critical books on the subject, finally concluding:

> But there is no evidence to warrant the belief, nor is there valid cause or need to believe, that the Framers possessed the ultimate wisdom and best insights on the meaning of freedom of expression. What they said is far more important than what they meant. It is enough that they gave constitutional recognition to the principle of freedom of speech and press in unqualified and undefined terms."[24]

If Jefferson endorsed a few "salutary" prosecutions for "seditious libel" at the state level—not by the federal government, as in the Alien and Sedition Acts— he may have been more concerned with state rights than the principle of freedom of expression. Such cases were few, the most prominent being Joseph Dennie of the *Port Folio* and Harry Croswell of the Hudson, New York, satirical *Wasp*, who printed that Jefferson had paid Callender for calling Washington "a traitor, a robber, a perjurer," among other epithets. Despite an eloquent defense by Alexander Hamilton, in which he pleaded for a continuance so Callender could make the eleven-day journey from Virginia to prove the truth of his allegations—denied by the judge—Croswell lost his case and appeal, but truth as a defense became more widely accepted if published "from good motives and for justifiable ends."[25]

In his later years, Jefferson reaffirmed his confidence in a free press serving a democratic society. He made this opinion most clearly in his well-known 1816 letter to Charles Yancey: "Where the press is free, and every man able to read, all is safe." Most indicative of all was Jefferson's letter to his old friend the Marquis de Lafayette, written in 1823—three years before Jefferson's death:

> But the only security of all, is in a free press. The force of public opinion cannot be resisted, when permitted freely to be expressed. The agitation it produces must be submitted to. It is necessary to keep the waters pure."[26]

As far as journalistic support was concerned, Jefferson was elected president in 1801 more because of the excesses of abuse in the Federalist press than because of positive support from Republican journals. Jefferson's Kentucky Resolutions, which attacked the Alien and Sedition Laws, became a critical weapon, almost the Republican platform for the election. The Republican newspapers rallied in defending the new president's policy of federal patronage, but they failed to provide an adequate defense for Thomas Paine when that battle-scarred warrior returned to the United States in 1802. This failure was significant because Paine embodied the undiluted—if sometimes extreme—political philosophy of the Jeffersonians, and the neglect of Thomas Paine on the part of some Republican editors revealed that the wellsprings of democratic philosophy were not as deep in the "Revolution of 1800" as some historians have believed. Paine died a forgotten man.

The Louisiana Purchase of 1803 provided the Republican press with an issue that was easily translated into vast popular approval, and in praising this momentous event the Republican editors learned how to lead rather than to thwart public opinion. But the maturity of Republican newspapers as a well-disciplined political force first became apparent with the editorial attitudes they struck on the controversy surrounding the Republican repeal of the Federalist judiciary act of 1801 and the attempted conviction of Justice Samuel Chase for "high crimes and misdemeanors." On both of these issues the Republican journals under consideration supported the administration without reservation and with practical unanimity, at the same time that the Republican ranks in Congress were badly divided. Some of the Republican newspapers—notably the Philadelphia *Aurora*—also exhibited a startling adherence to ethical principles in refusing to comment on the trial of Justice Chase while it was in progress in the Senate.

Aside from partisan motivations, one must also admire the efforts—unsuccessful though they were—of the leading Republican journals to grant Alexander Hamilton in death the same honest responses they had accorded him while living. One is repelled by the sentimental (and sometimes hypocritical) excesses of the Federalist press in lamenting Hamilton's untimely death, but had Jefferson's life suddenly ended sometime during his administration the Republican reaction to such an event would undoubtedly have been much the same.

As for the Embargo, the Republican press can hardly be censured for not obtaining greater support for a measure that was so inherently unpopular, but it must be noted that the Republican defense of the Embargo was not nearly as effective as the Federalist offense. Just as Jefferson's restriction of commerce tended to revive the Federalist Party in New England, it also reinvigorated the Federalist press everywhere. Moreover, Jefferson's relationship with the press appears at its worst during the bitter controversy over the Embargo policy. The president attempted to shroud the reasons for his decision in secrecy—an unjustifiable attitude in view of the profound consequences that the Embargo had for all Americans—and he never attempted to educate Republican editors or the public in the necessity for the Embargo, except through his messages to Congress and in replying to several petitions.

Indeed, on the basis of available evidence, one must conclude that once Thomas Jefferson was in office, he neglected to exert leadership over his partisan press. It is true that such leadership was still not regarded as one of the presidential functions, but other men high in public office—notably Alexander Hamilton and James Madison—were active in the journalistic battles of the period as a matter of course. Jefferson was overly scrupulous in his dealings with the press, for understandable reasons; he had been harmed by his famous letter to Philip Mazzei and by his introductory remarks to the American edition of Thomas Paine's *Rights of Man*. He had seen Hamilton's letter denouncing John Adams rebound on the Federalist Party, and he came to deplore the scurrility and abuse with which the newspapers of the period abounded.

The solidarity of the Republican press on the issues of patronage, judicial control, the Louisiana Purchase, and the Embargo indicates that leadership was forthcoming from some source. Through the years American historians have assumed that this leadership was provided by the administration's "semiofficial organ," the *National Intelligencer,* edited by Samuel Harrison Smith in Washington, D.C. While many items from the *National Intelligencer* were republished by other Republican journals across the land, these items were usually straightforward news accounts of congressional debates, presidential appointments, and so forth. The Philadelphia *Aurora,* on the other hand, seldom originated such items after the national capital moved to Washington; yet its editorial comments were republished in the Republican press at large with great frequency. Samuel Harrison Smith avoided personal partisan combat, but William Duane reveled in it. Duane defended Thomas Paine with great courage, while Smith said almost nothing. Duane attacked the hypocrisy of Republican eulogies on Hamilton's death, while Smith did not enter the discussion. Duane upheld the Embargo even in the hour of its defeat, while Smith issued no comment on the repeal of the measure.

In fact, the Jefferson administration was served by *two* newspapers—the sedate *National Intelligencer* in the national capital as official reporter and the robust *Aurora* in Philadelphia as unofficial partisan scrapper. Jefferson's extensive correspondence with William Duane from 1801 to 1809 indicates that the president himself had such an arrangement in mind.

One can assign the degree of leadership offered by other newspapers of the period. The leading political journals of Boston and all of New England were the Republican *Independent Chronicle* and the Federalist *Columbian Centinel.* In the South, Thomas Ritchie's *Richmond Enquirer* was fast becoming America's first regional newspaper. Within the Federalist press itself, the *Gazette of the United States,* edited by Enos Bronson in Philadelphia, fought mightily to retain its role as leading Federalist newspaper, but this distinction certainly passed to the *New-York Evening Post* sometime during Jefferson's administration, which makes William Coleman's approval of the Louisiana Purchase even more significant.

In many respects, Coleman was the most capable editor of the period among a group of competent men. The initial reaction by the *New-York Evening Post* to the Embargo revealed Coleman's breadth of vision and fair-mindedness. He was such a successful editor because he combined the erudition of Samuel Harrison Smith and Enos Bronson with the combative instincts of William Duane and

James Thomson Callender. The latter must remain an anomaly in the history of American journalism because his erratic course from Republican champion to Federalist hatchet man revealed more of his own personality than anything he wrote about, whether as reporter for the Richmond *Examiner* or as editor of the Richmond *Recorder*. Benjamin Russell, editor of the Boston *Columbian Centinel*, was a northern counterpart of the socially conscious Thomas Ritchie, and both men did much to enhance the role of the newspaper editor in a period when that role was just emerging. On the other hand, Abijah Adams of the Boston *Independent Chronicle* remains an elusive figure because the editorial policy of the *Chronicle* was determined largely by the independent writings of Benjamin Austin Jr.

On a broader scale, the Federalist assault in print was really a blessing in disguise for the Republicans because such attacks were counterproductive. In his second inaugural address, Jefferson declared, "Pride keeps them [the opposition] hostile; they brood over their angry passions and give them vent in the newspapers which they maintain. They still make as much noise as if they were the whole nation."

The idea of newspapers serving as a safety valve crops up frequently in the ruling Republican press and was aimed, of course, at the declining Federalists. There is a deeper issue here, however. As long as citizens could express themselves freely, they are less likely to take up arms. Thomas Jefferson expressed this idea best in a letter to Colonel Edward Carrington, written from Paris on January 16, 1787: "The way to prevent these irregular interpositions of the people, is to give them full information of their affairs through the channel of the public papers."

Conclusion

It is possible, of course, to assign too much political influence to the press in Jefferson's time, but the historical record indicates too little has been ascribed. Although newspapers were but part of the complex social and cultural landscape of the period, they are key to unlocking much that unfolded later. After all, why did Alexander Hamilton raise ten thousand dollars from his wealthy Federalist friends (one thousand dollars from his own pocket) to launch the *New-York Evening Post* on November 16, 1801, only months after Jefferson was inaugurated, if he did not expect to counter his rival politically?[1] This money was not used to establish a joint-stock company, but it was lent to the new editor, William Coleman, prevailing on the paper's sponsors eventually to cancel the notes they held. As Mott pointed out, "This was a common technique in the founding of political papers."[2] This was also a considerable amount of money at a time when, unlike today, newspapering was not a lucrative business. Contributors sought to convey political ideas, reap political rewards, and boost the political careers of their champions.

The most telling argument supporting the effectiveness of politically partisan newspapers during the age of Jefferson, however, was their sheer proliferation. Isaiah Thomas found only thirty-nine journals in all of the colonies in 1776, but this number had exploded to "upwards of three hundred and sixty" by June 1810, a year after Jefferson left office.[3] Thomas, whose work *The History of Printing in America* was published in 1810, may not have always been completely accurate, but the overview of this careful contemporary observer is invaluable. Thomas attributed this phenomenal growth of newspapers to the political climate of the times:

> A large proportion of the public papers at that date [1810] were established, and supported, by the two great contending political parties [Federalist and Republican] into which the people of these states are usually divided [*sic*]; and whose numbers produce an equipollence [equal power]; consequently, a great augmentation of vehicles [newspapers] for carrying on the political warfare have been found necessary.[4]

Newspapers at the time of Republican ascendancy were frequently referred to as "social engines." Gone or disappearing was the colonial printer who ran off a few sheets of a newspaper as a sideline, something else to sell in an apothecary or other shop. Although there were editors of stature in the late eighteenth century, the beginning of the early national period, printers who discovered they could channel public opinion—and thus became editors—did not come into their own until the Jeffersonian years. "Editorials" also began to appear at this time, although their function seems to have been more to emphasize the editor's views, which had been scattered through the paper, than to separate "news" from comment.

At the time printers were only slightly above wandering minstrels or mountebanks on the social scale, but as the press became recognized as part of the community, printers gained in prestige. As the Reverend Doctor Samuel Miller wrote in 1803 in his *A Brief Retrospect of the Eighteenth Century:*

> Instead, therefore, of being considered now, as they once were, of small moment in society, they have become immense moral and political engines, closely connected with the welfare of the state, and deeply involving both in its peace and prosperity.[5]

A better known observer of the newspaper scene, although referring more to the period of Andrew Jackson (who many, like William Duane, considered Jefferson's successor) was Alexis de Tocqueville, who visited the United States for nine months in 1831 and 1832 to study the prison system. In 1835 he published the first of four volumes of his masterwork, *De la démocratie en Amérique,* of which the first American edition of the translation appeared in 1838. Dumas Malone called his work "one of the best books ever written on the United States."[6] Here is what this astute Frenchman had to say about newspapers here (although he harbored some caveats as well):

> In America there is scarcely a hamlet which has not its own newspaper.
> . . . [The influence of journalism] in America is immense. It is the power which impels the circulation of political life through all the districts of that vast territory. Its eye is constantly open to detect the secret springs of political designs, and to summon the leaders to the bar of public opinion[7]

Although some writers still look askance at newspapers as historical sources, others have woven newspapers into their research with grace and acumen, as an index to public opinion or illuminating events in reconstructing the past. Among these are Dumas Malone, whose *Jefferson and His Time* (1948–81) won the Pulitzer Prize, and, earlier, Douglas Southall Freeman, who, with John Alexander Carroll and Mary Wells Ashworth, wrote *George Washington, A Biography* (1948–53). Freeman bridged the gap between journalism and history; he was also editor of the Richmond *News-Leader* at the time he was writing his biography of Washington. Other writers with newspaper experience before delving into history include such men as Allan Nevins, who wrote the definitive history of the *New-York Evening Post*. After all, those who respect the craft consider journalism at its best to be current history.

The American political press, with its colonial mercantile origins, did not begin with the presidency of Thomas Jefferson, of course. It was born in the struggle for independence, tempered in the adoption of the Constitution, and shaped by the political parties they brought into being in the first years of the republic. But the partisan press reached an intensity during the Jefferson years (1801–9) perhaps equaled but not surpassed in the later Jacksonian period (1829–37), long regarded as the culmination of the partisan press. Perhaps this aspect of Jefferson's presidency has been slighted by some because they do not recognize the idiom and context of this press, judging it by today's journalistic standards and practices. The press Thomas Jefferson knew was quite different. If one can get by the frequent coarse language and personal attacks in the public press of Jefferson's day, the issues and personalities stand out clearly. Editors spoke their minds in language that the people of the time could understand and indeed, at times, were entertained by. Many readers relished this political jousting, rooted in English satire, however crudely transported across the Atlantic.

Furthermore, to say that the people read only those partisan journals whose views they already shared, is also open to question. Taverns and coffeehouses and market stalls provided newspapers of all hues for readers who could not afford to subscribe to them. Thus, readers might soak up other ideas or modify their own attitudes. At least they might come up with viewpoints to challenge the other fellow's position. These animated conversations sometimes led to heated arguments and even fisticuffs. The age knew little entertainment other than that found in the taverns, and newspapers were very much part of this scene.

Tocqueville made the interesting observation, "In the United States each separate journal exercises but little authority, but the power of the periodical press is only second to that of the people."[8] In other words, the influence of one newspaper, such as William Duane's *Aurora*, reached beyond Philadelphia because its items were picked up and reprinted in Republican journals across the land. Duane and his *Aurora*, in a sense, became the leaders of the Republican press, which quoted the *Aurora* more frequently than any other Republican journal, at least during Jefferson's presidency.

Jefferson himself, although perhaps reluctant to enter the arena of partisan journalism, relied on Duane and never exposed himself to public scrutiny by writing for the newspapers. Nevertheless, Jefferson early recognized the power of the press to sway national opinion. With no apparent reservations, he rescued Philip Freneau from obscurity to edit the *National Gazette* and do battle with the powerful and entrenched Federalist *Gazette of the United States* when the capital was still in Philadelphia. This clash defined the emerging two-party American political system. Jefferson's anti-Federalists, later called Republicans and then Democrats, represented the farmers of the countryside and the wage-earners of the towns, both essential to Jefferson's concept of an agrarian democracy. The Federalists, at least as their opponents depicted them, were the wealthy and powerful of the cities and, as such, controlled the major newspapers.

In the bitterly fought election of 1800–1801, Jefferson himself reckoned that the Federalists controlled three-fourths of the nation's newspapers, adding that they were "swaying the government by their possession of the printing presses, which their wealth commands."[9] Yet in 1800 and 1801, the Federalists could not block Jefferson's election. Where then was the vaunted power of the press? The Federalist newspapers tended to protect their own interests and thus to alienate the lower classes, while the minority Republican newspapers offered the more potent message that resonated with the people. In the election that ultimately ratified Jefferson as our third president, the Federalist press failed, not the Republican. The Federalists may have won some of the newspaper battles, but the Republicans won the war.

In many respects, Jefferson's term in office was not only riddled by foreign threats—the possible involvement in the Napoleonic wars raging in Europe and the need to protect U.S. seamen everywhere—but also by partisan domestic scandals. It may surprise some to know that the return of Tom Paine from revolutionary France in 1802, which triggered the first all-out attack upon the Jefferson administration, was a more searing event than the later scandal concerning Sally Hemings. It was not that Tom Paine had sat in the French Assembly (Americans at that time rather liked revolutions) but that he had written *The Age of Reason,* deemed atheistic and un-American by many of his fellow countrymen. The rumors that Jefferson had fathered children by his slave Sally Hemings, pushed into print by James Thomson Callender of the *Richmond Recorder,* a defector from Republican ranks, created less of a stir at the time than the furor surrounding Tom Paine. In fact, even some of the Federalist editors would not reprint Callender's stories.

While these stories were unfolding—which, by the way, had no effect on Jefferson's landslide re-election in 1804—most Americans seemed torn between exclusive Federalism or inclusive Republicanism. This was not an easy decision, for newspapers—especially country weeklies—were about the only connection many citizens had with their federal government. Judging from the newspapers themselves, the Republican press wrote for the people, and the Federalists seemed to write for each other. The Federalists did become more caustic, however, as Jefferson's administration progressed, as they could see the Virginia Dynasty looming on the horizon. For the first time in their political experience, they were the "outs" wanting to get back "in."

There were "responsible" newspapers during this period, to use our terminology and concept of journalism, but they were few, mainly Jefferson's

National Intelligencer, which was well written but ineffective in the political battles of the day, and the *New-York Evening Post* of William Coleman, who wrote exceptionally well and, unlike his fellow Federalist or Republican editors, found that one could be both combative and civil.

The newspapers of the time, especially the Republican ones, fitted well into a raw land peopled by independent men and women. Some tend to think of these journals only in terms of the invective they spewed forth. But it can also be said that the newspapers of this period freely and openly reprinted items from other newspapers, some far away, as settlements pushed westward, creating a budding sense of nationhood. Isaiah Thomas made a very good point when he wrote in 1810:

> The extreme cheapness with which newspapers are conveyed by the mail, in the United States, added to the circumstance of their being altogether unencumbered with a stamp duty, or any other public restriction[,] renders their circulation more convenient and general than in any other country.[10]

Perhaps the final test of the effectiveness of newspapers, both Federalist and Republican, in the age of Jefferson rests on one basic fact. There were no "interpositions," as Jefferson called armed rebellions by the people, during his administration. Led by the disgruntled Federalists, the people aired their grievances in the public press or started newspapers of their own with cheap, hand-operated presses designed for the frontier. Some historians deplore the vituperation and invective that flooded the politically partisan press. To Mott, these years were the Dark Ages of American journalism. To me, they were the birth pangs of democracy.

Notes

Introduction

1. Elizabeth Janeway, *Between Myth and Morning* (New York: Morrow, 1974), 24.

2. J. G. A. Pocock, *Virtue, Commerce, and History: Essays on Political Thought and History, Chiefly in the Eighteenth Century* (Cambridge & New York: Cambridge University Press, 1985), 9.

3. Jerry W. Knudson, "Late to the Feast: Newspapers as Historical Sources," *Perspectives,* Newsletter of the American Historical Association 31 (October 1993): 9–11.

4. Wilson Carey McWilliams, *The Idea of Fraternity in America* (Berkeley: University of California Press, 1973), ix.

5. Lucy Maynard Salmon, *The Newspaper and the Historian* (New York: Oxford University, 1923), 491.

1. The Partisan Press, 1801–1809

1. Daniel J. Boorstin, *The Lost World of Thomas Jefferson* (New York: Holt, 1948), 5.

2. Isaiah Thomas, *The History of Printing in America: With a Biography of Printers & an Account of Newspapers,* ed. Marcus A. McCorison, 2nd ed. (New York: Weathervane Books, 1970), 14–17.

3. Washington, D.C., *National Intelligencer,* April 28, 1802.

4. Boorstin, *Lost World of Thomas Jefferson,* 6.

5. Frank Luther Mott, *American Journalism: A History of Newspapers in the United States through 260 Years, 1690 to 1950,* rev. ed. (New York: Macmillan, 1950), 167–80.

6. Merrill D. Peterson, *Thomas Jefferson and the New Nation* (New York: Oxford University Press, 1970), 408.

7. Ibid., 470.

8. Ibid., 469.

9. Ibid., 470.

10. Michael Lienesch, "Thomas Jefferson and the Democratic Experience: The Origins of the Partisan Press, Popular Political Parties, and Public Opinion," in *Jeffersonian Legacies,* ed. Peter S. Onuf (Charlottesville: University Press of Virginia, 1993), 336.

11. Philadelphia *Gazette of the United States,* April 16, 1801.

12. Ibid., 17.

13. Richmond *Recorder,* May 21, 1803.

14. Jay Fliegelman, *Declaring Independence: Jefferson, Natural Language, & the Culture of Performance* (Stanford: Stanford University Press, 1993), 123.

15. *New-York Evening Post,* September 21, 1804.

16. Joyce Appleby, *Thomas Jefferson* (New York: Holt, 2003), 8.

17. Mott, *American Journalism,* 169.

18. William E. Ames, *A History of the National Intelligencer* (Chapel Hill: University of North Carolina Press, 1972).

19. Philadelphia *Gazette of the United States,* July 1, 1801.

20. Ibid., June 23, 1801.

21. Boston *Independent Chronicle,* April 16, 1801.

22. Jerry W. Knudson, *In the News: American Journalists View Their Craft* (Wilmington, Del.: Scholarly Resources, 2000), 25–46.

23. Kim Tousley Phillips, *William Duane, Radical Journalist in the Age of Jefferson* (New York: Garland, 1989), 638.

24. Duane to Jefferson, January 23, 1809, in Worthington C. Ford, ed., "Letters of William Duane, 1800–1834," *Proceedings of the Massachusetts Historical Society,* 2nd ser., 20 (1906–7): 313–14.

25. Thomas, *History of Printing in America,* 17.

26. James Morton Smith, *Freedom's Fetters: The Alien and Sedition Laws and American Civil Liberties* (Ithaca, N.Y.: Cornell University Press, 1956), passim.

27. Philadelphia *Gazette of the United States,* August 10, 1801.

28. Washington, D.C., *National Intelligencer,* October 10, 1804.

29. Max Lerner, *America as a Civilization: Life and Thought in the United States Today* (New York: Simon & Schuster, 1957), 749–64.

30. Mott, *American Journalism,* 102.

31. Willard Grosvenor Bleyer, *Main Currents in the History of American Journalism* (Boston: Houghton Mifflin, 1927), 133.

32. Jerry W. Knudson, "Political Journalism in the Age of Jefferson," *Journalism History* 1 (Spring 1974): 20.

33. Bernard Mayo, ed. *Jefferson Himself: The Personal Narrative of a Many-Sided American* (Boston: Houghton Mifflin, 1942), 253 and 204.

34. Allan Nevins, *The Evening Post: A Century of Journalism* (New York: Boni & Liveright, 1922), 17.

35. Philadelphia *Gazette of the United States,* August 10, 1801.

36. Philadelphia *Aurora,* June 17, 1802.

37. Lyman Horace Weeks, *A History of Paper-Manufacturing in the United States, 1690–1916* (New York: Lockwood, 1916), 115.

38. Philadelphia *Aurora,* December 2, 1801.

39. Washington, D.C., *National Intelligencer,* December 11, 1801.

40. Ibid., January 14 and 16, 1801. See also January 19, 1801.

41. Ibid., January 14, 1801.

42. Space was not provided for reporters in the House of Commons until 1834. Official reporting was not adopted by the Senate until 1848 or by the House of Representatives until 1850. The first issue of the *Congressional Record* appeared on March 4, 1873. Elizabeth Gregory McPherson, "Reporting the Debates of Congress," *Quarterly Journal of*

Speech 28 (1942): 141–48. See also Frederic B. Marbut, "Early Washington Correspondents: Some Neglected Pioneers," *Journalism Quarterly* 25 (1948): 369–74 and 400.

43. Washington, D.C., *National Intelligencer,* January 8, 1802.

44. Ibid.

45. Republished in ibid., March 10, 1802.

46. *Richmond Enquirer,* November 7, 1806.

2. REPUBLICAN PRINTERS: "IMMIGRANT SCRIBBLERS"

1. Worthington Chauncey Ford, "Jefferson and the Newspaper," *Records of the Columbia Historical Society* 8 (1905): 98.

2. Paul Leicester Ford, ed., *The Writings of Thomas Jefferson,* 10 volumes (New York: Putnam, 1892–99), 9:316–17.

3. Kenneth Stewart and John Tebbel, *Makers of Modern Journalism* (New York: Prentice-Hall, 1952), 35.

4. William E. Smith, "Samuel Harrison Smith," *Dictionary of American Biography* [*DAB*], vol. 17, ed. Dumas Malone (New York: Scribners, 1928–58), 343–44.

5. Bernard Bailyn, *To Begin the World Anew: The Genius and Ambiguities of the American Founders* (New York: Knopf, 2003), 41.

6. Margaret Bayard Smith, *The First Forty Years of Washington Society in the Family Letters of Margaret Bayard Smith,* ed. Gaillard Hunt (New York: Scribners, 1906), 9.

7. Alfred McClung Lee, *The Daily Newspaper in America: The Evolution of a Social Instrument* (New York: Macmillan, 1937), 480.

8. Willard Grosvenor Bleyer, *Main Currents in the History of American Journalism* (Boston: Houghton Mifflin, 1927), 130.

9. Wilhelmus Bogart Bryan, *A History of the National Capital from Its Foundation through the Period of the Adoption of the Organic Act,* 2 vols. (New York: Macmillan, 1914, 1916), 1:355.

10. Margaret Bayard Smith, *First Forty Years,* 10, and Claude G. Bowers, *Jefferson in Power, the Death Struggle of the Federalists* (Boston: Houghton Mifflin, 1936), 3.

11. William E. Smith, "Samuel Harrison Smith," *DAB,* 17:343–44.

12. William E. Smith, "Margaret Bayard Smith," *DAB,* 17:318–19.

13. William E. Smith, "Samuel Harrison Smith," *DAB,* 17:344.

14. Frank Luther Mott, *American Journalism: A History of Newspapers in the United States through 260 Years, 1690 to 1950,* rev. ed. (New York: Macmillan, 1950), 178.

15. William E. Smith, "Samuel Harrison Smith," *DAB,* 17:344.

16. Jerry W. Knudson, "Political Journalism in the Age of Jefferson," *Journalism History* 1 (Spring 1974): 20.

17. Allen Culling Clark, "William Duane," *Records of the Columbia Historical Society* 9 (1906): 17–22.

18. Ibid., 22–23.

19. Claude G. Bowers, "William Duane," *Dictionary of American Biography* [*DAB*], vol. 5, ed. Allen Johnson and Dumas Malone (New York: Scribners, 1930), 467–68.

20. Ibid., 468.

21. Jeffrey L. Pasley, *"The Tyranny of Printers": Newspaper Politics in the Early American Republic* (Charlottesville: University Press of Virginia, 2001), 193.

22. Bureau of the Census, *A Century of Population Growth* (Washington, D.C.: U.S. Government Printing Office, 1909), 197, and *The Encyclopaedia Britannica*, 9th ed., 25 vols. (New York: Encyclopaedia Britannica Company, 1878), 18:738.

23. J. Thomas Scharf and Thompson Westcott, *History of Philadelphia, 1609–1884*, 3 vols. (Philadelphia: L. H. Everts, 1884), 1:507.

24. Philadelphia *Aurora*, April 23, 1800.

25. William Duane, *A Letter to George Washington, President of the United States, Containing Strictures on His Address of the Seventeenth of September, 1796, Notifying His Relinquishment of the Presidential Office* (Philadelphia: Printed for the author, 1796), 18.

26. Worthington C. Ford, ed., *The Writings of George Washington*, 14 vols. (New York & London: Putnam, 1889–93), 14:194–95.

27. The only editor actually indicted under the Alien Law was John D. Burk of the New York *Time Piece*. Mott, *American Journalism*, 148.

28. Pickering to John Adams, July 24, 1799, Pickering Papers, Massachusetts Historical Society, XI: 487; cited by James Morton Smith, *Freedom's Fetters: The Alien and Sedition Laws and American Civil Liberties* (Ithaca, N.Y.: Cornell University Press, 1956), 283.

29. A Federalist court in 1801 ruled that Duane was a British subject, and a suit by Levi Hollingsworth for libel was brought in a federal court for this reason. See Dumas Malone, *The Public Life of Thomas Cooper, 1783–1839* (New Haven, Conn.: Yale University Press; London: Oxford University Press, 1926), 151n6. Duane eventually took out naturalization papers to be safe. See James Morton Smith, *Freedom's Fetters*, 278n4.

30. Adams to Pickering, August 1, 1799. Charles Francis Adams, ed., *The Works of John Adams*, 10 vols. (Boston: Little, Brown, 1850–1856), 9:5.

31. The other men arrested were Samuel Cuming, a printer employed on the Philadelphia *Aurora*, and Robert Moore, a recent Irish immigrant. See Scharf and Westcott, *History of Philadelphia*, 1:496–97.

32. Quoted in Francis Wharton, *State Trials of the United States . . .* (Philadelphia: Carey & Hart, 1849), 379–80.

33. The opposition press insisted that only fifteen men had assaulted Duane. This account of the affair is drawn from the Philadelphia *Aurora*, April 14 and 27, 1799. The incident is also described in John Bach McMaster, *A History of the People of the United States*, 8 vols. (New York: Appleton, 1885), 2:438–39.

34. Philadelphia *Aurora*, February 19, 1800.

35. *Annals*, 6C, 1S, 117. The House defeated the Ross bill under the moderate leadership of John Marshall.

36. *Annals*, 6C, 1S, 122.

37. James Morton Smith, *Freedom's Fetters*, 298.

38. Ibid., 297–300.

39. Leonard W. Levy, *Jefferson and Civil Liberties: The Darker Side* (Cambridge: Harvard University Press, 1963), 57.

40. James Morton Smith, *Freedom's Fetters*, 284–88.

41. Jefferson to Duane, May 23, 1801, in Paul Leicester Ford, *Writings of Thomas Jefferson*, 8:5.

42. Undated MS. (1801) in ibid., 56.

43. Philadelphia *Gazette of the United States,* September 3, 1801. See also letters by "Juris Consultus" in the issues of September 4 and 8, 1801.

44. Clark, "William Duane," 25.

45. Simon Gratz Collection, Historical Society of Pennsylvania.

46. Quoted in William M. Meigs, "Pennsylvania Politics Early in This Century," *Pennsylvania Magazine of History and Biography* 4 (1893): 483.

47. Michael Leib to Dr. Rodney, Philadelphia, January 28, 1807, Simon Gratz Collection, Historical Society of Pennsylvania.

48. Jefferson to Monroe, Oct. 29, 1823, in Paul Leicester Ford, *Writings of Thomas Jefferson,* 10:275.

49. Quoted in Frank Luther Mott, *Jefferson and the Press* (Baton Rouge: Louisiana State University Press, 1943), 49.

50. John Quincy Adams, *Memoirs,* ed. Charles Francis Adams, 12 vols. (Philadelphia: Lippincott, 1874–77), 6:17, entry for June 11, 1822.

51. Meigs, "Pennsylvania Politics Early in This Century," 483.

52. Bowers, "William Duane," *DAB,* 5:468.

53. Philadelphia *Gazette of the United States,* January 27, 1801.

54. George Henry Payne, *History of Journalism in the United States* (New York & London: Appleton, 1920), 184.

55. David M. Matteson, "Abijah Adams," *Dictionary of American Biography* [*DAB*], vol. 1, ed. Allen Johnson (New York: Scribners, 1928), 35–36.

56. Ibid., 35.

57. Joseph T. Buckingham, *Specimens of Newspaper Literature: With Personal Memoirs, Anecdotes, and Reminiscences,* 2 vols. (Boston: Little, Brown, 1850), 1:267.

58. Boston *Independent Chronicle,* January 1, 1801.

59. "A Description of Duke's County," *Proceedings of the Massachusetts Historical Society,* 2nd ser., 4 (1855): 63; and Samuel Eliot Morison, "Benjamin Austin," *DAB,* 1:431–32.

60. Morison, "Benjamin Austin," *DAB,* 1:432.

61. Ibid., 1:431–32; Buckingham, *Specimens of Newspaper Literature,* 1:273–75; and the Boston *Independent Chronicle* for dates cited.

62. Morison, "Benjamin Austin," *DAB,* 1:432. See also *Trial of Thomas O. Selfridge . . . for Killing Charles Austin* (Boston: Russell & Cutter / Belcher & Armstrong / Oliver & Munroe, 1807); Thomas O. Selfridge, *Correct Statement of the Whole Preliminary Controversy between Tho. O. Selfridge and Benjamin Austin* (Charlestown, Mass.: Printed by Samuel Etheridge, 1807), and Benjamin Austin, *Memorial on the Grounds of Excusable Homicide to the Legislature of Massachusetts* (Boston, 1806).

63. Buckingham, *Specimens of Newspaper Literature,* 1:271.

64. C. C. Pearson, "Thomas Ritchie," *Dictionary of American Biography* [*DAB*], vol. 15, ed. Dumas Malone (New York: Scribners, 1935), 628.

65. Charles Henry Ambler, *Thomas Ritchie: A Study in Virginia Politics* (Richmond: Bell, 1913), 17.

66. Ibid., 19.

67. Ibid.

68. Pearson, "Thomas Ritchie," *DAB,* 15:629.

69. Ambler, *Thomas Ritchie,* 28–29.

70. *Richmond Enquirer,* May 13, 1806.

71. Pearson, "Thomas Ritchie," *DAB,* 15:28–29.

72. Ibid., 628.

73. *Editors of the Past,* address by Judge Robert W. Hughes at Charlottesville, Virginia, June 22, 1897. McGregor Collection, Alderman Library, University of Virginia.

74. Ambler, *Thomas Ritchie,* 293.

75. William Duane to an anonymous correspondent, Philadelphia, July 27, 1820. Vaux Papers, Historical Society of Pennsylvania.

76. *Richmond Enquirer,* June 4, 1805.

77. Duane to Jefferson, Philadelphia, May 10, 1801, in Worthington C. Ford, ed., "Letters of William Duane, 1800–1834," *Proceedings of the Massachusetts Historical Society,* 2nd ser., 20 (1906–7): 267.

78. Allan Nevins, *The Evening Post: A Century of Journalism* (New York: Boni & Liveright, 1922), 49.

79. Fred S. Siebert, Theodore Peterson, and Wilbur Schramm, *Four Theories of the Press* (Urbana: University of Illinois Press, 1956), 1.

80. H. W. Boynton, *Journalism and Literature* (Boston & New York: Houghton Mifflin, 1904), 23.

81. Edwin Emery and Henry Ladd Smith, *The Press and America* (New York: Prentice-Hall, 1954), 165.

82. A definitive statement of Jefferson's changing attitude toward newspapers may be found in Mott, *Jefferson and the Press.*

83. Jefferson to Duane, Monticello, May 31, 1824, *Historical Magazine,* 2nd ser., 4 (July 1868): 66.

3. FEDERALIST EDITORS: "MONUMENTAL COLUMNS"

1. Alfred McClung Lee, *The Daily Newspaper in America: The Evolution of a Social Instrument* (New York: Macmillan, 1937), 180.

2. Bernard A. Weisberger, *The American Newspaperman* (Chicago: University of Chicago Press, 1961), 39.

3. The source of the following biographical information on Enos Bronson is a manuscript written by Burton Alva Konkle in the Konkle Papers, Historical Society of Pennsylvania. Apparently this work is the only known record of Bronson's life.

4. Konkle Papers, Historical Society of Pennsylvania.

5. Frank Luther Mott, *American Journalism: A History of Newspapers in the United States through 260 Years, 1690 to 1950,* rev. ed. (New York: Macmillan, 1950), 122–23.

6. Philadelphia *Aurora,* April 10, 1801.

7. Philadelphia *Gazette of the United States,* November 2, 1801.

8. Timothy Dwight to Enos Bronson, Philadelphia, January 21, 1802, American Clergy, III, Dwight, Historical Society of Pennsylvania.

9. Daniel J. Boorstin, *The Lost World of Thomas Jefferson* (New York: Holt, 1948), 240.

10. William C. Dowling, *Literary Federalism in the Age of Jefferson: Joseph Dennie and "The Port Folio," 1801–1811* (Columbia: University of South Carolina Press, 1999), 49.

11. Herbert E. Sloan, *Principle and Interest: Thomas Jefferson and the Problem of Debt* (New York: Oxford University Press, 1995), 244–46.

12. Allan Nevins, *The Evening Post: A Century of Journalism* (New York: Boni & Liveright, 1922), 9–10.

13. Ibid., 13–14.

14. Ibid., 17. Another of the founders of the *Anti-Democrat* was Robert Goodloe Harper.

15. For a list of twenty-six original subscribers, suggesting the high social and financial standing of the *Post*'s early supporters, see ibid., 18–19.

16. Claude G. Bowers, "William Coleman," *Dictionary of American Biography* [*DAB*], vol. 4, ed. Allen Johnson and Dumas Malone (New York: Scribners, 1930), 294.

17. Ibid., 294–95, and Nevins, *The Evening Post*, 15–17.

18. *New-York Evening Post*, November 16, 1801.

19. Ibid.

20. Ibid., November 19, 1801.

21. George Henry Payne, *History of Journalism in the United States* (New York & London: Appleton, 1920), 191.

22. Charles H. Levermore, "The Rise of Metropolitan Journalism, 1800–1840," *American Historical Review* 6 (April 1901): 449.

23. Kenneth Stewart and John Tebbel, *Makers of Modern Journalism* (New York: Prentice-Hall, 1952), 36.

24. Philadelphia *Gazette of the United States*, November 18, 1801.

25. Republished in the *New-York Evening Post*, November 20, 1801.

26. Ibid.

27. Quoted in Nevins, *The Evening Post*, 20.

28. Republished in the *New-York Evening Post*, November 20, 1801.

29. Nevins, *The Evening Post*, 20.

30. Ibid.

31. Willard Grosvenor Bleyer, *Main Currents in the History of American Journalism* (Boston: Houghton Mifflin, 1927), 135.

32. Ibid., 133.

33. Quoted in Nevins, *The Evening Post*, 32.

34. Ibid., 32–33.

35. Ibid., 26–27. Jefferson's message to Congress appeared in the *Post* on December 12, 1801, but comment was reserved until December 17. "The Examination" by "Lucius Crassus" appeared on December 17, 21, 24, 26, 29, 31, 1801; January 2, 7, 12, 18, 19, February 3, 23, 27, March 2, 3, 19, and 20, 1802.

36. Nevins, *The Evening Post*, 27–28.

37. Mott, *American Journalism*, 185.

38. Philadelphia *Aurora*, July 1, 1802.

39. Nevins, *The Evening Post*, 51.

40. Ibid., 24.

41. Quoted in ibid., 23–24.

42. Mott, *American Journalism*, 131.

43. James Melvin Lee, *History of American Journalism*, rev. ed. (Boston & New York: Harper, 1923), 129–30.

44. Frederic Hudson, *Journalism in the United States, from 1690 to 1872* (New York: Harper, 1873), 147.

45. Frank W. Scott, "Benjamin Russell," *Dictionary of American Biography* [*DAB*], vol. 16, ed. Dumas Malone (New York: Scribners, 1935), 239–40.

46. Ibid., 239.

47. Mott, *American Journalism,* 131–32.

48. Hudson, *Journalism in the United States,* 151.

49. Joseph T. Buckingham, *Specimens of Newspaper Literature: With Personal Memoirs, Anecdotes, and Reminiscences,* 2 vols. (Boston, Little, Brown, 1850), 1:106.

50. Hudson, *Journalism in the United States,* 152.

51. Boston *Columbian Centinel,* March 4, 1801.

52. Hudson, *Journalism in the United States,* 148.

53. Boston *Columbian Centinel,* March 4, 1801.

54. Buckingham, *Specimens of Newspaper Literature,* 1:110–17.

55. Mott, *American Journalism,* 133.

56. Scott, "Benjamin Russell," *DAB,* 16:239.

57. Boston *Independent Chronicle,* October 8, 1801.

58. Scott, "Benjamin Russell," *DAB,* 16:239.

59. Stewart and Tebbel, *Makers of Modern Journalism,* 33.

60. Dumas Malone, "James Thomson Callender," *Dictionary of American Biography* [*DAB*], vol. 3, ed. Allen Johnson (New York: Scribners, 1929), 425–26.

61. Callender to Jefferson, October 26, 1798, Jefferson Papers, Library of Congress.

62. Quoted in Charles A. Jellison, "That Scoundrel Callender," *Virginia Magazine of History and Biography* 67 (July 1959): 296.

63. Worthington Chauncey Ford, "Jefferson and the Newspaper," *Records of the Columbia Historical Society* 8 (1905): 90.

64. Worthington Chauncey Ford, ed., *Thomas Jefferson and James Thomson Callender* (Brooklyn, N.Y.: Historical Print Club, 1897), 6. Jefferson gave Callender a total of $158.47.

65. Jellison, "That Scoundrel Callender," 296–97.

66. Alexander Hamilton, *Observations on Certain Documents Contained in Nos. V and VI of the "History of the United States for the Year 1796"* . . . (Philadelphia: Printed for John Fenno, 1797).

67. Callender to Jefferson, Raspberry Plain, Sept. 22, 1798, in Worthington Chauncey Ford, *Jefferson and Callender,* 10.

68. Callender to Jefferson, Raspberry Plain, Oct. 26, 1798, ibid., 11.

69. Ibid., 12.

70. Callender to Jefferson, Richmond, August 10, 1799, ibid., 15.

71. Ibid., 16.

72. Jefferson to Callender, Monticello, October 6, 1799, ibid., 18. Callender had sent sixteen pages of the *Prospect* on September 26, 1799, stating, "I will send all I print by the first opportunities, to Charlottesville," ibid., 17. He sent eight additional pages on October 7; sixteen on November 16; "50 or 60" soon after December 17, ibid., 19.

73. Callender to Jefferson, Richmond, Feb. 15, 1800, ibid., 20. "Some weeks ago, Mr. George Jefferson sent you a complete copy of the Prospect per post."

74. Ibid.

75. Callender to Jefferson, Richmond, March 14, 1800, ibid., 21.

76. Callender to Jefferson, Richmond, March 10, 1800, ibid., 20.

77. Quoted in James Morton Smith, *Freedom's Fetters: The Alien and Sedition Laws and American Civil Liberties* (Ithaca, N.Y.: Cornell University Press, 1956), 340.

78. Ibid., 340–41.

79. Richmond *Examiner,* May 9, 1800; quoted in James Morton Smith, *Freedom's Fetters,* 342.

80. James Morton Smith, *Freedom's Fetters,* 334–35. An account of the trial is given in Francis Wharton, *State Trials of the United States during the Administrations of Washington and Adams* . . . (Philadelphia: Carey & Hart 1849), 688–721, and the trial is described in Frederick Trevor Hill, *Decisive Battles of the Law* (New York & London: Harper, 1907), 1–26. See also John C. Miller, *Crisis in Freedom: The Alien and Sedition Acts* (Boston: Little, Brown, 1951), 210–20.

81. Monroe to Jefferson, May 27, 1800, and Jefferson abstract, May 28, 1800, Manuscript Letters of N. P. Trist to James Madison and Mrs. Dolley Madison, Virginia Historical Society.

82. James Morton Smith, *Freedom's Fetters,* 346.

83. Ibid., 356.

84. Quoted in ibid., 358.

85. Callender to Jefferson, Richmond Jail, September 13, 1800, in Worthington Chauncey Ford, *Jefferson and Callender,* 26–27.

86. Callender to Jefferson, Richmond Jail, October 1800, ibid., 29.

87. On October 11, 1800, Callender wrote to Jefferson: "For some time past, I have regularly sent you, as far as they were printed, the Sheets of the 2d volume of *The Prospect,* because I flattered myself, that although neither the stile nor matter could be exactly conformable to your ideas, or taste, yet that upon the whole, they would not be disagreeable. Whether I was right or wrong, or whether indeed you received my letters, I do not know." Ibid., 28. On November 17, 1800, Callender wrote: "I had foresworn pamphlets, as one always loses by them. But in truth I feel a kind of pride at this moment, to let them see I can write as well *here* as anywhere else." Ibid., 30.

88. Callender to Jefferson, Richmond Jail, February 23, 1801, ibid., 32.

89. Callender to Jefferson, Richmond, April 12, 1801, ibid., 33–34.

90. Ibid., 34.

91. Callender to Madison, Petersburg, April 27, 1801, ibid., 35–37.

92. Callender to Madison, Petersburg, April 27, 1801, ibid., 35.

93. Jefferson to Monroe, Washington, July 17, 1802, W. C. Ford, "Thomas Jefferson and Callender," *New England Historical and Genealogical Register* 51 (1897): 324.

94. Jefferson to Monroe, July 15, 1802, in Paul Leicester Ford, ed., *The Writings of Thomas Jefferson,* 10 vols. (New York: Putnam, 1892–99), 7:164.

95. James Truslow Adams, *The Living Jefferson* (New York: Scribners, 1936), 315.

96. See, for example, Pearl M. Graham, "Thomas Jefferson and Sally Hemings," *Journal of Negro History* 44 (1961): 89–103.

97. Richmond *Recorder,* November 17, 1802.

98. Ibid., March 16 and May 28, 1803.

99. Ibid., September 22, 1802.

100. Ibid., May 28, 1803.

101. Jerry W. Knudson, "Jefferson on the Couch Again," *Clio among the Media* 28 (Winter 1996): 1 and 11.

102. *Philadelphia Inquirer,* April 9, 1995.

103. J. G. A. Pocock, *Virtue, Commerce, and History* (New York: Cambridge University Press, 1985), 9.

104. Douglas L. Wilson, "Thomas Jefferson and the Character Issue," *Atlantic Monthly* 270 (November 1992): 57–74.

105. Washington, D.C., *National Intelligencer,* September 29, 1802.

106. See "TO J. T. CALLENDER," Washington, D.C., *National Intelligencer,* October 27, 1802, republished from the Richmond *Examiner.*

107. Philadelphia *Aurora,* September 15, 1802. See also the *Aurora* for July 15 and September 10, 1802, and "Hamilton—and Callender" in the issue of September 9, 1802. For comment on "Jefferson and Callender" by the *New-York Evening Post,* see the Richmond *Recorder,* August 18, 1802.

108. William M. Van der Weyde, ed., *The Life and Works of Thomas Paine,* 10 vols. (New Rochelle, N.Y.: Thomas Paine Historical Association, 1925), 8:4

109. Philadelphia *Gazette of the United States,* June 15, 1801.

110. Philadelphia *Aurora,* March 31, 1801.

111. Philadelphia *Gazette of the United States,* June 4, 1801.

4. ELECTION OF 1800–1801: ANGUISH AND TRIUMPH

1. Quoted in Margaret A. Blanchard, *History of the Mass Media in the United States: An Encyclopedia* (Chicago: Ftizroy Dearborn, 1998), 285.

2. Washington, D.C., *National Intelligencer,* February 16, 1801.

3. Ibid.

4. Philadelphia *Gazette of the United States,* February 16, 1801.

5. Ibid.

6. Washington, D.C., *National Intelligencer,* January 21, 1801.

7. Ibid.

8. Philadelphia *Gazette of the United States,* February 16, 1801.

9. Washington, D.C., *National Intelligencer,* December 15, 1800.

10. Ibid.

11. On this point, see John S. Pancake, "Aaron Burr: Would-Be Usurper," *William and Mary Quarterly,* 3rd ser., 8 (1951): 204–13. Burr's case is most ably presented in Nathan Schachner, *Aaron Burr, a Biography* (New York: Stokes, 1937). For the election of 1800, see also Morton Borden, *The Federalism of James A. Bayard* (New York: Columbia University Press, 1955); volume 4 of Irving Brant, *James Madison,* 6 vols. (Indianapolis: Bobbs-Merrill, 1941–61); and Charles A. Beard, *Economic Origins of Jeffersonian Democracy* (New York: Macmillan, 1949). I found no charge in the contemporary press that Jefferson had made a deal with the Federalists in order to obtain his election in the House of Representatives.

12. Washington, D.C., *National Intelligencer,* December 24, 1800. Italics added.

13. Ibid., January 5, 1801. See also, January 7, 1801.

14. Philadelphia *Aurora,* January 1, 1801.

15. Washington, D.C., *National Intelligencer,* January 1, 1801.

16. Boston *Independent Chronicle,* January 8, 1801.

17. Philadelphia *Aurora,* January 10, 1801. The eight states were listed as New Hampshire, Massachusetts, Rhode Island, Connecticut, New Jersey, Delaware, Maryland, and South Carolina.

18. Ibid.

19. Quoted in Bernard Fay, *The Two Franklins: Fathers of American Democracy* (Boston: Little, Brown 1933), 301.

20. For an excellent summary of the campaign, see Charles O. Lerche Jr., "Jefferson and the Election of 1800: A Case Study in the Political Smear," *William and Mary Quarterly,* 3rd ser., 5 (1948): 467–91.

21. Ibid., 490.

22. Ibid., 474.

23. Constance B. Schulz, "Of Bigotry in Politics and Religion, the Federalist Press, and the Syllabus," *Virginia Magazine of History and Biography* 91 (1983): 73–91.

24. Philadelphia *Aurora,* November 11, 1800.

25. Ibid.

26. Boston *Columbian Centinel,* January 7, 1801.

27. Philadelphia *Gazette of the United States,* January 31, 1801.

28. Boston *Columbia Centinel,* January 7, 1801.

29. Schachner, *Aaron Burr,* 200–201 and 203.

30. Quoted in Noble E. Cunningham Jr., *The Jeffersonian Republicans: The Formation of Party Organization, 1789–1801* (Chapel Hill: University of North Carolina Press, 1957), 245.

31. Republished in the Washington, D.C., *National Intelligencer,* February 20, 1801.

32. Philadelphia *Aurora,* February 20, 1801.

33. Philadelphia *Gazette of the United States,* February 20, 1801.

34. Ibid.

35. Philadelphia *Gazette of the United States,* February 21, 1801.

36. Boston *Independent Chronicle,* February 26, 1801.

37. Ibid.

38. Washington, D.C., *National Intelligencer,* February 18, 1801.

39. Philadelphia *Aurora,* February 20, 1801.

40. Willard Grosvenor Bleyer, *Main Currents in the History of American Journalism* (Boston: Houghton Mifflin, 1927), 132.

41. Noble E. Cunningham Jr., "Virginia Jeffersonians' Victory Celebrations in 1801," *Virginia Cavalcade* 8 (Summer 1958): 4.

42. Philadelphia *Gazette of the United States,* February 23, 1801.

43. Washington, D.C., *National Intelligencer,* February 27, 1801.

44. Boston *Independent Chronicle,* March 5, 1801.

45. Washington, D.C., *National Intelligencer,* March 6, 1801.

46. Ibid.

47. Ibid.

48. Philadelphia *Aurora,* March 6, 1801.

49. Ibid.

50. Ibid.

51. Philadelphia *Gazette of the United States,* March 9, 1801.

52. Philadelphia *Aurora,* March 9, 1801.

53. Ibid.

54. Ibid., March 10, 1801.

55. Boston *Columbian Centinel,* March 14, 1801.

56. Philadelphia *Aurora,* March 25, 1801.

57. Ibid., March 27, 1801.

58. Boston *Independent Chronicle,* April 27, 1801.

59. Boston *Columbian Centinel,* July 18, 1801.

60. Philadelphia *Aurora,* March 12, 1801.

61. Philadelphia *Gazette of the United States,* April 14, 1801.

62. Philadelphia *Aurora,* June 10, 1801.

63. Boston *Columbian Centinel,* January 3, 1801.

64. Philadelphia *Gazette of the United States,* January 10, 1801.

65. Boston *Columbian Centinel,* January 21, 1801.

66. Ibid.

67. Philadelphia *Aurora,* March 10, 1801.

68. Ibid.

69. Ibid., March 11, 1801.

70. Boston *Independent Chronicle,* March 30, 1801.

71. Republished in the Boston *Independent Chronicle,* September 7, 1801. See also April 16, 1801.

72. For contemporary comments on Jefferson's inaugural speech in this country, see the Washington, D.C., *National Intelligencer,* March 6 and June 29, 1801; the Philadelphia *Aurora,* March 7, 11, and 18, 1801; the Boston *Columbian Centinel,* March 18, 1801; and the Boston *Independent Chronicle,* March 26, April 13, and May 25, 1801.

73. Washington, D.C., *National Intelligencer,* May 27, 1801.

74. Ibid., July 22, 1801.

75. Republished in ibid.

76. Boston *Independent Chronicle,* May 25, 1801.

77. Ibid., June 18, 1801.

78. Ibid., July 30, 1801.

79. Ibid., November 12, 1801.

80. Philadelphia *Aurora,* December 16, 1801.

81. Boston *Independent Chronicle,* December 28, 1801.

82. Ibid., March 26, 1801.

83. Philadelphia *Gazette of the United States,* April 14, 1801.

84. Republished in the Philadelphia *Aurora,* November 13, 1800.

85. Washington, D.C., *National Intelligencer,* December 14, 1801.

86. Boston *Independent Chronicle,* September 3, 1801.

87. Lerche, "Jefferson and the Election of 1800," 491.

88. Cunningham, *Jeffersonian Republicans,* 247.

89. Stephen G. Kurtz, *The Presidency of John Adams: The Collapse of Federalism, 1795–1800* (Philadelphia: University of Pennsylvania Press, 1957), 406.

90. Lerche, "Jefferson and the Election of 1800," 490.

91. Cunningham, *Jeffersonian Republicans,* 248.

92. Philadelphia *Aurora,* March 17, 1801.

5. Tom Paine Comes Homes, 1802

1. Letter from Paine to Congress, September 30, 1805, quoted in Moncure Daniel Conway, *The Life of Thomas Paine; with a History of his Literary, Political and Religious Career in America, France, and England,* 2 volumes (New York & London: Putnam, 1892), 2:358.

2. Of the nine-man committee appointed earlier to form a new constitution for France, only Paine and Sieyes survived the Terror. "Thomas Paine in England and France," *Atlantic Monthly* 4 (December 1859): 701.

3. William M. Van der Weyde, ed., *The Life and Works of Thomas Paine,* 10 vols. (New Rochelle, N.Y.: Thomas Paine Historical Association, 1925), 8:4.

4. See the Philadelphia *Gazette of the United States* for July 16 and 21, 1801, and the Philadelphia *Aurora* for July 14, August 3 and 7, 1801.

5. Paine to Consul Rotch, July 8, 1802, probably his last letter from Paris before sailing for America, Van der Weyde, *Life and Works of Thomas Paine,* 1:421.

6. Paine to Jefferson, Paris, June 9, 1801, ibid., 420.

7. Ibid., 445.

8. Quoted in Alfred Owen Aldridge, *Man of Reason, the Life of Thomas Paine* (Philadelphia: Lippincott, 1959), 269.

9. Ibid.

10. Paul Leicester Ford, ed., *The Writings of Thomas Jefferson,* 10 vols. (New York: Putnam, 1892–99).

11. John Bach McMaster, *A History of the People of the United States,* 8 vols. (New York: Appleton, 1885), 2:595.

12. Crane Brinton, "Thomas Paine," *Dictionary of American Biography* [*DAB*], vol. 14, ed. Dumas Malone (New York: Scribner's, 1935) states that Paine "wisely" refused passage on a government ship (p. 163). However, Aldridge, *Man of Reason,* 271, asserts that "Actually Paine's correspondence reveals that he delayed his passage for reasons quite independent of events in America." Henry S. Randall, *The Life of Thomas Jefferson,* 2 vols. (New York: Derby & Jackson, 1858), 2:642, erroneously states that Paine "got ready and returned in the sloop of war."

13. McMaster, *History of the People of the United States,* 2:594–96. See also Philadelphia *Gazette of the United States,* July 27, 1801.

14. Henry Adams, *History of the United States of America during the First Administration of Thomas Jefferson,* 2 vols. (New York: Scribners, 1889), 1:318 and 317.

15. Aldridge, *Man of Reason,* 270.

16. Philadelphia *Gazette of the United States,* July 21, 1801.

17. Quoted in W. E. Woodward, *Tom Paine: America's Godfather, 1737–1809* (New York: Dutton, 1945), 309.

18. Quoted in Mary Agnes Best, *Thomas Paine, Prophet and Martyr of Democracy* (New York: Harcourt, Brace, 1927), 373.

19. Philadelphia *Gazette of the United States,* August 8, 1801.

20. G. Vale, *The Life of Thomas Paine, Author of "Common Sense," "Rights of Man," "Age of Reason," &c., &c., with Critical and Explanatory Observations on His Writings; and an*

Appendix Containing His Letters to Washington, Suppressed in His Works at Present Published in the Country (New York: Published by the author, 1841), 127.

21. Washington, D.C., *National Intelligencer,* July 29, 1801.

22. See Boston *Independent Chronicle,* July 30, 1801.

23. Quoted in Aldridge, *Man of Reason,* 273.

24. Republished in the *New-York Evening Post,* November 3, 1802.

25. Ibid.

26. Ibid.

27. Philadelphia *Aurora,* November 3, 1802.

28. Ibid.

29. Worthington C. Ford, ed., "Letters of William Duane, 1800–1834," *Proceedings of the Massachusetts Historical Society,* 2nd. ser., 20 (1906–7): 279.

30. Quoted in Hesketh Pearson, *Tom Paine, Friend of Mankind* (New York & London: Harper, 1937), 251.

31. Philadelphia *Aurora,* July 14, 1801.

32. Ibid., August 7, 1801.

33. *New-York Evening Post,* November 4, 1802.

34. Philadelphia *Gazette of the United States,* September 28, 1801.

35. Richmond *Recorder,* December 8, 1802.

36. Paine did hope to publish part 3 of the *Age of Reason,* then in manuscript form, but was unable to do so. The work was bequeathed to the wife of his French benefactor, M. Bonneville, who later reverted to Catholicism and mutilated Paine's manuscript. See Moncure D. Conway, "An Unpublished Letter of Thomas Paine," *Nation* 62 (February 6, 1896): 118.

37. Philadelphia *Aurora,* October 13, 1802.

38. Ibid., October 25, 1802.

39. Ibid., November 8, 1802.

40. *New-York Evening Post,* November 5, 1802.

41. Philadelphia *Gazette of the United States,* September 25, 1801.

42. This comment refers to a rumor in 1796 that Paine had died in France. On that occasion, James Cheetham, editor of the New York *American Citizen,* composed an epitaph: "Blasphemes the Almighty, lives in filth like a hog, / Is abandoned in death and interr'd like a dog." (Quoted in Conway, *Life of Thomas Paine,* 2:419.)

43. Philadelphia *Gazette of the United States,* September 7, 1801.

44. Boston *Columbian Centinel,* August 22, 1801.

45. Ibid.

46. Quoted in Woodward, *Tom Paine,* 310.

47. James Cheetham, *The Life of Thomas Paine, Author of Common Sense, The Crisis, Rights of Man, &c. &c. &c.* (New York: Printed by Southwick & Pelsue, 1809), 227.

48. William Plumer Jr., *Life of William Plumer, by His Son, William Plumer, Jr.* (Boston: Phillips, Samson, 1856), 242–43.

49. McMaster, *History of the People of the United States,* 2:620.

50. Aldridge, *Man of Reason,* 275.

51. Quoted in Randall, *The Life of Thomas Jefferson,* 2:644.

52. *New-York Evening Post,* October 15, 1802.

53. Philadelphia *Aurora,* December 9, 1802.

54. *New-York Evening Post,* January 10, 1803.

55. Republished in the Richmond *Recorder,* December 15, 1802.

56. Ibid., September 15, 1802.

57. Ibid., December 3 and 1, 1802.

58. Ibid., December 8, 1802.

59. Ibid.

60. Republished in ibid., September 15, 1802.

61. Ibid., December 8, 1802.

62. Republished in ibid., April 6, 1803.

63. Ibid., November 10, 1802.

64. Boston *Columbian Centinel,* July 25, 1801.

65. The eight letters appeared first in the Washington, D.C., *National Intelligencer,* November 15, 22, 29, December 6, 1802; January 25 and February 2, 1803; Philadelphia *Aurora,* March 12, 1803; and Trenton *True American,* April 21, 1803.

66. McMaster, *History of the People of the United States,* 2:620.

67. Washington, D.C., *National Intelligencer,* November 15, 1802.

68. *New-York Evening Post,* February 4, 1803.

69. Ibid.

70. Republished in the Richmond *Recorder,* April 16, 1803.

71. Philadelphia *Aurora,* December 9, 1802.

72. Philadelphia *Gazette of the United States,* August 13, 1801.

73. *New-York Evening Post,* October 1, 1802.

74. Ibid.

75. Philadelphia *Aurora,* November 29, 1802.

76. Ibid., December 7, 1802.

77. Ibid., December 16, 1802. See also the comments in the issue of December 27, 1802.

78. Paine had experienced vicious attacks before. Foremost among these were William Cobbett, *A Letter to the Infamous Tom Paine* (Philadelphia: William Cobbett, 1796), and Francis Oldys [George Chalmers], *The Life of Thomas Paine, the Author of Rights of Man, with a Defense of His Writings* (London: Printed for John Stockdale, 1791). James Cheetham's spurious *The Life of Thomas Paine* (New York: Printed by Southwick & Pelsue, 1809), published soon after Paine's death, cost Cheetham $150 for libeling Mrs. Bonneville, a low fine because the presiding judge thought the book "tended to serve the cause of religion." See Frank Smith, *Thomas Paine, Liberator* (New York: Stokes, 1938), 308.

79. Washington, D.C., *National Intelligencer,* November 15, 1802.

80. Ibid.

81. Philadelphia *Aurora,* December 9, 1802.

82. Ibid., December 7, 1802.

83. Aldridge, *Man of Reason,* 280.

84. William James Linton, *The Life of Paine* (London: Watson, 1841), 38.

85. Plumer, *Life of William Plumer,* 243.

86. Vale, *Thomas Paine,* 143. Charles R. King, *Life and Correspondence of Rufus King,* 6 vols. (New York: Putnam, 1894–1900), 4:182. Conway, *Life of Thomas Paine,* 2:326. Van der Weyde, *Life of Thomas Paine,* 435–436 and 444.

87. Joseph T. Buckingham, *Specimens of Newspaper Literature: With Personal Memoirs, Anecdotes, and Reminiscences,* 2 vols. (Boston, Little, Brown, 1850), 2:250.

88. *New-York Evening Post,* June 10, 1809.

89. Philadelphia *Aurora,* November 23, 1802.

90. Conway, *Life of Thomas Paine,* 2:361.

91. Quoted in Van der Weyde, *Life and Works of Thomas Paine,* 2:418.

92. Quoted in Conway, *Life of Thomas Paine,* 2:418. Grave robbers desecrated Paine's grave, and some of his bones and skull were on display in a London curio shop for some years.

6. LOUISIANA PURCHASE: "THIS NEW, IMMENSE, UNBOUNDED WORLD"

1. Quoted in Curtis M. Geer, *The Louisiana Purchase and the Westward Movement* (Philadelphia: Printed for subscribers by G. Barrie & Sons, 1904), 211.

2. Thomas M. Cooley, "The Acquisition of Louisiana," *Indiana Historical Publications* 2 (1895): 65.

3. Walter Robinson Smith, *Brief History of the Louisiana Territory* (St. Louis, Mo.: St. Louis News Company, 1904), 72.

4. [François] Barbe-Marbois, *The History of Louisiana, Particularly of the Cession of that Colony to the United States of America. . . .* (Philadelphia: Carey & Lea, 1830), 331–32.

5. E. Wilson Lyon, *The Man Who Sold Louisiana: The Career of François Barbe-Marbois* (Norman: University of Oklahoma Press, 1942), 121.

6. Quoted in Geer, *Louisiana Purchase,* 212.

7. Ibid., 213.

8. Ibid., 215.

9. Paul Leicester Ford, ed., *The Writings of Thomas Jefferson,* 10 vols. (New York: Putnam, 1892–99), 8:145.

10. Ibid., 147.

11. Philadelphia *Aurora,* March 26, 1802.

12. Ibid., March 29, 1802.

13. Ibid., March 30, 1802.

14. *New-York Evening Post,* April 3, 1802.

15. Philadelphia *Aurora,* June 14, 1802.

16. Washington, D.C., *National Intelligencer,* November 26, 1802.

17. Frederick J. Turner, "The Policy of France toward the Mississippi Valley in the Period of Washington and Adams," *American Historical Review* 10 (1904–5), 267–69.

18. Quoted in J. A. James, "Louisiana as a Factor in American Diplomacy, 1795–1800," *Mississippi Valley Historical Review* 1 (1914): 53–54.

19. Ibid., 54–55.

20. Washington, D.C., *National Intelligencer,* January 12, 1803.

21. Richmond *Recorder,* April 3, 1802.

22. Ibid., April 24, 1802.

23. Philadelphia *Aurora,* December 30, 1802.

24. *New-York Evening Post,* February 8, 1803.

25. Ibid., February 21, 1803.

26. Georges Oudard, *Four Cents an Acre,* trans. Margery Bianco (New York: Brewer & Warren, 1931), 287.

27. Quoted in E. Wilson Lyon, *Louisiana in French Diplomacy, 1759–1804* (Norman: University of Oklahoma Press, 1934), 215.

28. Lyon, *The Man Who Sold Louisiana*, passim.

29. Oudard, *Four Cents an Acre*, 291.

30. Lyon, *The Man Who Sold Louisiana*, 120–21.

31. Quoted in Oudard, *Four Cents an Acre*, 292.

32. James Alexander Robertson, *Louisiana under the Rule of Spain, France, and the United States* (Cleveland: Clark, 1911), 63.

33. Lyon, *Louisiana in French Diplomacy*, 227.

34. Ibid.

35. "Treaty between the French Republic and the United States, Concerning the Cession of Louisiana, Signed at Paris the 30th of April, 1803," *Louisiana Historical Quarterly* 2 (1919): 139–40.

36. Ibid., 140.

37. Ibid., 141–42.

38. Walter Robinson Smith, *Brief History of the Louisiana Territory*, 72.

39. Boston *Independent Chronicle*, June 30, 1803.

40. Washington, D.C., *National Intelligencer*, July 4, 1803.

41. Philadelphia *Aurora*, July 8, 1803.

42. Boston *Independent Chronicle*, July 4, 1803.

43. Ibid., July 11, 1803.

44. Boston *Columbian Centinel*, July 13, 1803.

45. Philadelphia *Aurora*, July 8, 1803.

46. Washington, D.C., *National Intelligencer*, quoted in the Boston *Independent Chronicle*, July 11, 1803.

47. Washington, D.C., *National Intelligencer*, July 8, 1803.

48. Boston *Independent Chronicle*, July 14, 1803.

49. Ibid., August 8, 1803.

50. Washington, D.C., *National Intelligencer*, July 11, 1803.

51. Ibid., July 13, 1803.

52. Boston *Columbian Centinel*, August 10, 1803.

53. Ibid., July 20, 1803.

54. Ibid., August 10, 1803.

55. John Bach McMaster, *A History of the People of the United States*, 8 vols. (New York: Appleton, 1885), 2:630.

56. Philadelphia *Aurora*, July 21, 1803.

57. Washington, D.C., *National Intelligencer*, August 17, 1803.

58. Ibid., August 1, 1803.

59. Ibid., January 16, 1804.

60. Ibid., January 30, 1804.

61. Ibid., August 19, 1803.

62. Walter Robinson Smith, *Brief History of the Louisiana Territory*, 73.

63. James K. Hosmer, *The History of the Louisiana Purchase* (New York: Appleton, 1902), 157.

64. Walter Robinson Smith, *Brief History of the Louisiana Territory*, 75.

65. Washington, D.C., *National Intelligencer*, January 27, 1804.

66. Walter Robinson Smith, *Brief History of the Louisiana Territory,* 76–77.

67. Washington, D.C., *National Intelligencer,* December 21, 26, 1803, and January 2, 1804.

68. E. O. Randall, "The Louisiana Purchase," *Ohio Archaeological and Historical Publications* 13 (1904): 248–62.

69. Oudard, *Four Cents an Acre,* 303.

70. Ibid., 304.

71. *New-York Evening Post,* December 31, 1803.

72. Everett Somerville Brown, *The Constitutional History of the Louisiana Purchase, 1803–1812* (Berkeley: University of California Press, 1920), 35.

73. Washington, D.C., *National Intelligencer,* February 2, 1804. For accounts of other celebrations, see the issues for March 2 and 5, 1804.

74. Ibid., January 30, 1804.

75. *New-York Evening Post,* July 5, 1803.

76. Ibid., November 5, 1803.

77. Ibid., November 7, 1803. See also issues for November 8, 9, 10, 12, 16, 17, 18, 19, and 21, 1803.

78. Ibid., November 28, 1803.

79. Ibid.

80. Washington, D.C., *National Intelligencer,* November 28, 1803.

81. Ibid., July 11, 1804.

82. Ibid., July 18, 1804.

83. Ibid., July 20, 1804.

84. Ibid., December 30, 1805.

85. Ibid., January 10, 1806.

86. Ibid., July 18, 1804.

87. Ibid., August 16, 1805.

88. Ibid., December 31, 1806.

89. Ibid., January 16, 1807.

90. *Richmond Enquirer,* February 19, 1805.

91. Ibid.

7. Duel at Weehawken

1. Harold C. Syrett and Jean G. Cooke, eds., *Interview in Weehawken: The Burr-Hamilton Duel, as Told in the Original Documents* (Middletown, Conn.: Wesleyan University Press, 1960), 160.

2. Henry Adams, *History of the United States of America during the First Administration of Thomas Jefferson,* 2 vols. (New York: Scribners, 1889), 2:191.

3. Allan Nevins, "Alexander Hamilton," *Dictionary of American Biography* [*DAB*], vol. 8, ed. Dumas Malone (New York: Scribners, 1950), 170–79; and Isaac Joslin Cox, "Aaron Burr," *DAB,* vol. 3, ed. Allen Johnson (New York: Scribners, 1929), 314–21.

4. Nevins, "Alexander Hamilton," *DAB,* 8:173.

5. Ibid., 174.

6. Samuel H. Wandell and Meade Minnigerode, *Aaron Burr,* 2 vols. (New York & London: Putnam, 1925), 1:273.

7. Allan McLane Hamilton, *The Intimate Life of Alexander Hamilton* (New York: Scribners, 1911), 384.

8. Quoted in Nathan Schachner, *Alexander Hamilton* (New York & London: Appleton-Century, 1946), 422.

9. Quoted in David Loth, *Alexander Hamilton: Portrait of a Prodigy* (New York: Carrick & Evans, 1939), 296.

10. Henry Jones Ford, *Alexander Hamilton* (New York: Scribners, 1920), 343.

11. William Graham Sumner, *Alexander Hamilton* (New York: Dodd, Mead, 1890), 246.

12. Syrett and Cooke, *Interview in Weehawken,* 99.

13. Louis M. Hacker, *Alexander Hamilton in the American Tradition* (New York, Toronto & London: McGraw-Hill, 1957), 221.

14. Holmes Alexander, *Aaron Burr, The Proud Pretender* (New York & London: Harper, 1937), 213.

15. Richard B. Morris, ed., *Alexander Hamilton and the Founding of the Nation* (New York: Dial, 1957), 603.

16. Quoted in Allan McLane Hamilton, *Intimate Life of Alexander Hamilton,* 399.

17. Schachner, *Alexander Hamilton,* 430.

18. *New-York Evening Post,* July 13, 1804.

19. Ibid.

20. Philadelphia *Aurora,* July 13, 1804.

21. Ibid., July 14, 1804.

22. Quoted in ibid., July 21, 1804.

23. Ibid.

24. Ibid., July 23, 1804.

25. Washington, D.C., *National Intelligencer,* July 18, 1804.

26. Boston *Columbian Centinel,* July 18, 1804.

27. Ibid., July 25, 1804.

28. *Richmond Enquirer,* July 21, 1804.

29. Ibid.

30. Boston *Independent Chronicle,* July 23, 1804.

31. *New-York Evening Post,* July 13, 1804.

32. Ibid.

33. Ibid.

34. Republished in ibid., July 17, 1804.

35. Ibid.

36. Anne Cary Morris, ed., *The Diary and Letters of Gouverneur Morris,* 2 vols. (New York: Scribners, 1888), 2:456–58.

37. *New-York Evening Post,* July 15, 1804.

38. Philadelphia *Aurora,* July 16, 1804. On July 17 the *New-York Evening Post*'s original announcement of Hamilton's death and account of the funeral procession were republished without comment. The duel correspondence was republished without comment on July 18 and 20; an account of the funeral was republished from the New York *American Citizen* on July 19, and the funeral oration from the *Post* on July 20.

39. Philadelphia *Aurora,* July 18, 1804.

40. *New-York Evening Post,* July 17, 1804.

41. Ibid.

42. Ibid.

43. Ibid.

44. Republished in ibid., July 17, 1804.

45. Benjamin Ellis Martin, "Transition Period of the American Press," *Magazine of American History* 17 (1887): 289–90.

46. *New-York Evening Post,* July 18, 1804.

47. Republished in ibid.

48. Ibid., July 19, 1804.

49. Republished in ibid.

50. Republished in ibid. For other eulogistic comments, see the issues of July 21 (*Albany Register* and the *Federal Ark*), July 23 (*National Aegis*), and July 31, 1804 (the *Balance, New-England Republican, Newport Mercury, Connecticut Gazette, Norfolk Gazette, Portsmouth Oracle,* the *Bee,* and the Philadelphia *Port Folio*).

51. Republished in the *New-York Evening Post,* July 19, 1804.

52. Ibid.

53. Ibid.

54. Ibid.

55. Ibid., July 21, 1804.

56. Ibid., July 23, 1804.

57. Boston *Independent Chronicle,* July 26, 1804.

58. Ibid.

59. *Richmond Enquirer,* July 25, 1804.

60. Boston *Independent Chronicle,* August 2, 1804.

61. Ibid.

62. Republished in ibid., August 6, 1804.

63. Boston *Columbian Centinel,* August 8, 1804.

64. Boston *Independent Chronicle,* August 9, 1804.

65. *New-York Evening Post,* July 31, 1804.

66. Ibid., July 20, 1804.

67. Republished in ibid.

68. Ibid.

69. Ibid., August 2, 1806.

70. Washington, D.C., *National Intelligencer,* August 8, 1804.

71. Alexander, *Aaron Burr, the Proud Pretender,* 217.

72. Republished in the *New-York Evening Post,* August 2, 1804.

73. Ibid., July 31, 1804.

74. Republished in ibid., July 20, 1804.

75. Republished in the *Richmond Enquirer,* August 8, 1804.

76. *New-York Evening Post,* September 1, 1804.

77. Ibid., August 20, 1804.

78. Ibid., August 25, 1804.

79. Charles Edwards, *Pleasantries about Courts and Lawyers of the State of New York* (New York: Richardson, 1867), 367; cited in Alexander, *Aaron Burr, the Proud Pretender,* 215.

80. James Parton, *The Life and Times of Aaron Burr* (New York: Mason, 1859), 616.

81. Arthur Hendrick Vandenberg, *The Greatest American, Alexander Hamilton* (New York & London: Putnam, 1921), 296.

82. Boston *Independent Chronicle,* July 26, 1804.

83. Washington, D.C., *National Intelligencer,* November 4, 1807.

8. ASSAULT ON THE JUDICIARY

1. Charles Warren, *The Supreme Court in United States History,* rev. ed., 2 vols. (Boston: Little, Brown, 1926), 1:190.

2. Henry Adams, *History of the United States of America during the First Administration of Thomas Jefferson,* 2 vols. (New York: Scribners, 1889), 2:152.

3. Ibid., 2:243.

4. Albert J. Beveridge, *The Life of John Marshall,* 4 vols. (Boston & New York: Houghton Mifflin, 1916–1919), 3:53.

5. Felix Frankfurter and James M. Landis, *The Business of the Supreme Court: A Study in the Federal Judicial System* (New York: Macmillan, 1927), 21 and 24–25.

6. Max Farrand, "The Judiciary Act of 1801," *American Historical Review* 5 (1899–1900): 682.

7. Ibid., 682–86.

8. Quoted in ibid., 683.

9. Ibid., 683; and Warren, *The Supreme Court in United States History,* 1:186.

10. Farrand, "Judiciary Act of 1801," 683–84.

11. William S. Carpenter, *Judicial Tenure in the United States, with Especial Reference to the Tenure of Federal Judges* (New Haven, Conn.: Yale University Press, 1918), 77.

12. Farrand, "Judiciary Act of 1801," 685–86. The best discussion of the merits of the act of 1801 is found in Frankfurter and Landis, *The Business of the Supreme Court,* 21–30; and an excellent summary of the debate for repeal is found in Homer Cary Hockett, *The Constitutional History of the United States, 1776–1826* (New York: Macmillan, 1939), 302–6. See also Andrew C. McLaughlin, *A Constitutional History of the United States* (New York & London: Appleton-Century, 1935), 288–93, as well as other works cited elsewhere in this chapter.

13. Warren, *Supreme Court in United States History,* 208, and Frankfurter and Landis, *Business of the Supreme Court,* 28 29n79.

14. Beveridge, *Life of John Marshall,* 3:50.

15. Hockett, *Constitutional History of the United States,* 305.

16. Carpenter, *Judicial Tenure in the United States,* 78.

17. Washington, D.C., *National Intelligencer,* January 20, 1802.

18. Ibid., February 5, 1802.

19. Ibid., March 5, 1802.

20. Republished in ibid., February 12, 1802.

21. Ibid., February 19, 1802.

22. Philadelphia *Gazette of the United States,* November 19, 1801.

23. Ibid.

24. Ibid., January 23, 1802.

25. Philadelphia *Aurora,* January 28, 1802.

26. Ibid., February 4, 1802.

27. Ibid., February 18, 1802.

28. Washington, D.C., *National Intelligencer,* July 14, 1802.

29. Henry Adams, *History of the United States,* 2:151.

30. Gustavus Myers, *History of the Supreme Court of the United States* (Chicago: C. H. Kerr, 1925), 246.

31. Henry Adams, *History of the United States,* 2:158.

32. Ibid., 2:153–59.

33. Richard B. Lillich, "The Impeachment of Justice Samuel Chase," *American Journal of Legal History* 4 (1960): 49.

34. Frederick T. Hill, *Decisive Battles of the Law* (New York & London: Harper, 1907), 6–7.

35. B. J. Lossing, *Biographical Sketches of the Signers of the Declaration of American Independence* (Philadelphia: Davis, Porter, 1860), 146–50, and Edward S. Corwin, "Samuel Chase," *Dictionary of American Biography* [*DAB*], vol. 4, ed. Allen Johnson and Dumas Malone (New York: Scribners, 1930): 34–37.

36. Paul Leicester Ford, ed., *Essays on the Constitution of the United States* . . . (Brooklyn, N.Y.: Historical Printing Club, 1892), 325–28.

37. Corwin, "Samuel Chase," *DAB,* 4:36.

38. Ibid.

39. Henry Adams, *History of the United States,* 2:147–48.

40. Quoted in ibid., 2:149.

41. Samuel H. Smith and Thomas Lloyd, *Trial of Samuel Chase,* 2 vols. (Washington, D.C.: Printed for Samuel H. Smith, 1805), 1:5–8.

42. Ibid., 8.

43. Ibid., 9.

44. Charles Evans, *Report of the Trial of the Hon. Samuel Chase* . . . (Baltimore: Printed by Samuel Butler & George Keatinge, 1805), 3.

45. Henry Adams, *History of the United States,* 2:226.

46. Everett Somerville Brown, ed., *William Plumer's Memorandum of Proceedings in the United States Senate, 1803–1807* (New York: Macmillan, 1923), 236.

47. Lillich, "Impeachment of Justice Samuel Chase," 60.

48. Ibid., 61.

49. Quoted in ibid., 68.

50. S. Butler, ed., *Columbian Eloquence, Being the Speeches of the Most Celebrated American Orators, as Delivered in the Late Interesting Trial of the Hon. Samuel Chase,* 3 vols. (Baltimore: Printed for S. Butler & S. Cole, 1806), 3:322.

51. Ibid., 361.

52. Lillich, "Impeachment of Justice Samuel Chase," 70.

53. Henry Adams, *History of the United States,* 2:240.

54. Corwin, "Samuel Chase," *DAB,* 4:37.

55. Washington, D.C., *National Intelligencer,* May 20, 1803.

56. *New-York Evening Post,* January 11, 1804.

57. Ibid., January 20, 1804.

58. Ibid., March 3, 1804.

59. Washington, D.C., *National Intelligencer,* April 4, 1804.

60. Ibid.

61. Ibid.

62. Ibid.

63. *New-York Evening Post,* December 7, 1804. See also December 12, 1804.

64. *Richmond Enquirer,* December 14, 1804.

65. Ibid., December 22, 1804.

66. Ibid., December 29, 1804.

67. *New-York Evening Post,* March 9, 1805.

68. Ibid., January 21, 1805.

69. Ibid., February 6, 1805.

70. Republished in ibid.

71. *Richmond Enquirer,* February 8, 1805.

72. *New-York Evening Post,* February 14, 1805.

73. Republished in ibid. See also the issues for January 9, February 9, 11, 21, 22, 23; and March 3, 1805; and the *Richmond Enquirer* for February 22 and 26, 1805.

74. Washington, D.C., *National Intelligencer,* March 1, 1805.

75. Boston *Columbian Centinel,* March 6, 1805.

76. Philadelphia *Aurora,* March 9, 1805.

77. *Richmond Enquirer,* March 12, 1805.

78. *New-York Evening Post,* March 6, 1805.

79. Republished in ibid.

80. Washington, D.C., *National Intelligencer,* March 20, 1805. For additional comments on Burr's conduct as presiding officer in the Senate, see the *New-York Evening Post* for March 11 and 12, 1805.

81. Beveridge, *Life of John Marshall,* 3:220.

82. Hockett, *Constitutional History of the United States, 1776–1826,* 314.

83. Charles A. Beard, *The Supreme Court and the Constitution* (New York: Macmillan, 1912), 126–27.

84. Lillich, "Impeachment of Justice Samuel Chase," 71.

85. Brown, *William Plumer's Memorandum,* 311.

86. *New-York Evening Post,* March 9, 1805.

9. The Embargo and Commercial Warfare, 1807–1809

1. Doron S. Ben-Atar, *The Origins of Jeffersonian Commercial Policy and Diplomacy* (New York: St. Martin's Press, 1993), 165.

2. Henry Steele Commager, ed., *Documents of American History,* 4th ed. (New York: Appleton-Century-Crofts, 1948), 199.

3. Washington, D.C., *National Intelligencer,* May 9, 1806.

4. Burton Spivak, *Jefferson's English Crisis: Commerce, Embargo, and the Republican Revolution* (Charlottesville: University Press of Virginia, 1979), 102.

5. Quoted in the Washington D.C., *National Intelligencer,* May 13, 1807.

6. Ibid., July 17, 1807.

7. Philadelphia *Gazette of the United States,* May 1, 1801.

8. Commager, *Documents of American History,* 202–3.

9. Louis Martin Sears, "The Middle States and the Embargo of 1808," *South Atlantic Quarterly* 21 (1922): 169.

10. *New-York Evening Post,* September 9, 1808.

11. Boston *Independent Chronicle,* December 24, 1807.

12. Washington, D.C., *National Intelligencer,* December 25, 1807.

13. Ibid., December 23, 1807.

14. Ibid., December 25, 1807.

15. Boston *Columbian Centinel,* December 30, 1807.

16. *New-York Evening Post,* December 26, 1807.

17. Ibid., December 29, 1807.

18. Ibid., December 26, 1807. See also the issues for December 29 and 31, 1807; January 2 and February 2, 1808.

19. Ibid., December 26, 1807.

20. Ibid., December 28, 1807.

21. Philadelphia *Gazette of the United States,* December 24, 1807.

22. Ibid., December 24, 1807.

23. *New-York Evening Post,* December 29, 1807.

24. Philadelphia *Aurora,* January 19, 1808.

25. Ibid., December 28, 1807.

26. Philadelphia *Gazette of the United States,* December 24, 1807.

27. Republished in the *New-York Evening Post,* December 29, 1807.

28. Philadelphia *Aurora,* January 19, 1808.

29. Quoted in the *New-York Evening Post,* January 25, 1808.

30. *Richmond Enquirer,* July 5, 1808.

31. *New-York Evening Post,* July 25, 1808.

32. Washington, D.C., *National Intelligencer,* August 1, 1808.

33. Ibid.

34. Ibid., August 15, 1808.

35. Ibid., August 24, 1808.

36. Ibid., October 28, 1808.

37. *New-York Evening Post,* September 23, 1808.

38. Ibid., September 26, 1808.

39. Ibid., December 10, 1808.

40. *Richmond Enquirer,* December 31, 1807.

41. Boston *Independent Chronicle,* December 31, 1807.

42. Republished in ibid.

43. *New-York Evening Post,* January 9, 1808.

44. Ibid., January 14, 1808.

45. Ibid., January 15, 1808.

46. Ibid., January 25, 1808.

47. Washington, D.C., *National Intelligencer,* January 25, 1808.

48. *New-York Evening Post,* February 4, 1808.

49. James Duncan Phillips, "Jefferson's 'Wicked Tyrannical Embargo,'" *New England Quarterly* 18 (1945): 468–69 and 472.

50. *New-York Evening Post,* March 12, 1808.

51. Ibid., April 4, 1808.

52. Ibid., September 29, 1808.

53. Ibid., April 21, 1808.

54. [William Cullen Bryant], *The Embargo, or Sketches of the Times: A Satire, by a Youth of Thirteen,* facsimile reproduction in Thomas O. Mabbott, *The Embargo* (Gainesville, Fla.: Scholars' Facsimiles & Reprints, 1955), 22–23.

55. *Richmond Enquirer,* May 21, 1808.

56. Washington, D.C., *National Intelligencer,* June 1, 1808.

57. *Richmond Enquirer,* June 3, 1808. For other numbers of this series, "Submission—Or—Embargo?" see June 7, 10, 17, 24, and July 1, 1808.

58. Washington, D.C., *National Intelligencer,* October 17, 1808.

59. Ibid., June 15, 1808.

60. *New-York Evening Post,* July 1, 1808.

61. Ibid., July 13, 1808.

62. Ibid., July 20, 1808.

63. Republished in the Washington, D.C., *National Intelligencer,* July 29, 1808.

64. Ibid., September 5, 1808.

65. Ibid.

66. Republished in ibid., September 28, 1808.

67. *New-York Evening Post,* September 9, 1808.

68. Ibid., September 15, 1808.

69. Ibid., September 9, 1808.

70. *Richmond Enquirer,* September 23, 1808.

71. Ibid., November 11, 1808.

72. Washington, D.C., *National Intelligencer,* June 27, 1808.

73. *New-York Evening Post,* July 29, 1808.

74. Ibid., September 9, 1808.

75. Ibid.

76. *Richmond Enquirer,* January 10, 1809.

77. Ibid., February 10, 1809.

78. *New-York Evening Post,* January 28, 1809.

79. Ibid., February 6, 1809.

80. Philadelphia, February 7, 1809, Simon Gratz Collection, Historical Society of Pennsylvania.

81. Boston *Independent Chronicle,* February 27, 1809.

82. Washington, D.C., *National Intelligencer,* March 3, 1809.

83. Philadelphia *Aurora,* republished in ibid., March 4, 1809.

84. Philadelphia *Aurora,* March 4, 1809.

85. Ibid.

86. Boston *Columbian Centinel,* March 8, 1809.

87. Boston *Independent Chronicle,* March 9, 1809.

88. Ibid., March 13, 1809.

89. Boston *Columbian Centinel,* March 8, 1809.

90. Ibid.

91. *New-York Evening Post,* March 9, 1809.

92. Washington, D.C., *National Intelligencer,* March 13, 1809.

93. Louis Martin Sears, *Jefferson and the Embargo* (Durham, N.C.: Duke University Press, 1927), vii–viii.

94. *New-York Evening Post,* January 28, 1809.

95. Spivak, *Jefferson's English Crisis,* 204.

96. Republished in the *New-York Evening Post,* April 7, 1809.

97. Washington, D.C., *National Intelligencer,* December 23, 1807.

10. JEFFERSON AND THE PRESS

1. Merrill D. Peterson, *Thomas Jefferson and the New Nation: A Biography* (London: Oxford University Press, 1970), 713.

2. Ibid., 931.

3. Worthington C. Ford, ed., "Letters of William Duane," *Proceedings of the Massachusetts Historical Society,* 2nd ser., 20 (1906–7): 311–83.

4. Jeffrey L. Pasley, "*The Tyranny of Printers*": *Newspaper Politics in the Early American Republic* (Charlottesville: University Press of Virginia, 2001), 299.

5. Worthington C. Ford, "Letters of William Duane, 1800–1834," 257–394; and Colonel William Duane, "Selections from the Duane Papers," *Historical Magazine,* 2nd ser., 4 (1868): 60–75. See also the Vaux Papers and the Simon Gratz Collection at the Historical Society of Pennsylvania, and the Thomas Jefferson Papers, Library of Congress.

6. Dumas Malone, *Jefferson the President: First Term, 1801–1805* (Boston: Little, Brown, 1970), 225. Malone cites Jefferson to Madison, Aug. 29, 1803, Madison Papers, 26: 27.

7. Peterson, *Thomas Jefferson,* 713.

8. Text of the Norvell letter, June 11, 1807, Andrew A. Lipscomb, ed., *The Writings of Thomas Jefferson,* 20 vols. (Washington, D.C.: Thomas Jefferson Memorial Association, 1903), 11:222–26. Excerpt from Frank Luther Mott, *Jefferson and the Press* (Baton Rouge: Louisiana State University Press, 1943), 54–55.

9. Adrienne Koch and William Peden, eds. *The Life and Selected Writings of Thomas Jefferson* (New York: Modern Library, 1998), 652.

10. Jerry W. Knudson, "Political Journalism in the Age of Jefferson," *Journalism History* 1 (Spring 1974): 20.

11. Philadelphia *Port Folio,* January 15, 1803.

12. Jefferson to Noah Webster Jr, December 4, 1790, in Julian P. Boyd, ed. *Jefferson Papers,* 31 vols. (Princeton, N.J.: Princeton University Press, 1950–2004), 18:132.

13. Quoted in Peter S, Onuf, "The Scholar's Jefferson," *William and Mary Quarterly,* 3rd ser., 50 (October 1993): 690–91.

14. Ibid., 680.

15. Annals of Congress, 1st Cong., 1st sess., 451.

16. Jefferson to Madison, August 28, 1789, *Papers of Jefferson,* 15:367.

17. Jefferson to Monsieur A. Coray, October 31, 1823. Lipscomb, *Writings of Thomas Jefferson,* 15:489.

18. Jefferson to McKean, February 19, 1803; quoted in Leonard W. Levy, *Legacy of Suppression: Freedom of Speech and Press in Early American History* (Cambridge, Mass.: Belknap Press of Harvard University Press, 1960), 300.

19. Jefferson to Kosciusko, Washington, D.C., April 2, 1802, in Paul Leicester Ford, ed., *The Writings of Thomas Jefferson,* 10 vols. (New York: Putnam, 1892–99), 10:309–10.

20. Quoted in Koch and Peden, *Selected Writings of Thomas Jefferson,* 381.

21. Quoted in Richard D. Brown, *Knowledge Is Power: The Diffusion of Information in Early America, 1700–1865* (New York: Oxford University Press, 1989), 269.

22. Lipscomb, *Writings of Thomas Jefferson*, 3:380–81.

23. Koch and Peden, *Selected Writings of Thomas Jefferson*, 426.

24. Leonard W. Levy, *Emergence of a Free Press* (New York: Oxford University Press, 1985), 148–49.

25. For a concise account of the Croswell trial, see Jerry W. Knudson, *In the News: American Journalists View Their Craft* (Wilmington, Del.: Scholarly Resources, 2000), 20–22.

26. Both quotes, Margaret A. Blanchard, *History of the Mass Media in the United States: An Encyclopedia* (Chicago: Ftizroy Dearborn, 1998), 284–85.

CONCLUSION

1. Frank Luther Mott, *American Journalism: A History of Newspapers in the United States through 260 Years, 1690 to 1950*, rev. ed. (New York: Macmillan, 1950), 184.

2. Ibid.

3. Isaiah Thomas, *The History of Printing in America: With a Biography of Printers & an Account of Newspapers*, ed. Marcus A. McCorison, 2nd ed. (New York: Weathervane Books, 1970) 17.

4. Thomas, *The History of Printing in America*, 17.

5. Samuel Miller, *A Brief Retrospect of the Eighteenth Century* (New York: T. & J. Swords, 1803) 2:255.

6. Dumas Malone and Basil Raugh, *Empire for Liberty*, vol. 1, *The Genesis and Growth of the United States of America* (New York: Appleton-Century-Crofts, 1960), 532.

7. Alexis de Tocqueville, *Democracy in America*, trans. Henry Reeve (New York: Random House, 2000), 1:213 and 215. This Random House edition was reprinted from the original text of the 1835 English edition. The book was retranslated by Francis Bowen in 1862.

8. De Tocqueville, *Democracy in America*, 1:215.

9. Jefferson to French Struther, Philadelphia, June 8, 1797, and Jefferson to Col. Arthur Campbell, Monticello, Sept. 1, 1797, both in Bernard Mayo, ed., *Jefferson Himself: The Narrative of a Many-Sided American* (New York: Houghton Mifflin Company, 1942), 253 and 204.

10. Thomas, *The History of Printing in America*, note 19.

Index